高等学校英语应用能力考试 B 级实战教程

主　审　张　瑜　刘恩华
主　编　陆晓华　李　爽
副主编　周卫东　顾卫华

苏州大学出版社

图书在版编目(CIP)数据

高等学校英语应用能力考试 B 级实战教程/陆晓华,李爽主编. —苏州:苏州大学出版社,2020.9
ISBN 978-7-5672-3306-5

Ⅰ.①高… Ⅱ.①陆… ②李… Ⅲ.①英语水平考试-高等职业教育-自学参考资料 Ⅳ.①H310.421

中国版本图书馆 CIP 数据核字(2020)第 179506 号

高等学校英语应用能力考试 B 级实战教程
陆晓华 李 爽 主编
责任编辑 周建兰
助理编辑 万才兰

苏 州 大 学 出 版 社 出 版 发 行
(地址:苏州市十梓街 1 号 邮编:215006)
宜兴市盛世文化印刷有限公司印装
(地址:宜兴市万石镇南漕河滨路 58 号 邮编:214217)

开本 787 mm×1 092 mm 1/16 印张 16 字数 360 千
2020 年 9 月第 1 版 2020 年 9 月第 1 次印刷
ISBN 978-7-5672-3306-5 定价:40.00 元

苏州大学版图书若有印装错误,本社负责调换
苏州大学出版社营销部 电话:0512－67481020
苏州大学出版社网址 http://www.sudapress.com
苏州大学出版社邮箱 sdcbs@suda.edu.cn

前　言

　　高等学校英语应用能力考试(Practical English Test for Colleges,简称PRETCO)是教育部高等教育司于1996年开始筹备,1998年开始启动,2000年正式开考的针对高职高专院校英语教学质量的水平考试,每年6月和12月各考一次。这项考试主要考核考生实际运用英语进行日常对话和涉外业务交际的能力,以促进高职高专英语教学向培养高等应用技术型人才的方向进行改革;同时为用人单位提供针对高职高专毕业生英语水平的评价标准,也提高学生进入人才市场的竞争力。作为一线教师,我们的眼光既要宏观,又要具体,既要关注世界的变化,更要关心身边的责任,而指导学生顺利通过考核是我们该有的担当。担当,就是关键时刻要站得出;担当,就是攻坚克难要拿得下。担当需要勇气,更加需要知识和能力。

　　为此,本书编写团队重新审视考纲,注重实战,用时代赋予的启示盘活考题,精准施策,努力打造在实战中主动发现问题、善于思考问题、勇于突破知识边界,不断挑战自我、攀登高峰,从而在更大的人生舞台上展现才华、贡献力量的育人环境,在立德树人背景下推动高职高专英语教学改革,促进高职高专英语教学质量的提高,加强对高职高专英语教学和考试工作的宏观管理和英语教学质量的监测。

　　本书的设计理念及学法指导如下。

　　一、砥砺实战硬功

　　万事万物都有规律可循,找到规律,就找到了问题的关键,问题也就迎刃而解了。考试也是一样的,摸索规律,掌握方法,就会达到事半功倍的效果。本书编写团队试图将试题的答题技巧以规律化呈现。本书分为六个章节,第一章为考试大纲,第二章至第六章根据B级考试题型分模块进行讲解,即"听力理解""词汇与结构""阅读理解""英译汉""写作/汉译英",每个章节又分为"题型综述""考点归纳""技巧点拨""实战演练"四个板块。考生在了解每个部分的题型特点和具体要求的基础上,有针对性地把握相关语言知识点和应试技巧,最后以2015—2019年的真题(共10套题)为素材进行实战演练,通过讲练结合的形式帮助考生系统掌握各项语言点,化解考试难点,考生可根据自身情况进行针对性的复习,尤其针对薄弱环节,可以反复练习。

　　二、锤炼精湛技能

　　本书编写团队以"教会学生运用方法去解决问题,比单纯掌握知识技能更为重要"为信条,在深入剖析考题的基础上,帮助考生深入掌握解题技巧,提高解题能力。

　　针对"听力理解"题型,本书推出"听前略读题目,预测内容+听中速记要点,锁定重点+听后综合考量,一锤定音"的解题模式,培养考生提取关键信息、整合信息和运用信息推测、分析、判断、理解的能力，从而提升听力水平。以此教会考生学会倾听，倾听人群的每一种声音，尊重每一条不同的意见。

针对"词汇与结构"题型，本书推出"点到为止找考点＋穿针引线想语法＋面面俱到融语境"的解题模式，培养考生特别关注语言形式与语言意义、语言功能、上下文语境等方面的关系，有意识地根据考生的不同认知水平进行词、句、篇的分层过渡训练。以此教会考生学会观察，观察社会的每一个角落，捕捉环境中的每一种信号。

针对"阅读理解"题型，本书推出"总，速读全文把握大局＋分，上下求索往返迂回＋总，检查核实各个击破"的解题模式，培养考生通过浏览全文抓住关键字眼，把握主旨，精通细节，并且做到与作者"将心比心"。以此教会考生学会思考，既要坚持实事求是、证据为先，又要秉持理想价值、伦理判断。

针对"英译汉"题型，本书推出"拎出一个英语大主干，抽筋留骨去皮毛＋得出一个汉语大骨架，接骨连筋添皮毛"的解题模式，指导考生翻译时既要忠实于原文，又要符合汉语的习惯，不可太拘泥。拘泥、刻板的翻译若死守原文语言形式，就会损害原文思想内容。以此教会考生在思潮涌动、舆论繁杂的世界中保持理性、客观、严谨，坚守理想、信仰、底线。

针对"写作/汉译英"题型，本书推出"明确考查意图，搭好句型框架＋确定时态语态，注意前后呼应＋注意英语思维，克服母语障碍＋学会适当变通，避免逐字翻译"的解题模式，培养考生具备行文流畅的能力，因为书面表达不是对词、句的简单堆砌和对意思的杂乱呈现，而是将词、句有机组合在一起，将意思有条理地表达出来。要想使所写的内容有整体性、连贯性，就要学会全面掌握并且灵活运用连接性过渡词等技巧，使句子之间的衔接顺畅。以此教会考生树立人文精神，让笔尖所到之处都能够传播知识、文化、科学、智慧。

三、强化打赢本领

本书编写团队本着"一书在手，考试无忧"的理念，创造性地对2015—2019年的10套真题的每个题型进行量化分析，对每个考点精准施策。例如，通过对2015—2019年10次考试中词汇与结构部分Section A的分析，我们可以看出这部分主要考查的知识点分布如下：

考查的知识点	时间									
	2015-6	2015-12	2016-6	2016-12	2017-6	2017-12	2018-6	2018-12	2019-6	2019-12
时态与语态	1		1		1	1	1	1		
词汇/词组辨析	3	3	5	5	4	4	5	5	1	3
从句	1	2	1		2	1		1	2	1
介词（词组）		2	1	1	1	1	1	1		
分词	1				1			1	1	1
连词	2	2	1			2	1		1	1
固定搭配	2	1		2	1	1			3	3

续表

考查的知识点	时间									
	2015-6	2015-12	2016-6	2016-12	2017-6	2017-12	2018-6	2018-12	2019-6	2019-12
形容词			1							
副词				1					1	1
虚拟语气							1			

注：数字表示考查的次数。

从数据分析中我们发现，这部分主要涉及动词短语、动词的现在分词与过去分词、动词辨析、名词辨析、形容词辨析、副词与介词及代词的辨析、副词与形容词的级等考点，考查学生运用词语的能力，要求考生了解考试所涉及的词汇知识和语法知识，并能够在做题的时候灵活运用。这部分的分数不容易获得，考生必须依靠平时的知识记忆和积累，并能够在实际解题过程中将各种应试技巧融会贯通才能得到高分。基于此，我们给出备考关注点：一方面，加强词汇积累，考生最好将大纲中的短语——弄懂并掌握，英语中有不少的惯用词语搭配、习惯表达法和特殊用法等，都需要考生特别注意。另一方面，学会自我总结。在长期的英语学习中，考生除了掌握各种词汇短语，还要懂得用自己的方法总结一些规则，方便自己记忆。这样，再通过"全真演练"，考生基本可以做到百战不殆。

为了更好地帮助考生提高听力，本书在听力理解部分附上了听力文件的二维码，考生可以不受时间和空间限制，随时随地用手机扫描二维码播放听力，反复多次进行练习。此外，附录部分涵盖了真题听力原文、答案与解析和答题卡样张，供考生做题自查和教师讲解之用。

衷心感谢一路支持的各位领导、老师、朋友和同学们，由于编写时间仓促和编者水平有限，书中若有错误或不足之处，敬请各位不吝赐教，以期改进！

编　者

2020年7月

目 录

第一章　考试大纲 ··· 1
第二章　听力理解 ··· 4
　　第一节　题型综述 ·· 4
　　第二节　考点归纳 ·· 5
　　第三节　技巧点拨 ·· 9
　　第四节　实战演练 ·· 12
第三章　词汇与结构 ·· 29
　　第一节　题型综述 ·· 29
　　第二节　考点归纳 ·· 29
　　第三节　技巧点拨 ·· 30
　　第四节　实战演练 ·· 45
第四章　阅读理解 ··· 60
　　第一节　题型综述 ·· 60
　　第二节　考点归纳 ·· 61
　　第三节　技巧点拨 ·· 65
　　第四节　实战演练 ·· 66
第五章　英译汉 ··· 108
　　第一节　题型综述 ·· 108
　　第二节　考点归纳 ·· 108
　　第三节　技巧点拨 ·· 110
　　第四节　实战演练 ·· 115
第六章　写作/汉译英 ··· 124
　　第一节　题型综述 ·· 124

第二节　考点归纳 ………………………………………………………… 125
　　第三节　技巧点拨 ………………………………………………………… 125
　　第四节　实战演练 ………………………………………………………… 133
附录 …………………………………………………………………………………… 143
　　附录一　听力原文 ………………………………………………………… 143
　　附录二　答案与解析 ……………………………………………………… 161
　　附录三　答题卡样张 ……………………………………………………… 245

第一章
考 试 大 纲

我国高等职业教育、普通高等专科教育和成人高等教育的教学目标是"以就业为目的，以市场为导向"，培养高级应用型、技术型人才，其英语教学应贯彻"实用为主，够用为度"的方针，既要培养学生具备必要的英语语言基础知识，更应强调培养学生运用英语进行有关日常和涉外业务工作的交际能力。高等学校英语应用能力考试就是为了检验高职高专学生是否达到所规定的教学要求而设置的考试。本考试以《高职高专教育英语课程教学基本要求（试行）》（以下简称《基本要求》）为依据，既测试语言知识也测试语言技能，既测试一般性语言内容也测试与涉外业务有关的应用性内容，并侧重后者，实用性内容约占60%。

考虑到目前我国高职高专学生英语入学水平的现状，《基本要求》将教学要求分为A级和B级，A级是标准要求，B级是过渡要求。高等学校英语应用能力考试也相对应地分为A级考试和B级考试。修完《基本要求》A级规定的全部内容的学生可参加A级考试；修完《基本要求》B级规定的全部内容的学生可参加B级考试。

考试方式为笔试和口试，分别进行。笔试测试考生的英语语言知识和听、读、译、写四种实用技能；口试测试考生以英语为工具进行日常和业务口头交际的能力。

客观性试题有信度较高、覆盖面广的优点，而主观性试题有利于提高测试的效度，能更好地检测考生运用语言的能力。为此，高等学校英语应用能力考试采用主客观题混合题型，以保证良好的信度和效度。

高等学校英语应用能力考试按百分制计分，满分为100分。60分及60分以上为及格；85分及85分以上为优秀。考试成绩合格者获得"高等学校英语应用能力考试"相应级别的合格证书。

高等学校英语应用能力考试（B级）（以下简称PRETCO-B）考试大纲

一、考试对象

PRETCO-B适用于达到高职教育英语课程基础要求的高等职业教育、普通高职高专教育、成人高等教育和本科独立学院非英语专业的学生。

二、考试性质

本考试的目的是考核考生的英语基础知识和语言技能,以及使用英语进行简单的涉外日常交际与业务交际的能力,其性质是教学水平考试。

三、考试方式与内容

考试方式为笔试,包括五个部分:听力理解、词汇与结构、阅读理解、翻译(英译汉)和写作/汉译英。

第一部分:听力理解(Listening Comprehension)

本部分测试考生理解所听问题并快速做出回答、理解简短对话和听写词语的能力。听力材料的朗诵语速为每分钟100词。听力材料以简单的涉外日常交际和涉外业务交际内容为主。词汇限于本大纲"词汇表"中B级范围。

本部分的得分占总分的24%。测试时间为25分钟。

第二部分:词汇与结构(Vocabulary & Structure)

本部分测试考生运用词语和语法知识的能力。测试内容包括职业教育英语课程涉及的基础词汇用法和基础语法。词汇范围限于本大纲"词汇表"中B级范围。

本部分的得分占总分的15%。测试时间为10分钟。

第三部分:阅读理解(Reading Comprehension)

本部分测试考生从书面文字材料获取信息的能力。总阅读量约为800词。本部分测试的文字材料包括一般性阅读材料(文化、社会、常识、科普、经贸、人物等)和简单的应用性文字材料(或图文),不包括诗歌、小说、散文等文学性材料;其内容能为各专业学生所理解。应用性文字材料(术语、简历、便条、广告、简短便函、日程表、单证等)占50%左右。

本部分主要测试以下阅读技能:

① 了解语篇和段落的主旨和大意;
② 掌握语篇中的事实和主要情节;
③ 了解语篇上下文的逻辑关系;
④ 了解作者的目的、态度和观点;
⑤ 根据上下文正确理解生词的意思;
⑥ 了解语篇的结论;
⑦ 进行信息转换。

阅读材料涉及的词汇限于本大纲"词汇表"中B级范围。

本部分的得分占总分的31%。测试时间为35分钟。

第四部分:英译汉(Translation—English into Chinese)

本部分测试考生将英语正确译成汉语的能力。所译材料为句子和段落,包括一般性内容(约占60%)和应用性内容(约占40%);所涉及的词汇限于本大纲"词汇表"中B级范围。

本部分的得分占总分的15%。测试时间为25分钟。

第五部分：写作/汉译英（Writing/Translation—Chinese into English）

本部分测试考生填写英文表格、书写应用性短文或将简短的汉语应用性文字翻译成英语的能力。

本部分的得分占总分的15%。测试时间为25分钟。

考试内容及安排如表1.1所示。

表1.1 测试项目、内容、题型、分值比重及时间分配表

序号	测试项目	题号	测试内容	题型	百分比	时间分配
Ⅰ	听力理解	1－24	问答、对话、会话、短文	4选1、填空	24%	25分钟
Ⅱ	词汇与结构	25－39	词汇用法、句法结构、词性等	4选1、填空	15%	10分钟
Ⅲ	阅读理解	40－62	术语、语篇（应用性文字）、图文	4选1、填空、匹配、简答	31%	35分钟
Ⅳ	（翻译）英译汉	63－67	句子、段落	句子(3选1)、段落翻译	15%	25分钟
Ⅴ	写作/汉译英		应用性文字(便条、通知、备忘录、简短便函、简历、申请表等)	填表、写短文、汉译英	15%	25分钟
合计		67＋1			100%	120分钟

第二章

听 力 理 解

第一节 题型综述

高等学校英语应用能力考试 B 级测试的第一部分为听力理解题（Listening Comprehension），共有 24 题，占总分的 24%，测试时间为 25 分钟，听力材料的语速约为每分钟 100 词。本部分测试要求考生能听懂涉及日常交际的结构简单、发音清楚、语速较慢的英语简短对话和陈述，理解基本正确。听力理解能力与词汇量、语法知识、阅读理解能力、阅读速度、背景知识以及一个人的记忆能力都有着密切的关系，其中阅读理解能力尤为重要。实践证明，在各类英语考试中，绝大部分听力得分高的考生的其他各项的成绩也很优秀。

B 级听力材料通常以日常交际和简单的业务交际内容为主（表 2.1）。听力理解部分要求掌握的技能为：① 理解所听材料的主旨和要点；② 理解具体信息；③ 理解所听材料的背景、说话人之间的关系等；④ 推断所听材料的含义。

表 2.1 交际范围表

类型	具体内容	
日常交际	课堂交流	
	日常生活	介绍,问候,感谢,致歉,道别,指路
		天气,学习,爱好,饮食,健康,旅行,交通,购物
业务交际	一般涉外活动	迎送,安排日程与活动,安排宿舍,宴请,陪同购物,游览,就诊
	一般涉外业务	面试,介绍公司/工厂（历史、现状）

听力理解主要由四个部分组成（表 2.2），包括 Section A、Section B、Section C 和 Section D。Section A 测试考生根据听到的问题做出简短回答的能力，共有 7 个问题，每个问题播放 2 遍，共 7 题，每题 1 分。Section B 测试考生理解短对话（Short Dialogue）的能力，共有 7 个短对话，每个短对话播放 2 遍，共 7 题，每题 1 分。Section C 测试考生理解长对话（Conversation）的能力，共有 2 个长对话，每个长对话播放 2 遍，共 5 题，每题 1 分。Section D

测试考生理解短文(Short Passage)的能力,共 1 篇短文,短文播放 3 遍,需要完成 5 个填空(单词或短语),每空 1 分。

表 2.2 听力理解题型

序号	题号	测试内容	题目数量/个	分值/分	播放次数/遍
Section A	1—7	回答问题	7	7×1′	2
Section B	8—14	理解短对话	7	7×1′	2
Section C	15—19	理解长对话	5	5×1′	2
Section D	20—24	理解短文	5	5×1′	3
合计			24	24	

第二节 考点归纳

一、简短回答问题

Section A 为简短回答问题,问题大多涉及日常生活中的常见话题,即衣、食、住、行、工作、学习等方面,涵盖了校园、公共场所、家庭、职场、时间、关系等。这部分题型要求考生平时积累日常交际常见的表达方式,包括单词、短语和句型。根据历年真题,2015—2019 年简短回答问题部分常考的话题有如下几种(表 2.3)。

表 2.3 2015—2019 年常考话题

序号	话题	时间									
		2019-12	2019-6	2018-12	2018-6	2017-12	2017-6	2016-12	2016-6	2015-12	2015-6
1	邀请	√	√				√				
2	建议					√		√	√		
3	工作或生活	√	√	√	√	√	√	√	√	√	√
4	求允和应答	√	√	√	√						
5	提供和应答	√	√	√					√		
6	问路和应答	√					√				
7	购物	√				√					
8	谈论天气		√								
9	询问日期、时间和应答					√	√				√

续表

序号	话题	时间									
		2019-12	2019-6	2018-12	2018-6	2017-12	2017-6	2016-12	2016-6	2015-12	2015-6
10	约会或预约		√		√		√				
11	校园或学习								√	√	
12	打电话							√			√

从表2.3可以得知,2015—2019年简短回答问题部分主要涉及工作或生活、求允或应答两个方面,其他话题如邀请、建议、提供、预约、问路、购物、打电话等也占一定比例。因此,考生应掌握常见的工作和生活场景词汇,熟知求允、邀请、建议等句型,如:May/Can/Could I…,Can/Would/Could you…,Shall we…,Would you please…,What do you think about/of…,Would you like…,Do you mind …等等。

二、理解短对话和长对话

理解短对话和长对话对应的题型分别是 Section B 和 Section C。其中短对话共 7 组,通常是一男一女各说一句,然后就对话内容提出一个问题,每个对话和问题各读 2 遍。长对话共 2 组,通常是一男一女各说几句,然后对话后设置 2~3 个问题,每个对话和问题各读 2 遍。对话题型的内容一般以日常交际为主,句子结构和内容都不太复杂,话题通常为日常交际,即介绍、致谢、问路、天气、学习、爱好、伙食和健康等。考生可根据所获取的相关信息,针对对话中的某些细节做出判断、选择。对话所涉及的考查题型主要包含以下几种。

1. 事实细节题

这类题型主要考查考生捕捉听力材料细节的能力,不能靠猜测或主观印象来答题。考查的细节一般包括时间、地点、人物、动作、原因、目的、数字等,可以通过预判选项来推测可能考到的问题,问题的答案一般在对话中可以被直接找到。常见的提问方式有"Why/What/Where/How…"。考生要留意文中的因果连词(如:because, so, since, due to)和转折连词(如:but, however, although, though),听到时间、数字等时要边听边做笔记。如:

M: I want to start a business, but where can I get the money?

W: You can apply for a bank loan.

Q: What did the woman advise the man to do?

2. 判断推理题

判断推理题是理解对话中最难的一种题型,要求考生不仅能够听懂对话的字面意思,还要能从中推测出说话人的言外之意、观点、态度等。常见的提问方式有"What does the speaker think about the problem?" "What does the man/woman suggest?" "What can we learn about the man/woman?"等。如:

M: Have you got the driving license?

W: No. I've just passed the road test.

Q：What can we learn from the conversation?

3．时间数字题

时间数字题属于细节题的一种,是历年听力考试中常见的题型之一,选项通常是时间或数字的形式。考生往往通过简单计算就能得出答案,常见的提问方式有"Where/When/How long/How many/How much/How old…"。如：

W：Will you spare me some time to discuss my marketing plan?

M：Sorry. I'm busy at the moment. How about this afternoon?

Q：When will the two speakers discuss the plan?

4．地点场景题

地点场景题一般考查对话发生的地点或场所,选项一般为地点状语。此类题目的答案一般不会直接出现在对话中,考生可以根据与地点相关的特定词汇推断出地点或场景。常见的提问方式有"Where does the conversation most probably take place?""Where are the two speakers?""Where is the man/woman?"等。如：

W：Where is No. 3 teaching building?

M：Go ahead and turn right. You will see a white building.

Q：Where are the two speakers?

5．身份关系题

此类题型主要考查说话者的职业、身份以及相互关系,答案通常不会直接出现在对话中,考生需要通过对话中的关键词进行推断,如听到 restaurant、order、menu、waiter 等单词时可联想到饭店场景,由此推断出说话者的身份或关系。常见的人物关系有夫妻(husband—wife)、父子(father—son)、母女(mother—daughter)、师生(teacher—student)、老板与秘书(boss—secretary)、雇主与雇员(employer—employee)、医生与病人(doctor—patient)、房东与租客(landlord—tenant)、采访者与被采访者(interviewer—interviewee)等。如：

W：Do you know Mr. Johnson has been promoted?

M：Yes. He is now our new manager.

Q：What can we learn about Mr. Johnson?

常用的对话场景词汇见表 2.4。

表 2.4　对话场景词汇

序号	场景	常用词汇
1	公司/办公室	department 部门;CEO 首席执行官;board of directors 董事会;sales department 销售部;secretary 秘书;type a letter 打印信件;printer 打印机;interview 面试;interviewer 面试官;interviewee 面试者;promotion 晋升,升职;resignation 辞呈;employer 老板;employee 员工;colleague 同事;client 客户;accountant 会计
2	银行	open an account 开账户;cash a check 兑付支票;withdraw 取款;deposit 存款;saving 储蓄;interest 利息;balance 余额;teller 出纳员;ATM 自动取款机;loan 贷款;currency 货币;credit card 信用卡

续表

序号	场景	常用词汇
3	校园	professor 教授;oral exam 口试;written exam 笔试;test/quiz 考试/测验;score/mark/grade 分数;credit 学分;subject 科目;library 图书馆;dormitory 宿舍;laboratory 实验室;lecture 讲座;required course 必修课;optional course 选修课;term paper 学期论文;scholarship 奖学金;diploma 学位证书
4	邮局	stamp 邮票;parcel 包裹;postage 邮资;envelop 信封;delivery 派送;telegram 电报;postcard 明信片;airmail 航空邮件,航空邮政;surface mail 平信;registered mail 挂号信;printed matter 印刷品
5	餐厅/饭店	order 点菜;menu 菜单;bill 账单;a table for two 两人桌;main course 主菜;bar 酒吧;buffet 自助餐;cafeteria 自助餐厅;pay 支付;snack 小吃;steak 牛排;hamburger 汉堡;change 零钱;tip 小费;waiter/waitress 侍应生;go Dutch AA 制;selling season 销售旺季
6	酒店/旅馆	check in/out 办理入住/离店手续;make a reservation 预订;register 登记;reception desk 前台;laundry 洗衣
7	理发店	barber(为男子理发的)理发师;hairdresser 美发师;beard/mustache 胡子;shampoo 洗发香波;hair spray 发胶
8	医院/诊所	physician 内科医生;surgeon 外科医生;doctor 医生;patient 病人;ward 病房;emergency room 急救室;operation 手术;diagnose 诊断;injection 注射;prescribe 开处方;pill 药丸;dentist 牙医;tablet 药片;take the temperature 量体温;visiting hours 探视时间;a sore throat 喉咙痛
9	机场	passport 护照;visa 签证;ticket 机票;boarding card 登机牌;flight 航班;safety belt 安全带;economic class 经济舱;first-class cabin 头等舱;take off 飞机起飞;land 飞机着陆;captain 机长;stewardess/airhostess 空姐;airline 航空公司;crash 坠机;transit passenger 过境旅客
10	电话	dial 拨号;busy line 电话占线;make a local call 打市话;operator 接线员;hold the line 别挂电话;hold on 别挂电话;make a long-distance call 打长途电话
11	商场	shop assistant 营业员;salesgirl/saleswoman 女售货员;customer/shopper 顾客;on sale 大减价;reduction 减少;bargain 便宜货;discount 折扣;department store 百货公司;supermarket 大型超市;receipt 收据;cashier 收银员
12	家庭	father 父亲;mother 母亲;husband 丈夫;wife 妻子;niece 侄女/外甥女;nephew 侄子/外甥;cousin 表兄弟姐妹;uncle 叔叔/伯父;aunt 阿姨/姑姑;granddaughter 孙女/外孙女;grandson 孙子/外孙

三、短文填空

Section D 是一篇短文,录音播放 3 遍,设有 5 个空格,需要考生根据所听到的内容将信息补充完整。根据题目要求,每个空格不能填写超过 3 个词。这部分除了考查考生的听力理解能力之外,还测试考生多方面的语言技能,如单词拼写能力、速记能力、语法基本功等。需要注意的是,听写部分没有提供任何选项,这就意味着答题有一定的难度。所填单词或词组都属于考试大纲词汇范畴,大多以实词为主,即主要是动词、名词、形容词等的填写。这部分题型的主要特点如下:

① 篇幅较长,信息量较大,材料涉及面较广;
② 句子语法结构相对复杂,长难句较多;
③ 难度增加,要求考生根据听到的内容填出确切的单词或短语,拼写无误;
④ 考查考生的综合能力,包括听力理解、单词拼写、速记、语法知识等方面。

第三节　技巧点拨

一、听力技巧综述

1．掌握有效的听力策略

最常见并且行之有效的听力策略是"精听"和"泛听"。

精听对考生真正打好英语听力基础至关重要。通过精听练习,学生不仅能够提高听力水平,还能极大地促进自身对词汇和语法的学习,可以说是一举两得。在实际练习过程中,精听的最佳练习方法就是听写练习,具体方法是:首先,选择一段听力材料,不看原文,先从头到尾总体听一遍,力求有一个整体概念;其次,一边听一边写,一定要力争做到把每个单词都写下来;最后,在对照答案修改完之后,再对照原文从头到尾听一遍,认真琢磨听不懂的地方或有错误的地方。

泛听是指广泛的听,目的在于在听力练习中掌握文章的整体意思。泛听锻炼考生对英语的总体把握能力,可以培养英语语感,激活耳朵的感应能力。

泛听要求考生在听力练习中以掌握文章的整体意思为目的,只要不影响对整体文章的理解,一个词、一个短语甚至一个句子听不懂也没关系。泛听练习的选材比较宽泛,听力试题、新闻、电影等都可作为泛听材料。进行泛听练习时,考生要尽量集中注意力,能够理解主要大意即可。

2．平时加强听力训练

听力能力的提高并非一朝一夕能做到的,需要平时一点一滴的积累。首先,要积累大量的词汇,尤其是 B 级听力高频词汇。词汇量的重要性不言而喻。有时可能仅仅因为一个关键词未听懂,考生对整个句子的理解就会产生偏差或错误,从而影响做题的正确性。

此外,学生在平时训练听力时要经常运用听力速记技巧,常见的速记方法有符号和缩写两种,如"↑up""↓down""←left""→right"" = equal""NY：NewYork""HK：Hong Kong""App：Application""Edu：Education"等。学生亦可发明创造自己能够看懂的符号或缩写,如"ex→expensive""eq→earthquake""ys→yesterday"等。

3．合理运用考试时间

听力理解题位于考试的第一部分,考生需要调整心情,尽快进入考试状态,集中注意力,避免由于紧张而出现大脑一片空白的情况。考试过程中,考生不要纠结于没有听懂的单词或短语,而应跟着录音往下听,抓住后面的信息;养成良好的听力习惯,边听边做记录,留意听音重点,排除干扰选项,最后做出正确选择。听力播放之前,考生要充分利用试音时间,快速熟悉播音员的语音、语调和语速,迅速浏览题目选项,找出关键词并做好标记。听力过程中,考生要善于捕捉关键词,比如人物、时间、地点、原因、目的、方式、数字等相关信息,运用速记技巧边听边做记录。一段听力材料播完之后,考生要快速确定答案,切忌听完之后反复纠结,以致错过下一题的信息。如果出现漏听或听不懂的情况,不要慌乱,必要时可以使用猜题技巧,如"视听一致"原则,即听到什么就选什么。

二、简短回答问题题型的听力技巧

此类题型是较为简单的一种听力题型,考生只需根据听到的问题给出简短回答。根据历年听力真题,这部分的问题主要有两类:一般疑问句和特殊疑问句。针对这两种句型的特点,考生可以采用不同的解题策略。

1. 一般疑问句

一般疑问句的结构是"助动词+主语+动词原形+其他成分?"。听到这类疑问句时,考生有时只需回答 Yes 或 No。肯定回答用"Yes,主语+do/does。",否定回答用"No,主语+do/does not。"。助动词也常用缩写形式,主要有 don't、doesn't、didn't 等。有时考生只需根据所问内容,给出确切的答案即可。如:

Q: May I have your name, please? (2017 年 6 月真题)

A. On Monday.　　　　　　B. John Smith.

B. Take it easy.　　　　　　D. It's too late.

【解析】题干是"能告诉我您的名字吗?",因此正确答案是 B 选项。

2. 特殊疑问句

特殊疑问句是指以特殊疑问词开头,对句中某一成分进行提问的句子。常用的特殊疑问词有 what、who、whose、which、when、where、how、why 等。回答特殊疑问句时,不能用 Yes 或 No,即不能问什么答什么,尤其是简略回答。做这类题时,考生要捕捉问题中的特殊疑问词,根据疑问词给出相对应的回答。如:

Q: Excuse me. Where is the information center? (2017 年 12 月真题)

A. It's over there.　　　　　B. Sorry to hear that.

C. That's all right.　　　　　D. It's wonderful.

【解析】题干是"打扰了,信息中心在哪里?",因此正确答案是 A 选项。

此外,考生平时要积累一些日常交际常用的词汇和表达方式,如关于天气、问路、购物、用餐、邀请、道谢、道歉、约会、祝贺、建议等方面,这样考试时就能应付自如。

三、理解短对话和长对话题型的听力技巧

理解对话是听力考试中最常见的一种题型,主要考查考生在一定的语境和情景中所表现出来的快速反应能力和推理判断能力。常用的考查题型有以下几种。

1．事实细节题

这类题型在听力考试中所占比重很大，考生在听的过程中要注意捕捉表示转折、因果、条件等关系的关联词语，如 however、but、as well as、not only ... but also、because、since、so、if、even if、though、although 等连接词。听到时间、数字、价格、人名、地名时，考生要及时做好记录。

2．判断推理题

这类题型测试考生在听力方面的综合素质。解题时，考生需要注意说话者的语音、语调，从而判断他们的意图、观点和态度；对会话中的否定结构要特别敏感，如 hardly、never、few、little、rather than、instead of、without 等否定词；要听清问题，注意提问中有没有 not 这个词。

3．时间数字题

这类试题都会涉及某些数字，一般要进行简单的运算。有时对话中只出现一个时间，有时出现两个或两个以上的时间，考生需要做好笔记，将听到的时间记录下来，同时注意表示动作发生先后的词，如 before、after、previous、former、meanwhile、finally、next、later 等。对于数字题，除了听清具体的数字，考生还应注意倍数、分数、百分比等词汇。

4．地点场景题

考生在听力过程中要留意对话中与地点相关的词汇，如听到 doctor、nurse、headache、fever 等词时可推断地点为医院；听到 teacher、student、campus、course、class 等词时会联想到学校的场景。此外，考生在平时进行听力训练时要注意积累常见的场景词汇。

5．身份关系题

解这类题时，考生需要注意对话中的称呼语，因为称呼语往往会直接暴露说话人的身份或说话人双方的关系，如"Mr."表示对方可能是自己的上司。其次，考生要捕捉体现某种人物关系或某种职业的相关词汇，注意说话人的语气和态度，比如师生、夫妻、老板与员工、家长与子女之间都有特定的说话方式和特点，抓住关键词就能找出人物之间的关系。

四、短文填空题的听力技巧

短文填空题要求考生听完3遍录音后填写出准确的单词或短语，这类题的解题技巧主要包括以下三点。

第一，快速浏览全文，理解短文大意，根据上下文和语法知识预测空格处要填的单词。

第二，边听边记，采用速记方法，迅速记下每一个听到的单词。如果遇到听懂词意但不会拼写单词的情况，可从上下文寻找是否有帮助、提示的地方。

第三，第一遍听的时候侧重短文大意，可以做简单记录；第二遍填写听到的单词或词组，把听不出来的单词先放一放，等第三遍播放时再记录；听最后一遍时要仔细检查、核对，确保大小写、单复数、时态语态等没有错误。

第四节 实战演练

2015年6月真题

Part I Listening Comprehension （25 minutes）

Directions：*This part is to test your listening ability. It consists of 4 sections.*

Section A

扫码获取听力音频

Directions：*This section is to test your ability to give proper responses. There are 7 recorded questions in it. After each question, there is a pause. The questions will be spoken **two times**. When you hear a question, you should decide on the correct answer from the 4 choices marked A), B), C) and D) given in your test paper. Then you should mark the corresponding letter on the Answer Sheet with a single line through the center.*

Example：You will hear：Mr. smith is not in. Would you like to leave a message?

You will read：A) I'm not sure.   B) You're right.
C) Yes, certainly.   D) That's interesting.

From the question we can learn that the speaker is asking the listener to leave a message. Therefore, **C) Yes, certainly** is the correct answer. You should mark C) on the Answer Sheet with a single line through the center.

[A] [B] [~~C~~] [D]

Now the test will begin.

1. A) You are late.   B) My pleasure.
   C) Fine, thanks.   D) Go ahead, please.

2. A) I'm John Smith.   B) Thank you.
   C) Not too bad.   D) It's over there.

3. A) Pass it to me, please.   B) Yes, of course.
   C) This way, please.   D) Don't worry.

4. A) All right.   B) Not at all.
   C) I'm fine.   D) It doesn't matter.

5. A) Here you are.   B) Thank you for coming.
   C) It's too late.   D) Yes, once a month.

6. A) Never mind.   B) Mind your steps.

C) Sure.　　　　　　　　　　　D) Don't mention it.

7. A) Long time no see.　　　　　B) Here it is.

　C) Coffee, please.　　　　　　D) No problem.

Section B

Directions: *This section is to test your ability to understand short dialogues. There are 7 recorded dialogues in it. After each dialogue, there is a recorded question. Both the dialogues and questions will be spoken **two times**. When you hear a question, you should decide on the correct answer from the 4 choices marked A),B),C) and D) given in your test paper. Then you should mark the corresponding letter on the Answer Sheet with a single line through the center.*

Now listen to the dialogues.

8. A) He missed the bus.　　　　　　B) He got to the wrong place.

　C) He forgot the time.　　　　　　D) He was sick.

9. A) By a gift card.　　　　　　　　B) By cheque.

　C) In cash.　　　　　　　　　　　D) By credit card.

10. A) The man's foreign language ability.　B) The man's education background.

　　C) The man's communication skill.　　D) The man's work experience.

11. A) She doesn't like her job.　　　　B) She has changed her job.

　　C) She is retired.　　　　　　　　D) She has quit her job.

12. A) From its advertisement.　　　　B) From its website.

　　C) From its newsletter.　　　　　D) From its sales people.

13. A) In a hospital.　　　　　　　　B) In a restaurant.

　　C) In a hotel.　　　　　　　　　D) In a supermarket.

14. A) Today.　　　　　　　　　　　B) Next Monday.

　　C) Tomorrow.　　　　　　　　　D) This Friday.

Section C

Directions: *In this section, there are 2 recorded conversations. After each conversation, there are some recorded questions. Both the conversations and questions will be spoken **two times**. When you hear a question, you should decide on the correct answer from the 4 choices marked A),B),C) and D) given in your test paper. Then you should mark the corresponding letter on the Answer Sheet with a single line through the center.*

Now listen to the conversations.

Conversation 1

15. A) Meet a friend.　　　　　　　　B) Visit a patient.

　　C) See a doctor.　　　　　　　　D) Look for a dentist.

16. A) He's caught a cold.　　　　　　B) He's got a headache.

C) He's got his leg broken.　　　　D) He's got a fever.

Conversation 2

17. A) Mrs. Green.　　　　　　　　B) Mrs. Smith.
　　C) Mr. Kale.　　　　　　　　　D) Mr. Black.
18. A) On Friday.　　　　　　　　B) On Thursday.
　　C) On Wednesday.　　　　　　D) On Monday.
19. A) Write a letter.　　　　　　　B) Arrange the meeting.
　　C) Send an email.　　　　　　D) Pass a message.

Section D

Directions: *In this section you will hear a recorded short passage. The passage is printed in the test paper, but with some words or phrases missing. The passage will be read **three times**. During the second reading, you are required to put the missing words or phrases on the Answer Sheet in order of the numbered blanks according to what you hear. The third reading is for you to check your writing.*

Now the passage will begin.

　　Good afternoon, ladies and gentlemen. Thank you very much for coming to our conference this afternoon. I'm Henry Johnson, the sales __20__ of Smart Toys. Now I'd like to introduce you to a completely __21__ of toy manufacture. Firstly, I'll talk about the market research which led to the __22__ of this product. Then I'll explain the production and our sales plan. Finally, I'll make some suggestions so that you can make this product a __23__. We are confident this new product will sell well in the __24__. At the end of my speech, we'll have a question-and-answer section.

2015 年 12 月真题

Part I　Listening Comprehension　(25 minutes)

扫码获取听力音频

Directions: *This part is to test your listening ability. It consists of 4 sections.*

Section A

1. A) Wonderful.　　　　　　　　B) Here you are.
　　C) Thank you.　　　　　　　　D) I'll take one.
2. A) You can't miss it.　　　　　　B) It takes too much time.
　　C) Nice to see you.　　　　　　D) Yes. It's John Smith.
3. A) How are you?　　　　　　　B) Yes, I do.
　　C) Here it is.　　　　　　　　D) My pleasure.
4. A) I'd love to.　　　　　　　　B) Take it easy.
　　C) Five more minutes, please.　　D) The department managers.

5. A) That's too late. B) On Monday morning.
   C) Not bad. D) 45 dollars.
6. A) Sure. B) Have a good time.
   C) Enjoy your dinner. D) Two single rooms, please.
7. A) On the third floor. B) No problem.
   C) Mind your steps. D) This way, please.

Section B

8. A) She moved to another city. B) She was tired of the job.
   C) The working condition was poor. D) The job was too challenging.
9. A) A pair of shoes. B) A pair of socks.
   C) A T-shirt. D) Blue jeans.
10. A) He's been late. B) He's got a cold.
    C) He's failed an interview. D) He's lost his job.
11. A) The flight time. B) The new model.
    C) The after-sales service. D) The meeting schedule.
12. A) It is a good working habit. B) It is helpful for learning.
    C) It is a waste of time. D) It is harmful to health.
13. A) The job is interesting. B) The boss is nice.
    C) The salary is good. D) The office is nice.
14. A) Making a work plan. B) Working on a new project.
    C) Having a training course. D) Asking for a pay rise.

Section C

Conversation 1

15. A) One night. B) Two nights.
    C) Three nights. D) Four nights.
16. A) Behind the building. B) In front of the building.
    C) Across the street. D) Near the shopping mall.

Conversation 2

17. A) A day off. B) A pay rise.
    C) A new position. D) A paid holiday.
18. A) Two years. B) Three years.
    C) Five years. D) Eight years.
19. A) To send an email to the general manager.
    B) To give the woman more responsibilities.
    C) To offer the woman a training opportunity.
    D) To discuss the matter with the managers.

Section D

Have you ever thought what keeps people happy in their work? We've recently __20__ a survey. Of course, salary is important. Apart from salary, what else makes people happy with their jobs? Now please look at the chart. You can see the __21__ factor is the opportunities to learn and grow. It represents __22__ percent of the people we asked. And 20 percent of the people say __23__ to achieve their goal is important. Our survey also shows that another two important factors are a good working relationship with co-workers and a good __24__ .

2016年6月真题

Part I   Listening Comprehension （25 minutes）

扫码获取听力音频

Directions: *This part is to test your listening ability. It consists of 4 sections.*

Section A

1. A) See you later.   B) In July.
   C) Hurry up.   D) Not too bad.

2. A) No, I didn't.   B) He's fine.
   C) You are right.   D) No worry.

3. A) I don't think so.   B) Very good.
   C) Of course not.   D) Not at all.

4. A) Never mind.   B) Take care.
   C) Here it is.   D) This way, please.

5. A) Yes, I am.   B) OK.
   C) Take it easy.   D) Go ahead.

6. A) Certainly.   B) Mind the steps.
   C) Fine, thanks.   D) Well done.

7. A) No, thanks.   B) You're welcome.
   C) Here you are.   D) Economy class.

Section B

8. A) The party.   B) The exhibition.
   C) The holiday.   D) The interview.

9. A) This afternoon.   B) Tonight.
   C) Right now.   D) Tomorrow.

10. A) Buy a gift.   B) Send a parcel.
    C) Book a ticket.   D) Rent an apartment.

11. A) He missed the bus.　　　　　　　B) He got lost.

　　C) His car broke down.　　　　　　 D) His bicycle was stolen.

12. A) Buy the new software.　　　　　 B) Ask Jack for help.

　　C) Stop using the software.　　　　 D) Help the woman.

13. A) He is the new manager.　　　　　 B) He is away on business.

　　C) He is on sick leave.　　　　　　 D) He is retired.

14. A) Ask his parents for help.　　　　　B) Start to save money.

　　C) Borrow money from his friends.　 D) Get a loan from the bank.

Section C

Conversation 1

15. A) She had a traffic accident.　　　　B) She drove too fast.

　　C) She ran the red light.　　　　　　D) She drove drunk.

16. A) Her credit card.　　　　　　　　 B) Her passport.

　　C) Her insurance policy.　　　　　　D) Her driving license.

Conversation 2

17. A) IT engineer.　　　　　　　　　　B) Sales manager.

　　C) Computer programmer.　　　　　 D) Office secretary.

18. A) A food company.　　　　　　　　B) A shipping company.

　　C) An IT company.　　　　　　　　 D) An auto company.

19. A) Next Monday.　　　　　　　　　B) This Thursday.

　　C) This month.　　　　　　　　　　D) Next month.

Section D

Ladies and gentlemen, good afternoon. First of all, let me __20__ to you for coming to the opening ceremony of our new branch office.

This branch is the 25th office we have __21__ so far. We are very happy that we have finally opened a branch in this city. This branch, we believe, will help __22__ the local economy. And our company will in turn benefit from doing business here. We promise that we will provide the __23__ to our customers. And, of course, we need your __24__ and cooperation.

2016年12月真题

Part I　Listening Comprehension（25 minutes）

Directions: *This part is to test your listening ability. It consists of 4 sections.*

Section A

扫码获取听力音频

1. A) Sorry, he's not in.　　　　　　　　B) Here you are.

C) Try again, please. D) Thank you.

2. A) Nice to see you. B) See you later.
   C) No, I don't. D) Take care.

3. A) See you next time. B) No, thanks.
   C) You are welcome. D) Press the button here.

4. A) Over there. B) Yes, I do.
   C) I like Chinese food. D) Tomorrow morning.

5. A) Never mind. B) Certainly.
   C) Only a week. D) My pleasure.

6. A) On the Internet. B) She's very nice.
   C) By bus. D) It's far away.

7. A) We are busy. B) Take it easy.
   C) It's expensive. D) He's very kind.

Section B

8. A) Earth Day. B) Mother's Day.
   C) Father's Day. D) Thanksgiving Day.

9. A) Flight numbers. B) Bus schedules.
   C) Banking services. D) Office hours.

10. A) How to book a flight. B) Where to sign the name.
    C) When to hand in the form. D) Whom to ask for help.

11. A) From newspapers. B) From the sales department.
    C) From magazines. D) From the website.

12. A) The development plan. B) The market share.
    C) Sales of a new product. D) Costs of advertising.

13. A) When to get the orders. B) Where to obtain the price list.
    C) How to pay for the goods. D) Whom to contact.

14. A) It has over 500 employees. B) It was started in 1998.
    C) It has several branches. D) It is located in Beijing.

Section C

Conversation 1

15. A) Making a sales plan. B) Preparing an annual report.
    C) Doing a market survey. D) Writing a business letter.

16. A) It costs much less. B) It saves time.
    C) Most old people like it. D) Most young people like it.

Conversation 2

17. A) He has got a summer job. B) He has lost his job.

        C) He has just visited a park.   D) He has been to the beach.

18. A) A sales person.   B) A tour guide.
    C) A manager assistant.   D) A computer programmer.

19. A) Because the salary is too low.
    B) Because she has to travel abroad frequently.
    C) Because the company is too small.
    D) Because a tour guide has to work long hours.

Section D

Good evening, ladies and gentlemen!

First of all, I'd like to __20__ a sincere welcome to you all, the new comers of our company. As you know, our company is one of the top 50 companies in the country and has a history of more than 100 years. I think you must __21__ being a member of such a great company. But we cannot __22__ tradition alone. We need new employees with new knowledge and creative __23__.

I would like to welcome you __24__, and from today, let's begin to work together.

2017年6月真题

Part I Listening Comprehension （25 minutes）

Directions: *This part is to test your listening ability. It consists of 4 sections.*

扫码获取听力音频

Section A

1. A) Let's have a break.   B) This way, please.
   C) Don't mention it.   D) No, thank you.

2. A) On Monday.   B) John Smith.
   C) Take it easy.   D) It's too late.

3. A) How do you do?   B) It doesn't matter.
   C) Yes, please.   D) Mind your step.

4. A) I'm afraid not.   B) Never mind.
   C) Hurry up.   D) Have a good time.

5. A) Go ahead, please.   B) Yes, I am.
   C) I'd love to.   D) He's from China.

6. A) Oh, I see.   B) Here it is.
   C) It's over there.   D) Yes, of course.

7. A) Go on, please.   B) Two dollars.
   C) Sure, I will.   D) Here you are.

Section B

8. A) About 150 years ago.   B) About 120 years ago.
   C) About 115 years ago.   D) About 100 years ago.

9. A) Boring.   B) Difficult.
   C) Interesting.   D) Satisfactory.

10. A) Its location.   B) Its development.
    C) Its population.   D) Its history.

11. A) It is modern.   B) It is crowded.
    C) It is small.   D) It is quiet.

12. A) She is in poor health.   B) She failed a test.
    C) She hasn't enough money.   D) She hasn't got any offer.

13. A) Show his ID card.   B) Fill in a form.
    C) Write a report.   D) Pay some money.

14. A) She has her leg broken.   B) She fell from a bicycle.
    C) She feels a back pain.   D) She has got a headache.

Section C

Conversation 1

15. A) An apartment with a good view.
    B) An apartment of two-bedrooms.
    C) An apartment on the ground floor.
    D) An apartment with central heating.

16. A) Near a subway station.   B) Near a hotel.
    C) In the downtown.   D) In the suburbs.

Conversation 2

17. A) To have better opportunities.   B) To improve his skills.
    C) To work fewer hours.   D) To get a higher salary.

18. A) For six years.   B) For five years.
    C) For three years.   D) For two years.

19. A) A professor.   B) A manager.
    C) An engineer.   D) A designer.

Section D

First of all, on behalf of all the people from our company, I would like to say "Thank you for ___20___ us to such a wonderful party". I think the music is ___21___, the food and wine are very nice, and the people here are all very kind. Also we've enjoyed meeting and ___22___ you, sharing the comfortable time together. We have really enjoyed ourselves. I hope we will be able to maintain the __23__ and make next year another great one together. Thank you again for the party. We've really had __24__.

2017年12月真题

Part I Listening Comprehension （25 minutes）

Directions: This part is to test your listening ability. It consists of 4 sections.

扫码获取听力音频

Section A

1. A）It's over there.　　　　　　　　　B）Sorry to hear it.
   C）That's all right.　　　　　　　　　D）It's wonderful.
2. A）Here you are.　　　　　　　　　　B）It doesn't matter.
   C）Yes, of course.　　　　　　　　　 D）Thank you.
3. A）You are right.　　　　　　　　　　B）It's great.
   C）Here is my card.　　　　　　　　　D）How are you?
4. A）It's far away.　　　　　　　　　　B）Take care.
   C）On Monday.　　　　　　　　　　　D）Sure.
5. A）Yes, please.　　　　　　　　　　　B）Mind your step.
   C）OK.　　　　　　　　　　　　　　　D）Tomorrow morning.
6. A）No, thanks.　　　　　　　　　　　B）It's fine.
   C）Sorry, wrong number.　　　　　　　D）Not at all.
7. A）Certainly.　　　　　　　　　　　　B）Hurry up.
   C）Don't mention it.　　　　　　　　　D）See you later.

Section B

8. A）His health.　　　　　　　　　　　B）His exam.
   C）His presentation.　　　　　　　　 D）His interview.
9. A）A local paper.　　　　　　　　　　B）A price list.
   C）A movie ticket.　　　　　　　　　 D）A name card.
10. A）Call John.　　　　　　　　　　　B）Visit the man.
    C）Ask for help.　　　　　　　　　　D）Write a report.
11. A）It is being painted.　　　　　　　B）It has been booked.
    C）It is too expensive.　　　　　　　D）It is too small.
12. A）Satisfied.　　　　　　　　　　　　B）Confident.
    C）Excited.　　　　　　　　　　　　 D）Nervous.
13. A）He has got a job offer.　　　　　　B）He failed his final exam.
    C）He will move to a new city.　　　　D）He wants to rent an apartment.

14. A) The man will travel on business.　B) The man has taken a computer test.

C) The woman has passed a road test.　D) The woman will take a language course.

Section C

Conversation 1

15. A) To make an appointment.　B) To ask about the man's order.

C) To confirm the delivery.　D) To complain about the service.

16. A) They are user-friendly.　B) They are newly developed.

C) They are popular abroad.　D) They are of high quality.

Conversation 2

17. A) It wouldn't start.　B) It ran out of gas.

C) It was broken.　D) It was missing.

18. A) It has to be charged.　B) It is still new.

C) It is of good quality.　D) It was bought a year ago.

19. A) To recharge it.　B) To repair it.

C) To return it.　D) To sell it.

Section D

I am Mike Wang, a real estate agent. I __20__ to sell this house in just 15 days. I would love to help you buy or sell. Properties in this area are __21__. If you have considered selling your home, I would love to speak with you and help you in any way __22__. If you are currently renting a home and would like to buy one, give me a call. Home ownership has many __23__ over renting and is not as difficult as many people think. Call me today and let me help you make __24__.

2018年6月真题

Part I　Listening Comprehension　（25 minutes）

Directions: *This part is to test your listening ability. It consists of 4 sections.*

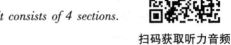

扫码获取听力音频

Section A

1. A) Oh, yes, please.　B) I like it very much.

C) Sit down, please.　D) Fine. And you?

2. A) Take care.　B) My pleasure.

C) It's great.　D) This way, please.

3. A) See you tomorrow.　B) OK, it doesn't matter.

C) Sorry, all our rooms are booked.　D) Here is the room key.

4. A) Have a nice day. B) Yes, please.
   C) Don't do it. D) Let's go.

5. A) Certainly. Is Friday OK? B) So long.
   C) Hurry up. D) Mind your steps.

6. A) Coffee, please. B) I'm fine, thank you.
   C) Your telephone number, please. D) Yes. Here you are.

7. A) Don't worry. B) All right.
   C) Good luck! D) Never mind.

Section B

8. A) By bus. B) On foot.
   C) By taxi. D) By bicycle.

9. A) A report. B) A project.
   C) A design. D) A plan.

10. A) He is an engineer. B) He is a doctor.
    C) He is a programmer. D) He is a manager.

11. A) Dealing with angry customers. B) Writing work reports.
    C) Giving presentations. D) Working on weekends.

12. A) To visit friends. B) To see a doctor.
    C) To take a holiday. D) To do business.

13. A) It had a flat tire. B) Its front window was broken.
    C) It was out of fuel. D) The engine didn't work.

14. A) Attend a job fair. B) Read newspapers.
    C) Visit the website. D) Ask her friends for help.

Section C

Conversation 1

15. A) To order a meal. B) To book a hotel room.
    C) To ask for sick leave. D) To report a case.

16. A) Her passport. B) Her smartphone.
    C) Her watch. D) Her computer.

Conversation 2

17. A) She has coughed a lot. B) She has a high fever.
    C) She has got a pain in the stomach. D) She has got a bad cold.

18. A) This morning. B) This afternoon.
    C) Last night. D) Yesterday.

19. A) Take her blood pressure. B) Give her some medicine.
    C) Perform an operation on her at once. D) Send her to the emergency room.

Section D

Volunteers are our heart and soul. Please come and help us build homes for __20__ low-income families. There is no experience needed and we supply the __21__. Just volunteer for a day. It's fun, rewarding and you can learn some __22__! If building isn't your thing, come and volunteer for one of our events or __23__. You must be __24__ 14 years of age to volunteer and those 15 years and under must come with a parent.

Come and sign up now to volunteer your time.

2018年12月真题

Part I Listening Comprehension (25 minutes)

Directions: This part is to test your listening ability. It consists of 4 sections.

扫码获取听力音频

Section A

1. A) Everything's OK.   B) I think so.
   C) It's a good idea.   D) I'll do that.

2. A) Sorry to hear that.   B) Hurry up.
   C) You are so nice.   D) Glad to meet you.

3. A) At 8:00 a.m.   B) You are right.
   C) Here you are.   D) I'd like to.

4. A) Have a good time.   B) It's fine.
   C) Take care.   D) Yes, it is.

5. A) Tomorrow morning.   B) It's not far away.
   C) It's over there.   D) Go ahead.

6. A) My pleasure.   B) Very good.
   C) Enjoy yourself.   D) How do you do?

7. A) Mind your steps.   B) Yes, please.
   C) See you later.   D) Nice to see you.

Section B

8. A) A sales meeting.   B) A New Year's Party.
   C) A product advertisement.   D) A new project.

9. A) From a newspaper.   B) From a TV ad.
   C) From a website.   D) From a friend.

10. A) A college professor.   B) A financial expert.
    C) A department manager.   D) A fashion designer.

11. A) Working on a report.　　　　　　　B) Giving a lecture.
    C) Traveling on business.　　　　　　D) Meeting with a customer.
12. A) He missed the bus.　　　　　　　　B) He was sick.
    C) He forgot the meeting time.　　　D) He came to the wrong room.
13. A) A sports event.　　　　　　　　　　B) A traffic accident.
    C) A forest fire.　　　　　　　　　　　D) Road repairs.
14. A) Good.　　　　　　　　　　　　　　　B) Difficult.
    C) Challenging.　　　　　　　　　　　　D) Boring.

Section C

Conversation 1

15. A) Looking for a job.　　　　　　　　B) Traveling abroad.
    C) Writing a term paper.　　　　　　D) Working on a project.
16. A) Do some shopping.　　　　　　　　B) Watch a football match.
    C) Go fishing.　　　　　　　　　　　　D) Visit their friends.

Conversation 2

17. A) Sales Manager.　　　　　　　　　　B) Marketing Manager.
    C) Project Manager.　　　　　　　　　D) Research Manager.
18. A) Next Tuesday.　　　　　　　　　　　B) Next Wednesday.
    C) Next Thursday.　　　　　　　　　　D) Next Friday.
19. A) By bicycle.　　　　　　　　　　　　B) By car.
    C) By bus.　　　　　　　　　　　　　　D) By subway.

Section D

When I need gas for my car, I pull into a gas station right around the corner from my house and use my gas card. Years ago, full-service gas stations were very __20__. However, things have changed. Now, most gas stations are self-service centers. Personally, I __21__ fill the car up with gas every time I stop. I generally __22__, but more and more gas stations accept credit cards. As gas prices are __23__, I'm now thinking about buying a more fuel-efficient vehicle or just __24__ to work.

2019年6月真题

Part I Listening Comprehension (25 minutes)

Directions: *This part is to test your listening ability. It consists of 4 sections.*

Section A

扫码获取听力音频

1. A) Let's go now.　　　　　　　　　　　B) Don't mention it.

C) Sit down, please.   D) Yes, I am.
2. A) Yes, it is.   B) All right.
   C) Sure, I will.   D) Never mind.
3. A) Nice.   B) Sure.
   C) I think so.   D) Yes, please.
4. A) Take it easy.   B) Not at all.
   C) No, thank you.   D) See you later.
5. A) No problem.   B) Go ahead.
   C) Here you are.   D) Take care.
6. A) Glad to meet you.   B) Mind your head.
   C) Very nice.   D) Quite convenient.
7. A) See you again.   B) Don't be late.
   C) Don't worry.   D) I'd love to.

Section B

8. A) She is an operator.   B) She is a doctor.
   C) She is a nurse.   D) She is a driver.
9. A) To go to study abroad.   B) To pay for her debt.
   C) To move to another city.   D) To raise money for her business.
10. A) A new product design.   B) After-sales service.
    C) The sales plan.   D) The pay raise.
11. A) See a doctor.   B) Place an order.
    C) Book a ticket.   D) Reserve a room.
12. A) Planning a budget.   B) Doing an experiment.
    C) Discussing a new design.   D) Having an interview.
13. A) Online.   B) In a job fair.
    C) From a magazine.   D) On TV.
14. A) She is over the speed limit.   B) She is smoking while driving.
    C) She is making a phone call.   D) She is on the wrong way.

Section C

Conversation 1

15. A) To apply for a job.   B) To ask for leave.
    C) To cancel an appointment.   D) To change an order.
16. A) 180.   B) 118.
    C) 100.   D) 80.

Conversation 2

17. A) Sports shoes.   B) Sun glasses.

C) A sun hat. D) A T-shirt.

18. A) He is a regular customer. B) He is one of her friends.
    C) He is the manager of the store. D) He is a new customer of the store.

19. A) 300 dollars. B) 240 dollars.
    C) 200 dollars. D) 140 dollars.

Section D

Thank you very much for meeting with me yesterday about our project. I really appreciate your help. And we'll take your suggestions into consideration when we __20__ for the next year. It was __21__ to have someone like you who has had experience with similar projects. I appreciate your taking the time out of your busy schedule to __22__ me. I'll __23__ to send you a follow-up when this project is completed. Please let me know if I can __24__ the favor and when.

2019 年 12 月真题

Part I Listening Comprehension （25 minutes）

扫码获取听力音频

Directions: *This part is to test your listening ability. It consists of 4 sections.*

Section A

1. A) Sure. B) Take care.
   C) Mind your step. D) It's kind of you.

2. A) Never mind. B) You're welcome.
   C) OK. D) Don't mention it.

3. A) None of your business. B) Here you are.
   C) I'm fine. D) It doesn't matter.

4. A) Not at all. B) It's over there.
   C) This way, please. D) No problem.

5. A) All right. B) Glad to see you.
   C) Go along the street. D) Take it easy.

6. A) Yes, please. B) No idea.
   C) Yes, I can. D) Good luck.

7. A) On foot. B) On Sunday.
   C) By bus. D) In cash.

Section B

8. A) A flight. B) A table.
   C) A meeting room. D) A movie ticket.

9. A) He has been promoted.　　　　　　　B) He has passed the road test.
　　C) He has bought a new car.　　　　　　D) He has got a job offer.
10. A) To visit his friend.　　　　　　　　　B) To see off a customer.
　　C) To meet his parents.　　　　　　　　D) To pick up his luggage.
11. A) It was too crowded.　　　　　　　　B) It was too far away.
　　C) It was too large.　　　　　　　　　　D) It was too noisy.
12. A) Serious.　　　　　　　　　　　　　　B) Friendly.
　　C) Hard-working.　　　　　　　　　　　D) Open-minded.
13. A) Make a complaint.　　　　　　　　　B) Apply for a job.
　　C) Place an order.　　　　　　　　　　　D) See a doctor.
14. A) Sign a contract.　　　　　　　　　　 B) Tour the city.
　　C) Meet new clients.　　　　　　　　　 D) See his friends.

Section C

Conversation 1

15. A) Computer science.　　　　　　　　　B) Big data in marketing.
　　C) The importance of education.　　　　D) The latest software.
16. A) He will be away on business.　　　　 B) He will meet his lawyer.
　　C) He has been busy with his paper.　　D) He will pay a visit to his parents.

Conversation 2

17. A) It can't start.　　　　　　　　　　　　B) Its keyboard doesn't work.
　　C) Its screen is broken.　　　　　　　　D) It gives no sound.
18. A) Three days ago.　　　　　　　　　　B) Six days ago.
　　C) A month ago.　　　　　　　　　　　D) Three months ago.
19. A) His ID card.　　　　　　　　　　　　B) His business card.
　　C) His receipt.　　　　　　　　　　　　D) His address.

Section D

　　I should say that teaching English in China is a real job, and the schools ___20___ you to be professional and you have to ___21___. If you don't meet their requirements, it is easy to get fired. But with ___22___ and the right attitude, it will be a very good experience where you will ___23___ about China and yourself! I am so happy that I took this ___24___ when I had it, and the memories will be with me for the rest of my life.

第三章 词汇与结构

第一节 题型综述

高等学校英语应用能力考试 B 级的第二部分为"词汇与结构",主要测试考生运用词语和语法知识的能力,测试范围限于《基本要求》中的"词汇表"B 级(2 500 词)和"语法结构表"所规定的全部内容。《基本要求》提到,通过高职高专教育英语课程的学习,学生在词汇和语法上应该达到下列要求。

1.词汇

认知 2 500 个英语单词(包括入学时要求掌握的 1 000 个词)以及由这些词构成的常用词组,对其中 1 500 个左右的单词能正确拼写、英汉互译。

2.语法

掌握基本的英语语法规则,在听、说、读、写、译中能正确运用所学语法知识。

词汇与结构部分的分值占总分的 15%,测试时间为 10 分钟。题型分为选择题(Section A)和填空题(Section B)。选择题共 10 题,占 10%;填空题共 5 题,占 5%。词汇部分主要考查同义词和近义词辨析、固定搭配、词性转换等;结构部分主要考查非谓语动词、时态、语态、从句、虚拟语气、主谓一致、强调句型等。

第二节 考点归纳

一、Section A

根据 2015—2019 年的 10 次考试的真题,这部分主要考查的知识点分布见表 3.1。

表 3.1 2015—2019 年 Section A 考查知识点分布情况

考查知识点	时间									
	2015-6	2015-12	2016-6	2016-12	2017-6	2017-12	2018-6	2018-12	2019-6	2019-12
时态与语态	1		1		1	1	1	1		
词汇/词组辨析	3	3	5	5	4	4	5	5	1	3
从句	1	2	1	1	2	1	1	2	2	1
介词(词组)		2	1	1	1	1	1	1	1	
分词	1				1			1	1	
连词	2	2	1			2	1		1	1
固定搭配	2	1		2	1	1			3	3
形容词			1							
副词					1				1	1
虚拟语气							1			

注:数字表示考查的次数。

这部分考查的重点是词汇或词组辨析,从句、介词(词组)、连词等也是常考的知识点。词汇或词组辨析,结合语境,主要考查从固定搭配上去辨析。从句、连词主要考查句子之间的逻辑关系。基于此,在备考过程中,一方面考生要扩大词汇量,加强对单词或者词组意义及用法的深度理解,譬如通过查看单词或词组的英语释义,体会单词或词组在具体语境中的使用。另一方面,考生要注意在句子或段落中去理解、识记单词和词汇的意义和用法,在语境中去体会句子与句子、段落与段落之间的逻辑关系。

二、Section B

Section B 的词形转换部分主要考查实词的用法,主要集中在动词、名词、形容词和副词四大词类上,考查内容包括动词的时态及语态变化、动词转名词、形容词转副词、形容词转名词、形容词比较级、固定搭配等。

第三节 技巧点拨

《基本要求》的语法部分要求考生要掌握基本的英语语法规则,在听、说、读、写、译中能正确运用所学语法知识。我们对高等学校英语应用能力考试 B 级中常考的一些语法要点进行梳理,以满足备考所需。

一、动词的时态与语态

严格来说,我们所称的时态包括"时"或者"时"与"体"的结合。英语中的"时"主要有两种:现在时和过去时;"体"一般包括进行体和完成体。通过两两组配,我们就可以推演出英语中常见的几种时态,见表3.2。

表3.2 英语常见的时态

体	时	
	现在	过去
进行	现在进行	过去进行
完成	现在完成	过去完成

常见的几种时态的用法如下所示。

1．一般现在时

一般现在时主要表示习惯性的行为或动作。如:

He goes to work by bus every day. 他每天乘公交车去上班。

How often do you wash your hair? 你多久洗一次头发?

2．一般过去时

一般过去时主要用于表示以下几种情况。

① 在过去某一确定时间完成了的行为或动作。如:

He went to work by bike yesterday. 他昨天骑自行车上班的。

② 时间不确定,又可以分为两种情况。

一是动作持续了一段时间,但现在已经结束。如:

He worked in that bank for four years. 他在那家银行工作了四年。(现在已不在那家银行工作了)

二是在过去一段时间的某一刻发生的行为或动作,现在已经结束了。如:

Did you ever hear him sing? 你曾听过他唱歌吗?

③ 表示过去的习惯性动作。如:

He always carried an umbrella. 他总是拿着一把伞。

3．现在进行时

① 表示现在正在发生的动作或行为。如:

What's the baby doing? 小宝宝在干什么?

He's tearing up the drawing. 他在撕画。

② 表示现阶段正在发生的事情,但不一定是在说话的时候。如:

He is teaching French and learning Chinese. 他在教法语和学中文。

4．过去进行时

① 表示过去持续了一段时间的动作或行为,但确切的时间界限不清楚或者不重要。如:

He was repairing his bike. 他在修理自行车。

••••——•••• (——表示过去进行时所表示的动作或行为)

② 跟表示时间点的状语连用,表示在那个时间点之前发生,并有可能在那个时间点之

后还会持续的动作或行为。如：

At eight he was having breakfast. 八点的时候他正在吃早饭。

③ 当过去进行时跟过去时连用时,过去进行时表示的动作或行为在过去时所表示的动作或行为之前发生,并有可能在它之后还会继续。如：

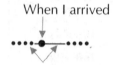

Tom was talking on the phone.

5. 现在完成时

现在完成时是考生感到难以把握的一个时态,一方面是因为汉语中没有相应的表达形式,另一方面是因为现在完成时所表示的事件发生在过去,但跟现在有关联,考生经常容易将它跟一般过去时混淆。我们在这里主要围绕现在完成时的形式和意义,以及它跟一般过去时的差别来展开说明。

(1) 现在完成时的形式：has/have + done

(2) 现在完成时的意义

现在完成时的时间概念有时是不明确的。我们关心的是现存的结果,或者过去发生的事对现在的影响。因此,现在完成时可以看作回顾到过去的现在时。

在英语中,现在完成时有以下两种用法。

① 表示始于过去并持续到现在(也许还会持续下去)的动作。其中动词一般是持续性动词,如 keep、live、read、write、walk、run、go 等。如：

I saw Sophia in May and I haven't seen her since. 我 5 月份见过索菲亚,此后我就没有再见过她了。(从 5 月份往后就没见过索菲亚,至今也没见到过)

I have smoked since I left school. 我离开学校后就一直在抽烟。

② 表示在过去不确定的时间里发生过或未发生过的动作,该动作与现在有某种联系。如：

I have read the instructions but I don't understand them. 我看过说明书,但是我没看懂。(看说明书是过去的动作,没看懂是现在的结果)

The lift has broken down. 电梯坏了。(结果:我们得走楼梯)

(3) 一般过去时与现在完成时的区别

① 一般过去时的时间概念是明确的；现在完成时的时间概念有时是不明确的。如：

I haven't seen him this morning. 我今天上午没见过他。(直到此刻还没见过他,此刻还是上午)

I didn't see him this morning. 我今天上午没有见到他。(上午已经过去了)

② 一般过去时表示的动作发生在过去,该动作已经结束；现在完成时表示的动作还在延续。如：

I've lived here for five years. 我在这里住了 5 年了。(我仍然住在这里)

I lived here for five years. 我在这里住过 5 年。(我现在不住在这里了)

如果用时间轴来表示,如下所示:

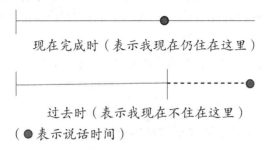

(●表示说话时间)

6. 过去完成时

过去完成时作为与现在完成时相对应的过去形式,表示在过去说话时已经发生的动作或行为。

① 动作或行为在说话的时候或者之前停止了。如:

By the end of last term, we had learned 3,000 new words. 到上学期期末,我们已经学了 3 000 个新单词。

② 动作或行为一直持续到说话的时候。如:

He said he had worked in that factory since 1990. 他说自从 1990 年以来他就在那家工厂工作。

③ 表示"过去的过去"。如:

He had served in the army for ten years; then he retired and married. His children were now at school. 他在部队服役了十年,然后就退役了,结婚了。他的孩子现在在上学。

它们之间的区别图示如下:

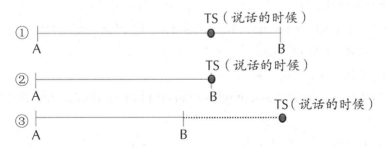

(●表示说话的时候,A 表示动作开始的时间,B 表示动作结束的时间)

① 表示动作或行为持续到说话的时候,还有可能会继续持续下去;
② 表示动作或行为在说话的时候或者正好在说话之前停止了;
③ 表示动作或行为在说话之前已经停止了,也就是"过去的过去"。

二、定语从句

定语从句所修饰的名词或者名词短语被称为先行词。定语从句位于先行词之后,起到修饰和限定先行词的作用。定语从句分为限定性定语从句和非限定性定语从句。

(一) 限定性定语从句

限定性定语从句通过对先行词进行描述,将其与同类的其他名词区别开来。如:
The man who told me this refused to give his name. 告诉我这件事的那个人拒绝说出他的名字。

who told me this 是定语从句,如果将它省去,我们就不知道谈论的是哪个人了。

1. 关系代词

限定性定语从句需要关系代词来引导。按照先行词是物还是人,关系代词在定语从句中作主语、宾语或者表示所属关系,关系代词的分类见表3.3。

表3.3 限定性定语从句的关系代词的分类

	作主语	作宾语	表示所属关系
先行词为人	who	whom/who	whose
	that	that	
先行词为物	which	which	whose/of which
	that	that	

(1) 先行词为人

① 关系代词在句中作主语。如:
Is he the man who wants to see you? 他就是想见你的人吗?(who 在从句中作主语)
在 all、everyone、everybody、no one、nobody 和 those 之后,也可以用 that。如:
Everyone who/that knew him liked him. 知道他的人都喜欢他。

② 关系代词在句中作宾语。如:
He is the man who/whom/that I saw yesterday. 他就是我昨天见的那个人。(who/whom/that 在从句中作宾语)
The friend with whom I was traveling spoke French. 跟我一起旅行的朋友说法语。(介词之后,关系代词用 whom 或 that)

③ 关系代词表示所属关系。如:
They rushed over to help the man whose car had broken down. 那人的车坏了,大家都跑过去帮忙。

(2) 先行词为物

① 关系代词在句中作主语。如:
This is the picture which/that caused such a sensation. 这就是那幅引起轰动的画。

② 关系代词在句中作宾语。如:
This is the photo that/which I took. 这是我拍的照片。
This is the pan in which I boiled the milk. 这是我煮了牛奶的锅。
在 all、everything、little、much、none、no 和 no 组成的复合词,以及最高级之后,一般用 that 或者省略关系代词,不用 which。如:
This is the best hotel (that) I know. 这是我所知道的最好的宾馆。

③ 关系代词表示所属关系。如：

Please pass me the book whose cover is green. = Please pass me the book the cover of which is green. 请递给我那本绿皮的书。

2．关系副词：when, where, why

关系副词可以看作由"介词＋关系代词"转化而来。

（1）when = in/on which（指时间）

the year when (= in which) he was born

the day when (= on which) they arrived

（2）where = in/at which（指地点）

the hotel where (= in/at which) they were staying

（3）why = for which（指原因）

The reason why (= for which) he refused is ...

（二）非限定性定语从句

非限定性定语从句位于一个确定的名词之后，它们不对名词进行定义，只是为其补充一些信息。与限定性定语从句不同，它在句中并不是必不可少的，即使被省略也不会对句子意思的理解带来混乱。在句中，逗号将它跟先行词隔开。

1．关系代词

非限定性定语从句的关系代词与限定性定语从句的关系代词略有不同，that 不能用于非限定性定语从句中。非限定性定语从句的关系代词的分类见表3.4。

表 3.4　非限定性定语从句的关系代词的分类

	作主语	作宾语	表示所属关系
先行词为人	who	whom/who	whose
先行词为物	which	which	whose/of which

（1）先行词为人

① 关系代词作主语。如：

Peter, who had been driving all day, suggested stopping at the next town. 彼得开了一天的车，建议到下一个城镇停一停。

② 关系代词作宾语。如：

Peter, whom everyone suspected, turned out to be innocent. 大家都怀疑彼得，但最后证明他是无辜的。

Mr. Jones, for whom I was working, was very generous about overtime payments. 我为琼斯先生工作，他对加班费很慷慨。

③ 表示所属关系。如：

This is George, whose class you will be taking. 这是乔治，你们将会上他的课。

（2）先行词为物

① 关系代词作主语。如：

The 8:15 train, which is usually very punctual, was late today. 8 点 15 分的火车, 一向非常准时, 今天晚点了。

② 关系代词作宾语。如:

Those books, which you can get at any bookshop, will give you all the information you need. 这些书你可以在任何一家书店买到, 可以提供给你所需要的任何信息。

His house, for which he paid $100,000, is now worth $500,000. 他花了 10 万美元买的房子, 现在值 50 万美元了。

③ 表示所属关系。如:

The car, whose handbrake wasn't reliable, began to slide backwards. 这辆车的刹车不灵, 车开始向后滑了。

④ which 可以指代整个句子。如:

The clock struck thirteen, which made everyone laugh. 钟敲了 13 下, 大家都笑了。

三、主动语态与被动语态

1. 被动语态的构成

主动语态与被动语态是就动词的形式而言的。主动语态的被动语态形式主要是将"to be"转变成跟主动语态动词同样的时态, 然后再加上过去分词。

在主动句中, 动词的主语是执行动作的人或物。如:

John cooked the food last night. 约翰昨天晚上做了饭。

在被动句中, 动作是对主语执行的。主动动词的主语变成被动动词的"施事者", 在句中一般不出现。如果要提到"施事者", 前面要用介词 by, 置于句末。如:

The food was cooked last night. 饭是昨天晚上做的。

My grandfather planted this tree. →This tree was planted by my grandfather. 这棵树是我爷爷种的。

现在时、过去时、完成时的被动形式示例如表 3.5 所示。

表 3.5 被动语态

时态	主动语态	被动语态
现在时	We keep the butter here. 我们把黄油放在这里。	The butter was kept here. 黄油被放在这里。
过去时	They broke the window. 他们打破了窗子。	The window was broken. 窗子被打破了。
完成时	People have seen wolves in the streets. 人们在街上看到过狼。	Wolves have been seen in the streets. 狼曾在街上被看到过。

2. 被动语态的主要用法

① 动作的执行者很清楚, 无须指出。如:

The streets are swept every day. 街道每天都有人扫。

The rubbish hasn't been collected. 垃圾还没被收走。

② 不知道、不确切地知道, 或者忘了是谁做了某事。如:

The minister was murdered. 部长被谋杀了。
My car has been moved! 我的车被挪动过!
③ 对动作更感兴趣,而不关心谁做了某事。如:
The house next door has been bought (by Mr. Jones). 隔壁房子被人买走了。
④ 出于心理原因。
说话的人用被动语态主要是为一些不愉快的事情开脱责任。如:
Employer: Overtime rates are being reduced/will have to be reduced. 加班费要扣减。
如果是愉快的事情,一般会用主动语态。如:
We are going to increase overtime rates. 我们准备增加加班工资。
⑤ 用于"have + 宾语 + 过去分词"结构。如:
Do you have your windows cleaned every month? 你们每个月都要请人打扫窗户吗?

四、现在分词与过去分词

1. 现在分词

(1) 形式

动词原形 + -ing,如:working, loving, sitting。

(2) 用法

① 组合成进行时。如:

You've been dreaming. 你一直在做梦。

② 作形容词。如:

running water 自来水

leaking pipes 漏油管道

③ 用于"have + 宾语"结构之后。如:

I won't have him cleaning his bike in the kitchen. 我不会让他在厨房里清洗自行车的。

④ 用在间接引语中起补充说明作用。如:

He told me to start early, reminding me that the roads would be crowded. 他告诉我早点出发,还提醒我路上会堵车。

⑤ 用于感官动词,如 see、hear、feel、smell、listen to、notice、watch 等之后。如:

Didn't you hear the clock striking? 你难道没听到钟声吗?

I watched them rehearsing the play. 我看到他们在那里排演戏剧。

⑥ 替代"主语 + 动词主动形式"。如:

He opened a drawer and took out a diary. = Opening a drawer, he took out a diary. 打开抽屉,他拿出一本日记本。

2. 过去分词

(1) 主动形式:having + 过去分词

主要用于强调第一个动作完成之后,第二个动作才开始。一般指两个动作之间有间隔或者第一个动词要经过一段时间。如：

Having failed twice, he didn't want to try again. 失败过两次,他再也不想去试了。

Having been his own boss for such a long time, he found it hard to accept orders from another. 当了这么长时间的老板,他很难接受别人的命令。

(2) 被动形式:动词原形 + -ed 或 + -d

① 作形容词。如：

stolen money 被偷的钱

a written report 书面报告

fallen leaves 落叶

② 替代"主语 + 动词被动形式"。如：

She enters. She is accompanied by her mother. = She enters, accompanied by her mother. 她在母亲的陪同下走了进来。

五、状语从句

1. 原因状语从句

原因状语从句一般回答"Why …?"的问题,并由 because、as、seeing(that)和 since 来引导。如：

As/Because/Since you can't type the letter yourself, you'll have to ask Susan to do it for you. 既然你自己不能用打字机打这封信,那你就请苏珊替你打吧。

As/Because/Since it was too dark to go on, we camped there. 由于天色太晚难以继续,我们就在那里露营了。

2. 结果状语从句

结果状语从句描述结果,可由"so + 形容词"后面的 that 来引导,回答如"How (quick) …?"的问题。如：

His reactions are so quick (that) no one can match him. 他的反应如此敏捷(以至于)无人比得上他。

结果状语从句也可由"so + 副词"后面的 that 来引导,回答如"How (quickly) …?"的问题。如：

He reacts so quickly (that) no one can match him. 他反应如此敏捷(以至于)无人比得上他。

结果状语从句也可由"such (a) + 名词(或形容词 + 名词)"后面的 that 来引导,回答如"What's … like?"的问题。如：

They are such wonderful players (that) no one can beat them. 他们都是出色的运动员,没有人能战胜他们。

3. 让步状语从句

让步状语从句使句子具有对比的因素,因此有时也被称为对比从句。它们一般由

although、considering(that)(就……而论,考虑到)、though、even though(即使)、even if(即使)、no matter how(不管如何)等连词引导。如:

Although/Though/Even though/Even if you don't like him, you can still be polite. 尽管/即使你不喜欢他,你还是要有礼貌。

No matter what you do, don't touch this switch. 不管你干什么,都不要碰这个开关。

Patient as he was, he had no intention of waiting for three hours. 尽管他很有耐心,但他也无意等三个小时。

4. 目的状语从句

目的状语从句回答"What ... for?"及"For what purposes ...?"的问题,可由 so that(以便)、in order that(以便)、in case(以免)、lest(免得)、for fear(that)等连词来引导。

当主句中的动词为现在时、现在完成时或将来时时,so that 和 in order that 后面可以跟 may、can 或 will。so that 比 in order that 用得更为普遍。如:

I've arrived early so that/in order that I may/can/will get a good view of the procession. 我到得很早,以便我可以/能/会好好看看那行进的队伍。

当主句中的动词为一般过去时、过去进行时或过去完成时时,so that 和 in order that 后面跟 should、could、might 或 would。如:

I arrived early so that/in order that I should/could/might/would get a good view of the procession. 我到得很早,以便我可以/能/会好好看看那行进的队伍。

在目的状语从句中,我们任何时候都可以用 in order that 来代替 so that;而在结果状语从句中则不可以。如:

We arrived early so that (in order that) we could/should/might/would get good seats. 我们到得早,以便找到好座位。(我们是为了找到好座位而早到的)

We arrived early, so that we got good seats. 我们到得早,因此我们找到了好座位。(我们找到了好座位是到得早的结果)

5. 比较状语从句

比较状语从句经常回答"How ...?"的问题,后面跟着或暗含着 in relation to 或 compared with。(如: How quick is he in relation to/compared with ...? 较之于……他有多快?)

比较状语从句包括"as + 形容词 + as"(和……一样)、"as + 副词 + as"(和……一样)、"not so/as ... as"(和……不一样)、"-er than"(比……更)、"more ... than"(比……更多)、"less ... than"(比……更少)、"the ... the ..."(越……,越……)等结构。

当句子里两个动词相同,时态也一样时,第二个动词可以被省略,比较状语从句就成了含蓄的从句。如:

He answers as quickly as his sister (does). 他回答得和他妹妹一样快。

His sister is quicker than he (is). 他妹妹比他敏捷。

He moves more slowly than his sister (does). 他行动起来比他妹妹慢。

The more you practise, the better you get. 你练得越多,效果越好。

六、名词从句

试比较：

He told me about the cancellation of the match. 他告诉了我关于比赛取消的事。

He told me that the match had been canceled. 他告诉我比赛取消了。

cancellation 是名词,that the match had been canceled 是从句(具有限定动词)。整个从句所起的作用相当于一个名词,因而被称为名词从句。

像任何名词一样,名词从句也可作动词的主语,但更多被用作动词的宾语,或用作系动词 be 或其他动词如 seem 和 appear 的补语。如：

I know that the match will be canceled. 我知道比赛将被取消。(作宾语)

That the match will be canceled is now certain. 比赛将被取消现在是确定无疑的了。(作 be 的主语)

从陈述句中引出的名词从句一般为"that 从句"(有时为"what 从句"),但连词 that 常被省略。名词从句可以与其他从句连接在一起,相当于一个名词。

(1) 作主语

Money doesn't grow on trees. This should be obvious. 金钱不会从树上长出来。这该是显而易见的。

That money doesn't grow on trees should be obvious. 金钱不能从树上长出来应该是显而易见的。

我们倾向于避免使用这种结构,尽量用 it 开头,后接 be、seem 等。如：

It is obvious (that) money doesn't grow on trees. 显而易见,金钱是不会从树上长出来的。

(2) 作动词宾语

名词从句作动词宾语时,前面的 that 常被省略,特别是在非正式语体中。如：

Everybody knows (that) money doesn't grow on trees. 众所周知,金钱是不会从树上长出来的。

(3) 同位语从句

同位语从句可跟在 the fact that 等结构的后面。使用诸如 the fact that 和 the idea that 的说法可以避免出现用 that 开头造句的笨拙结构。如：

The fact that his proposal makes sense should be recognized. 应当承认他的建议是有道理的。

I heard the news that our team had won. 我听到了我们队获胜的消息。

可以跟同位语从句的名词通常有 news、idea、fact、promise、question、doubt、thought、hope、message、suggestion、word、possibility、decision 等。如：

I've come from Mr. Wang with a message that he won't be able to see you this afternoon. 我从王先生那里来,他让我告诉你他今天下午不能来看你了。

英语中引导同位语从句的通常有连词 that、whether,连接代词 what、who,以及连接副词

how、when、where 等。但 if 不能引导同位语从句。如：

He must answer the question whether he agrees with it or not. 他必须回答他是否同意这样一个问题。

（4）跟在描写感情的形容词之后

I'm afraid (that) we've sold out of tickets. 对不起,我们的票已经卖光了。

I'm pretty sure (that) he'll agree. 他会同意的,对此我相当有把握。

七、虚拟语气

英语中的语气分为陈述语气、祈使语气、虚拟语气、疑问语气和感叹语气五类。虚拟语气是说话者用来表示假设或难以实现的情况,所陈述的是一个条件,不一定是事实,甚至完全与事实相反。此外需要表达主观愿望或某种强烈的感情时,我们也可用虚拟语气。虚拟语气通过谓语动词的特殊形式来表示。

1. were 型虚拟语气

（1）用于非真实性条件句中

① 对现在或将来的虚拟

$\begin{cases} \text{if 从句:过去时,表示需要具备的条件} \\ \text{主句:would/should,表示可能的结果} \end{cases}$

If I was taller, I would become a policeman. 如果我个子再高一点,我就当警察了。

If you took a taxi, you'd get there quicker. 如果你叫一辆出租车,你就会快点儿到那儿。

② 对过去的虚拟

$\begin{cases} \text{if 从句:过去完成时,表示想象的条件} \\ \text{主句:would have/should have,表示想象的结果} \end{cases}$

If it had rained, we would have stayed at home. 要是下雨,我们就会待在家里了。

If I had not got married, I would still have been living abroad. 如果我没结婚,我就仍然住在国外。

（2）用于 wish/as if/as though/would rather 后的从句中

从句中虚拟语气的时态参照非真实性条件从句的变化,如果是对现在或将来情况的虚拟,从句的谓语动词用过去时;如果是对过去情况的虚拟,从句的谓语动词用过去完成时。见表 3.6。

表 3.6 虚拟语气的时态

wish*/as if/as though/would rather 虚拟情况	从句谓语动词的时态
与现在事实相反	did (were)
与过去事实相反	had done
与将来事实相反	did (were)

注:wish 表示与将来事实相反时,从句谓语动词也用"should/would/could + do"的形式,其实也是 did (were)

的形式,情态动词采用过去时。

I wish I knew his address. 我希望我知道他的地址。

I wish (that) I hadn't spent so much money. = I'm sorry I spent so much money. 我希望我没花那么多钱就好了。

He behaves as if he owned the place. 他表现得好像这地方为他所有似的。

He talks about Rome as though he had been there himself. 他谈起罗马好像他亲自去过一样。

Ann wants to tell Tom, but I'd rather she didn't (tell him). 安想告诉汤姆,但我宁愿她不告诉他。

I'd rather you had come yesterday. 我倒希望你昨天来了。

当 would rather 后从句中的主语跟句子主语不一致时,从句的谓语动词采用虚拟语气。如果主句的主语与从句的主语一致,would rather 后接动词原形。如:

I would rather invest time in my daughter than in the kitchen. 我宁愿把时间花在我女儿身上也不愿花在厨房里。

2. be 型虚拟语气

从句中的谓语动词用"should + do"结构时,should 可被省略,所以我们称这种从句为 be 型宾语从句。

(1) 用于表示建议、要求、命令等动词或名词后的名词从句中

这类动词主要有 suggest、advise、propose、recommend、demand、require、request、ask、order、command、decide、prefer、urge 等,以及它们相应的名词,包括 suggestion、advice、proposal、recommendation、demand、requirement、request、order、decision、desire 等。如:

He suggested that we should leave early. 他建议我们早点动身。

The doctor advised that he change his job. 医生劝他换工作。

I suggest that we (should) have lunch right now. 我建议我们现在就吃午饭。

The situation required that he be present. 这种情形需要他在场。

He agreed with my suggestion that we should change the date. 他同意我提出的更改日期的建议。

(2) 用于"It is + 形容词 + that"结构中

第一,表示情绪、观点的形容词或名词也要用虚拟语气,包括 necessary、important、impossible、natural、strange、surprising 等。在"It is + 形容词 + that + 主语从句"结构中,从句的谓语动词常用"should + 原形",且 should 的省略要视情况而定。如:

Do you think it is necessary that he (should) apply for the position? 你认为他有必要应聘那个职位吗?(should 表示"建议"的语气,可省略)

It is strange that such a person should be our friend. 奇怪的是这样一个人会成为我们的朋友。(should 表示"竟然"的语气,不可省略)

第二,礼貌委婉地表达情况的紧迫性可用虚拟语气。表示紧迫性的形容词包括

advisable、best、critical、desirable、essential、imperative、important、necessary、urgent、vital 等。如：

It's vital that you make a decision right now. 你立刻就做决定是至关重要的。

It is essential that we tackle this thorny problem. 我们很有必要处理这个棘手问题。

八、词形转换

做词形转换题时考生需要考虑两点：一是形式，二是意义。考生要对句子进行语法分析，判断需要转换的单词在句中充当什么成分以及需要被转换成何种词性；同时还需要结合上下文语义，判断转换的单词需要采用何种语法形式。

1．动词

动词主要涉及时态和语态、动名词和固定搭配。

例 1 I was told that their project（complete）_____ last week as scheduled.

【解析】从句缺少谓语动词，据此判断 complete 在句中作谓语。状语 last week 提示 complete 要用过去时。同时，project 与 complete 之间是动宾关系，所以 complete 还要被转换成被动语态。正确答案就是 was completed。

例 2 We are pleased to have you visit us and look forward to（meet）_____ you next week.

【解析】look forward to 表示"期待，期盼"，to 是介词，后面的动词要变成动名词。正确答案是 meeting。

例 3 The designers from our firm are ready（assist）_____ you throughout the whole process.

【解析】be ready to do sth. 是固定搭配，后接动词原形，所以 assist 要变成动词不定式 to assist。

例 4 Photography has changed our way of（view）_____ the world.

【解析】介词后常接名词或者动名词构成介宾结构，由于 view 后接了宾语 the world，view 要变成动名词形式 viewing。

2．名词

名词主要用于两种情况：一是用于介词之后，二是用于"a/the+（形容词）+名词"结构。

例 5 The project is still under（discuss）_____, and practical solutions are expected to be found.

【解析】由空格前的介词 under 可知，空格处需要填名词，以组成介宾结构。此处空格处要填 discussion。

例 6 It is possible that we reach a long-term（agree）_____ with the company.

【解析】根据"a+形容词+名词"结构可以判断空格处需要填一个名词，agree 相应地要变成 agreement。

此外，动词变名词主要通过加后缀的方式，常见的名词后缀有四种：一是"-ment"，如：development、movement、government；二是"-ion"，如：suggestion、discussion、education；三是"-al"，如：proposal、arrival；四是"-ing"，如：swimming、reading。

3. 形容词

形容词主要用于两种结构中：一是"连系动词+形容词"，二是"(much/far)+形容词比较级+than"结构。

例7 As a newcomer, almost everything in the company seems to be (interest)_____ to me.

【解析】be 在句中充当连系动词，后面要接形容词，interest 相应地要变成形容词 interesting。

例8 It seems to me that his solution is much (effective)_____ than mine.

【解析】根据 than 可以判断，这是一个比较句，空格处要填比较级，由于从句的谓语动词是连系动词 be，空格处需要填入形容词，effective 无须改变词性，只需变成比较级即可。由于 effective 是多音节形容词，比较级相应地要变成 more effective。

4. 副词

副词在句中作状语，主要修饰谓语成分或整个句子。从语法结构上来说，副词在句中可有可无，对句子主要结构不会造成任何影响，但对句子的意义理解会产生一定的影响。判断一个单词是副词的一个标准就是：去掉空格处，从语法结构上来说，这句话还是完整的。

例9 The bank loan has (great)_____ strengthened our financial position in the industry.

【解析】如果去掉空格，这句话就变成"The bank loan has strengthened our financial position in the industry."。从语法结构上来说，这句话的主谓宾各种语法成分齐全。据此可以判断空格处应填入单词的词性应是副词，greatly 作状语，修饰谓语动词 strengthen。

附：常见前缀及后缀表

表3.7 常见前缀

前缀	意义	举例
anti-	反,反对	antisocial
auto-	自己的	autobiography
bio-	生物的	biology
co-	共同的	cooperate
counter-	相反,反对	counterattack
de-	除去	defrost
dis-	不,相反	dishonest
e-	因特网上的或使用因特网的	e-business
en-	使,使处于……状态	enlarge, endanger
mis-	错误地	misunderstand
non-	表示否定	nonstop
tele-	远距离的	telescope
trans-	横穿,横贯	transpacific

表 3.8 常见后缀

名词后缀			
后缀	举例	后缀	举例
-age	passage	-ance	assistance, dependence
-ancy, -ency	expectancy, efficiency	-hood	childhood
-ion, -tion, -ation	confession, collection, observation	-ment	arrangement, development
-ness	kindness, happiness	-ty, -ity	cruelty, purity
动词后缀			
-en	fasten, shorten	-fy, -ify	satisfy, simplify
-ize, -ise（英）	modernize, standardize		
形容词后缀			
-able, -ible, -ble	acceptable, divisible	-al	environmental, exceptional
-ful	beautiful, careful	-ic, -ical	atomic, economical
-ish	bluish, childish	-ive	attractive, effective
-less	careless, homeless	-ly	daily, manly
-ous	dangerous, famous	-some	troublesome, handsome
-y	dirty, thirsty		
副词后缀			
-ly	completely, really	-ward(s)	backward(s), afterward(s)
-wise	clockwise, likewise		

第四节 实战演练

2015 年 6 月真题

Part Ⅱ Vocabulary & Structure （10 minutes）

Directions: *This part is to test your ability to construct correct and meaningful sentences. It consists of 2 sections.*

Section A

Directions: *There are 10 incomplete sentences here. You are required to complete each statement by choosing the appropriate answer from the 4 choices marked A), B), C) and D). You* should mark the corresponding letter on the Answer Sheet with a single line through the center.

25. I am very happy to declare that this year's sales target _____ ahead of time.
    A) achieved   B) has achieved
    C) has been achieved   D) had been achieved

26. The new traffic rules will become _____ from the first day of 2016.
    A) comfortable   B) excellent
    C) challenging   D) effective

27. The news quickly spread throughout the campus _____ he won the first prize in the competition.
    A) which   B) what
    C) that   D) who

28. The delivery of the goods was _____ because of the snow storm.
    A) worked out   B) put off
    C) turned on   D) taken in

29. When _____, the project will help to greatly improve the environment in the community.
    A) finished   B) to finish
    C) finishing   D) finish

30. The task will not be fulfilled _____ we get help from other departments.
    A) if   B) unless
    C) since   D) when

31. Vitamin B enables the body to _____ full use of the food taken in.
    A) make   B) reach
    C) put   D) bring

32. These construction workers are required to participate _____ the safety training program.
    A) at   B) with
    C) in   D) to

33. We'll send the memo in advance _____ all people can have enough time to get prepared.
    A) in case   B) so that
    C) as if   D) ever since

34. Congratulations on the great _____ you've made since last year.
    A) progress   B) measure
    C) appointment   D) sense

Section B

Directions: *There are 5 incomplete sentences here. You should fill in each blank with the proper form of the word given in brackets. Write the word or words in the corresponding space on the Answer Sheet.*

35. It is hard (guess) _____ what comments the manager will make on the design.
36. Payment can (make) _____ online from your checking or saving account.
37. This type of loan is (frequent) _____ used for this purpose.
38. It is possible that we reach a long-term (agree) _____ with the company.
39. I must admit that the situation is (difficult) _____ than I thought it would be.

2015 年 12 月真题

Part II Vocabulary & Structure (10 minutes)

Directions: *This part is to test your ability to construct correct and meaningful sentences. It consists of 2 sections.*

Section A

25. Some of the employees in the company are _____ to work at flexible hours.
    A) taken   B) achieved
    C) allowed   D) formed

26. Please call us for more information as our website is currently _____ construction.
    A) under   B) by
    C) of   D) with

27. _____, the sales manager began his report with the statistics of last month's sales.
    A) By now   B) As usual
    C) So far   D) At most

28. We really appreciate our working environment, in _____ there was open, friendly workplace communication.
    A) how   B) what
    C) whom   D) which

29. A company meeting provides an opportunity to _____ ideas and discuss any problems that come up within the workplace.
    A) reach   B) share
    C) take   D) lead

30. Big changes have taken place at the Marketing Department _____ the new manager came.

A) before B) after
C) since D) while

31. He said he would continue to support us _____ we didn't break the rules.

   A) as well as B) as soon as
   C) as far as D) as long as

32. The school was _____ in 1929 by a Chinese scholar.

   A) established B) placed
   C) imagined D) made

33. We have reached an agreement _____ we should invest in the Internet-related business.

   A) what B) where
   C) that D) as

34. _____ the excellent service, guests can enjoy delicious food in our restaurant.

   A) In place of B) In addition to
   C) In charge of D) In case of

Section B

35. We are looking forward to (receive) _____ your early reply.

36. The main purpose of (educate) _____ is to teach students to think for themselves.

37. I was told that their project (complete) _____ last week as scheduled.

38. It is (general) _____ believed that about 14% of new cars can have electrical problems.

39. As a newcomer, almost everything in the company seems to be (interest) _____ to me.

2016年6月真题

Part II Vocabulary & Structure (10 minutes)

Directions: *This part is to test your ability to construct correct and meaningful sentences. It consists of 2 sections.*

Section A

25. When I changed my job, I had to _____ to another apartment.

   A) gather B) post
   C) master D) move

26. We are looking for a secretary _____ speaks Chinese fluently.

   A) who B) which

C) whom   D) whose

27. This record will help your safety officer _____ what the problem is.
    A) bring up   B) put on
    C) find out   D) take in

28. The more you concentrate on training, _____ the results will be.
    A) good   B) better
    C) the better   D) the best

29. This workshop is to cope _____ the challenges we have faced worldwide.
    A) at   B) with
    C) of   D) in

30. The traditional stores have found it difficult to _____ with online shops recently.
    A) argue   B) begin
    C) meet   D) compete

31. According to the report, the local economy had _____ rapid growth over that period.
    A) practiced   B) experienced
    C) controlled   D) connected

32. _____ the website in Chinese, there is an English version provided.
    A) In addition to   B) As a result of
    C) On behalf of   D) For the purpose of

33. Last year some additional measures _____ to protect customers' personal information by our company.
    A) are taken   B) were taken
    C) have been taken   D) will be taken

34. Sales have shown some improvement _____ we launched the new product last year.
    A) until   B) unless
    C) since   D) although

Section B

35. Be (care) _____ while crossing the roads and remember that they drive on the left in England.

36. The new suitcase at the exhibition (design) _____ by a Chinese company.

37. The related information can help you to operate the machine (efficient) _____.

38. The project is still under (discuss) _____, and practical solutions are expected to be found.

39. According to the report, the North American health market (grow) _____ at a rate of about 7.4% in 2025.

2016年12月真题

Part II Vocabulary & Structure (10 minutes)

Directions: *This part is to test your ability to construct correct and meaningful sentences. It consists of 2 sections.*

Section A

25. The Internet allows rural school children _____ about what is happening in the world.
    A) to learn   B) learning
    C) learn   D) learned

26. The grocery store has been closed down since no one wanted to _____ the business.
    A) put up   B) give off
    C) take over   D) bring about

27. The CEO said that it would never be _____ late to apologize for its poor service.
    A) much   B) too
    C) so   D) very

28. The president gave a detailed _____ of his proposal at the meeting.
    A) explanation   B) search
    C) balance   D) word

29. Last year the employees in our department were so busy _____ they were not able to take a vacation.
    A) which   B) what
    C) who   D) that

30. Their talks next week are expected to focus _____ business management.
    A) on   B) with
    C) in   D) of

31. There are no openings at present, so the company will not _____ anybody.
    A) handle   B) lead
    C) hire   D) dismiss

32. I wanted to know when and where we should _____ our assignments.
    A) set back   B) fall into
    C) take off   D) hand in

33. We considered _____ to California at first, but decided not to in the end.
    A) move   B) moving
    C) to move   D) moved

34. Australia has its own _____ identity, which is very different from that of Britain.

   A) busy B) central
   C) capable D) cultural

Section B

35. (Surprising) _____, the team was able to finish the task two weeks ahead of schedule.

36. The designers from our firm are ready (assist) _____ you throughout the whole process.

37. It seems to me that his solution is much (effective) _____ than mine.

38. Your strong determination to improve services has left a deep (impress) _____ on us.

39. We are pleased to have you visit us and look forward to (meet) _____ you next week.

2017年6月真题

Part II Vocabulary & Structure (10 minutes)

Directions: *This part is to test your ability to construct correct and meaningful sentences. It consists of 2 sections.*

Section A

25. It was not until yesterday _____ they decided to re-open the business talk.

   A) when B) which
   C) that D) as

26. We have to _____ the cost of setting up a new hospital in that area.

   A) work out B) put on
   C) fill up D) carry on

27. We need to _____ an eye on all the activities to make sure that people stay safe.

   A) catch B) keep
   C) take D) bring

28. The local government has always placed a strong emphasis _____ education and vocational training.

   A) with B) for
   C) on D) to

29. Don't take the wrong turn before you _____ the railway station.

   A) have B) run
   C) keep D) reach

30. The team doesn't mind _____ at weekends as long as they can finish the task.
    A) worked   B) working
    C) to work   D) work

31. We are a non-profit company _____ team members are from all over the country.
    A) whose   B) that
    C) which   D) what

32. The meeting room is so small that it can hold 20 people _____.
    A) at last   B) at first
    C) at most   D) at once

33. She gave us a detailed _____ of the local government's new health-care proposal.
    A) impression   B) explanation
    C) education   D) communication

34. Linda _____ her training in a joint company by the end of next month.
    A) finishes   B) has finished
    C) had finished   D) will have finished

Section B

35. We were impressed by the (suggest) _____ you made at yesterday's meeting.

36. The (long) _____ Charles has lived in this city, the more he likes it.

37. If you want to learn some terms related to your field, you will find this book might be (help) _____.

38. No one is allowed (smoke) _____ in public buildings according to the new regulation.

39. The new president (ask) _____ some tough questions by the reporter in the interview yesterday.

2017年12月真题

Part II Vocabulary & Structure (10 minutes)

Directions: *This part is to test your ability to construct correct and meaningful sentences. It consists of 2 sections.*

Section A

25. We regard customer complaints as an opportunity to _____ our service.
    A) bring   B) receive
    C) improve   D) obtain

26. We took advantage of its sports facilities _____ staying at the hotel.

A) although B) while
C) until D) unless

27. It has been decided that Mr. Li will _____ the company when the CEO retires.
A) put off B) call for
C) bring about D) take over

28. The study shows that some students have difficulty _____ long English texts.
A) reading B) read
C) to read D) to be read

29. If you _____ your mind, please call me at this number before Saturday.
A) changed B) would change
C) had changed D) change

30. Having obtained the college diploma, he _____ a position in that company.
A) carried on B) took in
C) applied for D) put on

31. It is the management _____ has to make sure its staff are not overworked.
A) what B) that
C) which D) whose

32. Most people in this region think that they should _____ heavy industry.
A) develop B) supply
C) take D) make

33. _____ you are a first time buyer or not, we will offer you a good price today.
A) Whatever B) Whenever
C) Whether D) However

34. Our purchase decisions are generally made _____ the basis of price, delivery dates and after-sales service.
A) with B) over
C) in D) on

Section B

35. We promise (give) _____ you a reply within five workdays.

36. The bank loan has (great) _____ strengthened our financial position in the industry.

37. Photography has changed our way of (view) _____ the world.

38. That new model of the machine is not likely to go into (produce) _____ before late 2022.

39. Anyone applying for a visa to China (require) _____ to have finger prints.

2018年6月真题

Part II Vocabulary & Structure (10 minutes)

Directions: *This part is to test your ability to construct correct and meaningful sentences. It consists of 2 sections.*

Section A

25. Let's find people with computer skills to _____ a team for the project.
    A) look up   B) ring up
    C) give up   D) make up

26. If I were you, I _____ the company's website for more detailed information.
    A) would visit   B) will visit
    C) visit   D) have visited

27. No company can afford to bear the _____ of customer confidence.
    A) stress   B) loss
    C) worry   D) hurry

28. _____ she has been working in China for only two years, she speaks fluent Chinese.
    A) When   B) If
    C) Although   D) Until

29. We have read this instruction many times and we are _____ with all the steps we should take.
    A) similar   B) useful
    C) helpful   D) familiar

30. Employees would like to work under team leaders who _____ good examples.
    A) turn   B) put
    C) do   D) set

31. Turn to us for legal advice at any time _____ you need it.
    A) when   B) how
    C) where   D) why

32. Your pay raise will in part _____ your work experience and skills.
    A) carry on   B) take on
    C) depend on   D) put on

33. You are required to enter the name of the city in which your company _____.
    A) locates   B) located
    C) is locating   D) is located

34. Tourists can get the latest information of our city _____ the help of our local tour guides.

   A) on B) with C) under D) for

Section B

35. Patients can be treated in many (difference) _____ settings with various approaches.
36. After taking the training course, they have performed their duties much (well) _____ than before.
37. Only by (create) _____ a clean environment can we truly encourage more tourists to come.
38. This research paper focuses on (health) _____ lifestyles for elderly people.
39. Our new manager (expect) _____ to deliver a speech at tomorrow's meeting.

2018年12月真题

Part Ⅱ Vocabulary & Structure （10 minutes）

Directions：*This part is to test your ability to construct correct and meaningful sentences. It consists of 2 sections.*

Section A

25. If Mary had _____ the situation to Tom, he would have understood it.

   A) supplied B) explained C) charged D) thrown

26. I'm pleased to receive your letter of April 10th, _____ for our catalogue and price-list.

   A) ask B) asked C) to ask D) asking

27. _____ your trip is short or long, we can work out a schedule for you.

   A) Whether B) What C) How D) Which

28. The project team _____ people from different departments of the company.

   A) falls into B) brings about C) consists of D) results from

29. In the survey, we asked the workers about things _____ made their work harder to do.

   A) what B) that C) who D) this

30. We'd like to make an _____ with your manager to further discuss the contract.

   A) opportunity B) influence
   C) appointment D) experiment

31. About a quarter of American adults say that they _____ a book in whole in the past year.

   A) will not read B) do not read
   C) would not read D) have not read

32. We should be _____ of cultural differences while doing foreign trade.

   A) aware B) active
   C) friendly D) hopeful

33. This study has found some key factors _____ employees' stress in their work.

   A) turning down B) leading to
   C) taking off D) carrying out

34. The company can now focus its attention _____ developing its latest car model.

   A) in B) with
   C) at D) on

Section B

35. This APP allows you (see) _____ the departures and arrivals of all the flights.

36. We assure you that your order will (deliver) _____ within 5 workdays.

37. If you choose not to receive those emails, please let us know by (send) _____ us a message.

38. We are responsible for the installation and repair of the (equip) _____.

39. If you find any product that is (cheap) _____ than ours in other stores, please contact us.

2019年6月真题

Part II Vocabulary & Structure (10 minutes)

Directions: *This part is to test your ability to construct correct and meaningful sentences. It consists of 2 sections.*

Section A

25. _____ the robots were able to have hands like ours, we would still need to design a way to control them.

   A) Even if B) As if
   C) Just because D) Now that

26. Sometimes finding an ideal job is _____ difficult that you need to find another path to your goal.
    A) much B) such
    C) very D) so

27. In fact, it was this project _____ made me interested in computer science.
    A) that B) who
    C) when D) what

28. My goal right now is to find a position at a company _____ I can grow and take on new challenges over time.
    A) that B) which
    C) where D) whom

29. I came across this website when _____ a job search online.
    A) to do B) done
    C) was doing D) doing

30. Remember to dress properly and take _____ of your personal appearance when attending a job fair.
    A) concern B) attention
    C) care D) focus

31. We will keep in _____ with you throughout your job search via our Customer Service Centre.
    A) relation B) touch
    C) link D) connection

32. They are seeking candidates who have _____ least 1 to 5 years of experience in sales.
    A) in B) for
    C) at D) on

33. In most cases, when you make a purchase online, your rights are the same _____ those when you buy things in a shop.
    A) with B) like
    C) for D) as

34. Our homeowner policy does not cover damage _____ poor maintenance.
    A) putting out B) resulting from
    C) showing off D) taking off

Section B

35. If you fail (provide) _____ certain information when requested, we may not be able to offer you the service.

36. Machine learning engineering is developing (gradual) _____ as time goes by.

37. In recent times, machines are (smart) _____ than they used to be years ago.

38. Clients (ask) _____ to give feedback on the performance of our employees and their skills.

39. You can go directly to our chain store in your city to have the device (fix) _____.

2019 年 12 月真题

Part II Vocabulary & Structure (10 minutes)

Directions: *This part is to test your ability to construct correct and meaningful sentences. It consists of 2 sections.*

Section A

25. If you receive several job _____ during your job searching, how do you choose the best one?
    A) relations   B) regulations
    C) benefits   D) offers

26. When _____ wisely, these loans can help you achieve your dreams.
    A) use   B) to use
    C) used   D) using

27. If you want to visit the museum, you have to book your visit at least 2 days _____ advance.
    A) on   B) in
    C) for   D) with

28. _____ average, call center workers in this company make between $9 and $14 an hour.
    A) On   B) With
    C) Over   D) To

29. The mechanical trouble has prevented them from finishing the task on _____.
    A) duty   B) order
    C) time   D) plan

30. Just before the plane _____, the passengers were told there was an engine issue.
    A) turned on   B) took off
    C) set out   D) put down

31. We finally came to the conclusion _____ it was difficult to combine the two techniques.

A) which B) who
C) where D) that

32. The interviewer asked me to explain in _____ why I applied for the position.
    A) difficulty B) detail
    C) base D) belief

33. The customer service has refused to refund my money to me _____ it is their fault.
    A) as if B) ever since
    C) even though D) in case

34. I could never watch any movie more than once, _____ good it is.
    A) however B) whichever
    C) whatever D) wherever

Section B

35. (Surprising) _____, 70 percent of visitors will return for another holiday.

36. At that time, Jane (encourage) _____ to begin learning Chinese with her Chinese friends.

37. Please use this form to request an (appoint) _____ with a primary care provider.

38. Frankly speaking, the lecture is much (interesting) _____ than expected.

39. If you don't mind (wait) _____ 7-10 days, we can send you a personal check.

第四章

阅读理解

第一节 题型综述

高等学校英语应用能力考试 B 级测试的第三部分为阅读理解题(Reading Comprehension),该部分有 5 篇阅读语篇,共 23 道题,占总分的 31%,测试时间为 35 分钟。

阅读理解部分的语篇一般分为两种类型:一是以科普、人文、社会、常识、金融、经贸等为主的一般性材料;二是以广告、函电、合同、摘要、单证等为主的应用性材料。阅读总量大约为 800 词。本部分测试的文字材料以一般性阅读材料和实用性文字或图文材料为主(表 4.1)。

表 4.1 文字材料类型表

类型	具体内容
一般性阅读材料	科普、人文、社会、常识、金融、经贸等(不包括诗歌、小说、散文等文学性材料)
实用性文字或图文材料	术语、简历、便条、业务信函、广告、产品使用说明书、厂家介绍、产品维护、合同、电子邮件、传真、摘要、序言等

阅读理解材料包括四种题型(表 4.2)。第一篇阅读材料和第二篇阅读材料的题型相同,是阅读理解的主干题,也是传统的四选一客观题,差别在于第一篇文字材料之后有 5 个问题要解答,第二篇多是图文材料之后有 3 个问题要解答,只是语篇呈现形式和题目数量上有变化,解答要求一样,都要求考生根据对阅读材料内容的理解,从每道题的四个选项中选出一个正确的答案。第三篇阅读是摘要填空题,考生需要根据阅读材料的信息将正确的答案填入 5 个题目的空格处,但要注意每空不能超过 3 个单词。第四篇阅读是匹配题,主要是对专业词汇和术语的考查,考生要从英文列表中找出 10 个相应的汉语含义。第五篇阅读则是简答题,这部分通常为应用文,考生要使用 3 个以内的英文单词回答 5 个问题。

表4.2 阅读理解题型及分值分布

序号	题号	测试形式	题目数量/个	分值/分
Task 1	40—44	传统的四选一客观题	5	5×2′
Task 2	45—47	传统的四选一客观题	3	3×2′
Task 3	48—52	摘要填空题	5	5×1′
Task 4	53—57	匹配题	5	5×1′
Task 5	58—62	简答题	5	5×1′
合计			23	31

阅读理解部分要求掌握的技能有:了解语篇和段落的主旨和大意;掌握语篇中的事实和主要情节;理解语篇上下文的逻辑关系;了解作者的目的、态度和观点;根据上下文正确理解生词的意思;理解语篇的结论;进行信息转换。

第二节 考点归纳

2015—2019年,PRETCO-B真题的阅读理解部分的考查范围广、内容新,涉及实用性文字材料和涉外业务活动的诸多方面,详见表4.3。

表4.3 2015—2019年阅读理解常考内容

时间	阅读任务				
	Task 1	Task 2	Task 3	Task 4	Task 5
2019-12	沃尔顿女士对创业的解读	面对火灾的注意事项	BIZSHOT 2020的通知	营销术语	一则汽车保险的介绍
2019-6	在宾馆住宿时节省费用的介绍	琼斯清洁服务公司的宣传广告	Norris & Stevens公司提供的服务广告	质量控制术语	一则公司退货政策和对于有缺陷的或者受损物品的调换政策的介绍
2018-12	*Power Show.com*网站的介绍	公司业务变更的公告	增加公司业务量的三种广告方式	工作场所安全术语	一份使用保险卡的注意事项说明
2018-6	Home Solutions 保险介绍	推迟"总裁杯"高尔夫球比赛的通知	药品公司Prime的经营业务介绍	公共标识术语	一封煤气公司依照联邦法律要求开展安全检查的信函
2017-12	创办公司的准备事项介绍	活动邀请广告	团体定期参加人寿保险的商业广告	国外旅行术语	一则招聘地面维护工人的广告

续表

时间	阅读任务				
	Task 1	Task 2	Task 3	Task 4	Task 5
2017-6	行李检查的通知	西摩海洋探索中心发布的招募讲解员志愿者的广告	对患者进行调查的说明	安全管理术语	一份 ITaP 教学实验室的使用守则
2016-12	E-medical(电子医疗)介绍	夏季地铁实习项目的广告	会议邀请函	广告产业术语	一封要求退换商品的投诉信
2016-6	参加志愿活动需要的技能和收获介绍	小型企业发展研讨会的广告	新客户在线报告系统的备忘录	高铁术语	一封提议开展业务合作的商务电子邮件
2015-12	成功开办餐馆的注意事项说明	圣·查尔斯大街社区发布的车库旧物出售广告	Best Buy Express Service 公司业务的简介	道路标识术语	一则 Public Storage 公司的业务简介
2015-6	国外旅行的人身财产安全说明	马里兰社区联络处的招聘广告	Chevron 能源公司的简介	公司网站术语	公司首席执行官写给全体员工的一封信
总述	200 词左右的文字材料	应用性图文材料,如海报、通知等	应用性文字材料,如公司介绍、邀请函、内部通知、备忘录等	术语	函电、通知、说明、广告等应用性文字

从表 4.3 可以看出,在 2015—2019 年的 10 套题中,50 篇阅读理解考查的特点是以应用文为主,突出实用性,特别是 Task 3 的摘要填空题和 Task 5 的简答题,都是以应用文为主,涉及涉外业务活动和产品说明的诸多方面,是特定职业场景中的与就业有关的职业英语,主要考查学生的专业交际的语言能力。

考生应该熟悉 B 级考试中阅读理解的题型,通过梳理历年考点,理清相关类型题的答题技巧。能力加技巧,两者搭配,才能事半功倍。

一、单选题

阅读理解题的前两项任务都是单选的形式,常出现的考点题型有事实细节题、词义推断题、主旨大意题三种。

1. 事实细节题

事实细节题考查考生对文章内容的把握。

例如:2019 年 6 月真题第 41 题

41. One piece of advice to hotel guests is _____.
   A) to use all the hotel entertainment equipment
   B) to take your family members along with you
   C) to take advantage of the common extras included in the rate

D) to enjoy as many facilities provided by the hotel as possible

【解析】这道题的考点是具体的建议。这是一道事实细节题。由题干中的 One piece of advice to hotel guests 和题文同序原则定位到文章第二段第三、四句。定位句提到，能够帮助节省费用的通常的额外服务包括免费的早餐、Wi-Fi 和儿童餐，在宾馆住宿期间，要好好利用这些额外服务。选项 C 中 take advantage of 和 the common extras 与原文的表述基本一致。由此可以确定 C 项"利用包含在房费里面的额外服务"为本题的答案。

做这种题目时，考生应该带着问题从文章中找出相关信息。考生应在阅读前先浏览问题，在阅读时找出主要事实细节，这样在解答时可回看自己画出的重点，省时高效。

2．词义推断题

词义推断题考查考生对文章中出现的关键词、短语或句子含义的把握。

例如：2016年6月真题第41题

41. By saying "stretching your wings at work" (Para. 2), the author means "_____".

　　A) reducing your work time

　　B) getting pay raise more easily

　　C) making full use of your abilities

　　D) avoiding making similar mistakes

【解析】这道题的考点是理解短语的意思。这是一道语义推断题。由题干中的 stretching your wings at work(Para. 2)定位到文章第二段。定位段提到，一旦在志愿岗位上获得了这些技能，你可能会感觉更加舒服自在，因为你"在工作中伸展你的翅膀"。根据后文 gained these skills(获得这些技能)可知，"在工作中伸展翅膀"是指在工作中发挥能力。stretching your wings 的字面意思是"伸展翅膀"，在本句中引申为"大展宏图"，即"充分发挥自己的能力"。由此可以确定 C 项"充分发挥自己的能力"为本题的答案。

做这种题目时，考生应该充分利用上下文来取得其确切含义，绝对不可孤立地根据单个词语的字面意思做出推断。

3．主旨大意题

主旨大意题考查学生准确找出文章主题或中心思想的能力。

例如：2019年6月真题第44题

44. The passage is mainly about how to _____.

　　A) best enjoy room service in hotel

　　B) save money while staying in a hotel

　　C) choose a hotel in a university district

　　D) make use of common extras in a hotel

【解析】这道题的考点是对全文主旨的归纳。这是一道主旨大意题。本文主要介绍了在宾馆住宿时节省费用的三个妙招：尽可能地利用额外优惠；居住在市中心之外的宾馆或者高校周围的宾馆；到宾馆外面的饭店就餐。因此可以确定 B 项"在宾馆住宿时节省费用"为本题的答案。

做这种题目时,考生要想抓住文章的主干,掌握文章的结构,了解作者的意图,就要进行限时阅读,其间要精力集中。

二、填空题

第三篇和第五篇阅读理解是填空和回答问题的形式。文章多属于应用性文体,包括求职信、邀请信、投诉信、电子邮件、招聘广告、说明书等。在填写答案的时候,题目都要求不能超过 3 个单词。这两篇阅读理解基本上是考查对原文的一个复述,题目难度不大。

例如:2019 年 6 月真题第 48 题

48. Paying online via PayLease, a leading _____ company

【解析】这道题的考点是对原文的复述。通过关键词"Paying online via PayLease, a leading"和 company 定位到第一段第一、二句。定位句指出,Norris & Stevens 愿意帮助居民通过 PayLease 公司进行网上支付,PayLease 是财产管理行业处于主导地位的支付处理公司。通过对比题干和原文可知,空格处应该填入 PayLease 公司的业务范围。因此,可以确定本题的答案为 payment processing。

做这种题目时,考生要根据关键词定位,结合空格前后的内容,回到文章中去寻找同义或一样的内容,然后根据原文,找到空格处缺少的内容,原样填写即可。这部分的考题基本遵循命题顺序性原则。

三、匹配题

第四篇阅读理解的题型比较特殊,属于中英文词条的一一对应题型。此题要求找出中文词条所对应的英文翻译,考查学生对某一领域的单词的掌握情况。比如,2019 年 6 月真题的第四篇阅读理解考查的就是质量控制的相关术语。

例如:2019 年 6 月真题第 53 - 57 题

53.(quality control)质量控制　　　　　(consumer safety)消费者安全

54.(inspection certificate)检验证书　　　(quality engineering)质量工程

55.(quality level)质量等级　　　　　　(inspection cost)检验成本

56.(quality inspector)质检员　　　　　(supply chain)供应链

57.(sample size)样本大小　　　　　　(appearance check)外观检查

做这种题时,考生要先看一下"Directions"的第一句,结合题目中给出的中文意思,可以确定短语或专业术语的主题,然后利用排除法找出相应的英语选项。遇到不认识的单词或者短语也没关系,可以通过构词法来推断其中一个单词的大概意思,逐渐明确选择目标。这种题要求考生平时多观察周围生活中常出现的词汇,比如餐馆、医院、汽车、景点、停车场、电影院里经常出现的标语,都有可能成为考查的词汇,所以考生一定要注重对日常生活中应用性词汇的积累。对任何语言的学习都是一个循序渐进的过程,再宏伟瑰丽的建筑,都是靠一砖一瓦累积而成,而词汇就是语言学习中的基本因素。

第三节　技巧点拨

一、阅读技巧综述

1. 掌握有效的阅读方法

最常见并且行之有效的阅读方法是快速阅读法和读题找答案法。

快速阅读法就是运用略读、速读、跳读等阅读技巧进行阅读训练，在短时间内找出文章的关键词、主题句等。在实际做题的过程中，考生把表示五个"W"和一个"H"的词和句子画出来。文章的第一段一般也是文章的核心，考生要重点阅读，遇到不认识的词不要停下来，可以先跳过去，继续读完全文，可以根据上下文来猜生词的大概含义。一般说来题目排列的顺序是按照文章结构来安排的，所以在考试的过程中，考生可以通过阅读题干来推测文章所要陈述的内容，也可以通过阅读选项来帮助理解原文材料。

读题找答案法就是先读试题，然后再读原文，带着问题在文中找答案。考生要阅读题干，判断题目问的是客观信息还是主观选择。客观信息可以从文章中直接找出答案，而主观选择的题目则需要考生判断题目是考查文章的感情基调、隐含的观点，还是文章的主旨。做这类题时，考生要对文章进行全面梳理才能得出答案。考生要了解试题和选项所包含的信息，有针对性地对文章进行略读，对信息进行快速定位，再对信息进行分析对比和整合，排除干扰，得出正确答案。这种方法可以加强阅读的针对性，提高准确率。

2. 平时加强阅读训练

考生在平时的练习中除了积累词汇量，还应该多注意阅读能力的提高和做题技巧的总结。当考生掌握了充足的词汇量，熟读各种应用性文体，尤其是商务英语的文章时，在考试时就能沉着冷静地分析和理解文章，那么，分数都会逐步提高，并且个人整体的英语水平也会有很大提高。

3. 合理运用考试时间

在高等学校英语应用能力考试B级中，阅读理解的测试时间是35分钟。按5篇阅读理解进行分配，每篇必须在7分钟内完成，所以考生应尽量掌握好做题的节奏，在6分钟内完成一个语篇的所有题目并完成涂卡，用1分钟来检查。

二、解题技巧分解

1. Task 1 & Task 2

这两道题是传统的四选一单选题，考查对文章的主旨大意、事实细节和语义推断等的把控能力。一般来说，文章的每一段的第一句就是每一个段落的主题句，考生可以通过读第一段、每段的第一个句子和最后一段，快速确定文章的主题，因为这类文章都要求第一段提出观点、突出中心,下面的段落都是进行论证。最后一段往往是对第一段的总结和呼应,并强调文章的主题。同时,在阅读的过程中,考生可以把与题干相关的信息画出来,采用查读法,到原文中直接查找问题的答案,分析选项和原文是否相符即可。

2. Task 3

本题是摘要填空题,考查学生抓住主要信息、综合运用、读与写的能力。本题为一篇短文,里面含有5个小题,需要注意,每道题的答案不能超过3个单词。做这类题的时候,考生要将重点放在文章所传达的重要信息上,可以在阅读的过程中在文章中标注出来,不要花费大量的时间去理解某个词或句,只要了解其中包含的信息即可。这类应用性阅读的文章一般有较为固定的格式和常用句型。答题时考生可以先大概浏览一下原文,了解文章的类型,确定是广告、合同、通知,还是简介等,然后再了解所要填写的具体内容。按照题中的关键词去原文找答案时,大部分的题可以在文章中直接找出答案,有一些则需要考生进行转换或归纳。

3. Task 4

本题是匹配题,将17个英文术语和10个汉语相匹配,不是一一匹配,所以要求考生具备识别判断能力,将不相关的英文术语排除。这类术语一般包括应用性的各种列表、目录、说明或标语等。这类题是阅读理解题型中较为简单的题型,但是考生也要注意认真阅读题目要求和例子,先把熟悉和知道的题目匹配好,这样就可以缩小选择范围,遇到有生词的内容时,尽量先对熟悉的词进行判断。学生在平时要多注意积累这方面的相关材料的解题技巧。

4. Task 5

本题是简答题,主要考查学生对应用性文章的理解能力,这道题中的5个小题也需要用不超过3个词或短语的文字回答。这类题型的答题技巧和Task 3的答题技巧相似,总结起来也是分为三个步骤:判断类型→找出关键词和出处→进行归纳转换和删减。

第四节 实战演练

2015年6月真题

Part Ⅲ Reading Comprehension (35 minutes)

Directions: This part is to test your reading ability. There are 5 tasks for you to fulfill. You should read the reading materials carefully and do the tasks as you are instructed.

■ Task 1

Directions: After reading the following passage, you will find 5 questions or unfinished statements, numbered 40 to 44. For each question or statement there are 4 choices marked A), B), C) and D). You should make the correct choice and mark the corresponding letter on the Answer Sheet with a single line through the center.

It is important for us to know how to stay safe while traveling in foreign countries. We've all heard the stories of travelers having their wallets(钱包) stolen or finding themselves in the wrong part of town. So you have to be more careful than usual, when traveling abroad.

Remember to carry a small amount of cash and a copy of your ID with you at all times. There is no need to bring large amounts of cash with you. When shopping, use your credit card instead. Keep your wallet in your front pocket so that there is no way someone's hand could get in there without your noticing it.

Travel with a friend, business partner if possible. It is always better to travel in pairs than to go alone. Know where you're going. Look at the map before you leave the hotel so that you know where you're going and how to get there.

Lock your valuables(贵重物品) either in the safe in your hotel room or in the main hotel safe.

Be aware of your surroundings. Look around when walking, and avoid keeping your head low.

40. When shopping abroad, you are advised to _____.
    A) use online services   B) use a credit card
    C) pay by check   D) pay in cash

41. To keep your wallet safe, you'd better _____.
    A) hold it in your hand   B) leave it in the hotel safe
    C) put it in your front pocket D) keep it in your shoulder bag

42. To know where you are going, you are advised to _____.
    A) ask the police for detailed information
    B) look at the map before leaving the hotel
    C) always travel with your business partner
    D) have a smart phone with you while traveling

43. Where should you keep your valuables while staying in a hotel?
    A) In the hotel safe.   B) In your pockets.
    C) In your traveling bag.   D) In a bedside container.

44. Which of the following can be the title for the passage?
    A) How to Ask Ways While Traveling.   B) How to Shop in a Foreign Country.
    C) Protect Your Personal Information. D) Stay Safe While Traveling Abroad.

Task 2

Directions: *The following is a notice. After reading it, you will find 3 questions or unfinished statements, numbered 45 to 47. For each question or statement there are 4 choices marked A), B), C) and D). You should make the correct choice and mark the corresponding letter on the Answer Sheet with a single line through the center.*

Maryland Community Connection Proudly Presents:
Careers and Opportunities Job Fair
Monday, May 12, 2014
9:00am–4:00pm

Maryland Community Connection is expanding and we are looking for YOU!
Please send your resume to
info@marylandcommunityconnection.org
NO PHONE CALLS PLEASE

Interviews will be held on site for qualified candidates. Please arrive dressed professionally.

We are more than willing to train the right person!

Actively Seeking
- Entry Level Positions–Working with people with disabilities
- Manager of Community Services
- Transportation Specialist
- Director of Human Resources
- Director of Quality Assurance
- Summer Employment
  (Duration 8–12 Weeks)

MCC requires that you be atleast 18 years of age and have your own vehicle for the positions listed

MARYLAND COMMUNITY CONNECTION

4401 Nicole Drive
Lanham, MD 20706
Phone: 301-583-1158
Fax: 301-583-1320
E-mail: info@marylandcommunityconnection.org
Web: marylandcommunityconnection.org
Facebook: Maryland Community Connection
Twitter: @MDCantConnection

Do you have what it takes to help others?
Maryland Community Connection helps individuals with disabilities become Extraordinary members in their communities!

45. To apply for a position advertised, you should _____.
    A) make a phone call to the organization B) visit the organization in person
    C) send your resume online   D) sign up for registration

46. When they are selected, the right persons will be _____.
    A) shown around the company   B) provided with training
    C) given a welcome party   D) sent to work abroad

47. Job candidates are advised to be dressed professionally as they are likely to _____.
    A) sign a job contract   B) give a presentation
    C) help the disabled people   D) attend an interview on site

Task 3

Directions: *Read the following passage. After reading it, you should complete the information by filling in the blanks marked 48 to 52 (**in no more than 3 words**) in the table below. You should write your answers on the Answer Sheet correspondingly.*

Chevron

Chevron is one of the world's leading energy companies. Our highly skilled global workforce consists of about 64,500 employees, including more than 3,200 service station employees.

In 2013, Chevron's average net production was nearly 2.6 million oil-equivalent barrels(桶) per day. About 75% of that production occurred outside the United States. Chevron had a global production of 1.96 million barrels of oil per day at the end of 2013.

We care about the environment and are proud of the many ways in which our employees work to safeguard (保护) it. Our efforts to improve on our safe work environment continue to pay off. We recognize that the world needs all the energy we can develop, in every potential form. That's why our employees work responsibly to develop the reliable energy the world needs.

Chevron
One of the world's leading energy companies

Workforce: about __48__ employees

Production in 2013:
1) nearly __49__ oil-equivalent barrels per day
2) about 75% of the production outside __50__
3) a __51__ production of 1.96 million barrels of oil per day

Environment & Safety:
1) care about the environment and safeguard it
2) work responsibly to develop the __52__ the world needs

Task 4

Directions: *The following is a list of column titles used on a company's website. After reading it, you are required to find the items equivalent to (与……等同) those given in Chinese in the table below. Then you should mark the corresponding letters in order of the numbered blanks, 53 through 57, on the Answer Sheet.*

A -- Our Business
B -- Our Customers
C -- Customer Training
D -- About Us

E —————————————————— Career Development
F —————————————————— Select Region
G —————————————————— Contact Information
H —————————————————— Site Map
I —————————————————— Privacy Statement
J —————————————————— Terms of Use
K —————————————————— Company History
L —————————————————— Campus Recruiting
M —————————————————— Career Guide
N —————————————————— Press Releases
O —————————————————— Social Media
P —————————————————— Personal Investing
Q —————————————————— Financial Reporting

Examples:（L）校园招聘　　　　　　（N）新闻发布

53. ( )客户培训	( )公司历史	
54. ( )职业指导	( )使用条款	
55. ( )选择地区	( )财务报告	
56. ( )联系信息	( )社交媒体	
57. ( )职业发展	( )网站地图	

Task 5

Directions: *Read the following letter. After reading it, you are required to complete the answers that follow the questions (No. 58 to No. 62). You should write your answers (**in no more than 3 words**) on the Answer Sheet correspondingly.*

March 5, 2015

Dear Employees,

　　Please join me in welcoming Jim Johnson as our newest team member. Jim has become the General Manager since March 4. He will be in charge of a new project that can take our business to the national level.

　　Jim used to be the Vice President in ABC company for the years. In that position, he looked for opportunities for improvement, made suggestions and helped make decisions.

　　There will be a staff lunch in the meeting room at 12:30 on March 6. Please come and introduce yourselves. Pizza and soft drinks will be provided. If you can't attend, stop by Jim's office any time next week. He will be in the new office on the second floor.

　　Thank you.
　　Best Regards.

John Davis, CEO

58. Who has joined the company?

　　_____

59. What was his position in ABC company?

　　_____

60. What will the staff members do at the lunch party?

　　They will meet the new General Manager and _____ themselves.

61. If one can't come to the lunch party, what might they do?

　　They might visit the General Manager at his office any time _____.

62. Where is Jim Johnson's new office?

　　It's on _____.

2015 年 12 月真题

Part Ⅲ　Reading Comprehension (35 minutes)

Directions: *This part is to test your reading ability. There are 5 tasks for you to fulfill. You should read the reading materials carefully and do the tasks as you are instructed.*

Task 1

Starting a restaurant can be rewarding but challenging. Here are some steps to help you to make your restaurant business a success.

First, take a look at the restaurants that will be your competition. Learn what your competitors(竞争者) are serving and use the information to create a restaurant that will stand out among them. Speak to people to understand what type of restaurant they would like to have in the area.

Next, you will need to make a decision as to what kind of food you plan to offer. Choosing your target customers will help determine what type of food you will offer.

Research the different types of menus and select the menu items that will be right for your restaurant.

Deciding on the building and its location is also important for your success. Make sure that the building is easily found and reached. It is important to be located in an area that will attract customers.

Finally, do plenty of public relations work and advertisement of the restaurant opening. Consider having some special discounts and door prizes on the day of the grand opening.

40. According to the passage, the first step in starting a restaurant is to _____.

　　A) find a suitable location　　　　B) set up your profit goal

　　C) learn much about your competitors　　D) advertise the opening of your restaurant

41. By choosing your target customers, you can _____.

   A) learn how much you can charge for each dish

   B) decide on what kind of food to offer them

   C) know the cost of running the restaurant

   D) predict how many customers will arrive

42. Which of the following is important when you choose a building for your restaurant?

   A) There are no other restaurants nearby.

   B) It is easy for customers to visit.

   C) There is a parking lot available.

   D) It is popular with tourists.

43. On the day of the opening of your restaurant, you are advised to _____.

   A) show customers around the building   B) invite some important persons

   C) offer some special discounts   D) make an opening speech

44. The passage is mainly about _____.

   A) how to choose a restaurant location   B) how to cut restaurant running costs

   C) how to attract customers   D) how to start a restaurant

Task 2

45. Which of the following is advertised in the poster?

   A) An arts exhibition.   B) A furniture shop.

   C) A sport event.   D) A garage sale.

46. According to the poster, the money to be raised will be given to _____.

   A) a high school   B) a teen center

   C) a local hospital   D) a local newspaper

47. If you register before April 17, the registration fee is _____.

   A) $20   B) $25   C) $30   D) $35

Task 3

Using Best Buy Express Service is easy. Just follow the Purchasing Guide. Or contact us if you need more help. Please call 1-866-Best Buy with your questions.

The prices of Best Buy Express Service are updated daily from *BestBuy.com*.

All Best Buy Express transactions(交易) are safe and secure. Any personal information you give us will be handled in the strictest confidence according to our Privacy Policy available at *www.bestbuy.com*. $2,000 limit per transaction.

If something is not right with your purchase, simply return your item(s) to one of our Best Buy stores in the United States. Returns will only be processed starting from the day following your purchase. Best Buy will be pleased to exchange or give you a refund in any Best Buy store in the United States. The sales receipt will be required to process a return.

Best Buy Express Service

How to use: follow the __48__

How to contact: call __49__

Prices of products: updated __50__ from *BestBuy.com*

Security & Privacy:

1) Personal information: handled in the strictest confidence
2) Per transaction limit: $2,000

Returns:

1) where to return: any Best Buy store in the United States
2) when to process returns: from the day following __51__
3) what to be required to process a return: __52__

Task 4

A -------------------------------- Don't follow too closely

B -------------------------------- Keep distance

C -------------------------------- Accident area

D -------------------------------- Road closed

E -------------------------------- Road work ahead

F -------------------------------- Two-way traffic

G -------------------------------- One-way traffic

H -------------------------------- Bend ahead

I -------------------------------- Bus lane

J -------------------------------- Electronic toll collection(ETC)

K ———————————————— Service area
L ———————————————— No passing
M ———————————————— No parking
N ———————————————— Dead end
O ———————————————— No horn
P ———————————————— Falling rocks
Q ———————————————— Slow down at exit

Examples：(Q) 出口慢行　　　　　　　　(M) 禁止泊车

53. ( ) 单向行驶	( ) 事故多发区
54. ( ) 电子收费	( ) 小心岩石滑落
55. ( ) 前方弯道	( ) 服务区
56. ( ) 保持车距	( ) 公交车专用车道
57. ( ) 禁止鸣笛	( ) 前方道路封闭

Task 5

Public Storage is an international self-storage company. It rents spaces, ranging from closet-sized (橱柜大小的) units to ones that can hold the contents of a five-bedroom house. We offer indoor and outdoor business units to ones that can hold the contents of a five-bedroom house. We offer indoor and outdoor business units—some with climate control—that have drive-up, walk-up and elevator access and convenient access hours.

Once you find the right storage space, reserve (预订) the self-storage unit online for free. Feel free to inspect the space and meet the property manager before renting the storage unit. When you're ready to pack, we've got everything you need, including the moving supplies.

Once you move in, you keep the only key to your self-storage unit, which you can access on your schedule. All of our business storage agreements are month-to-month, and you can change your storage unit space and location without penalty (惩罚). Easy and flexible—that's what you can expect from Public Storage.

58. What kind of business units does Public Storage offer?

    Public Storage offers _____ business units.

59. How can customers reserve the self-storage unit?

    They can reserve it _____ for free.

60. What are you advised to do before renting the storage unit?

    To inspect the space and meet _____.

61. What will Public Storage promise to do if you get ready to pack?

    They will provide everything, including _____.

62. When can customers keep the key to their self-storage unit?

As soon as they _____.

2016 年 6 月真题

Part Ⅲ　Reading Comprehension (35 minutes)

Directions: *This part is to test your reading ability. There are 5 tasks for you to fulfill. You should read the reading materials carefully and do the tasks as you are instructed.*

Task 1

Volunteering gives you the opportunity to practice important skills used in the workplace. If you're considering a new career, volunteering can help you get experience in your area of interest and meet people in the field.

You might feel more comfortable <u>stretching your wings at work</u> once you've gained these skills in a volunteer position.

Volunteering offers you the chance to try out a new career without making a long-term effort. It is also a great way to gain experience in a new field. You can volunteer directly at an organization that does the kind of work you're interested in. Your volunteer work might also introduce you to professional organizations that could be of benefit to your career.

Volunteer work is unpaid, but this does not mean the skills you learn are basic. Many volunteering opportunities provide a wide range of training. Volunteering can also help you build upon skills you already have and use them to benefit the greater community. For instance, if you hold a successful sales position, you can further develop and improve your public speaking, communication, and marketing skills.

40. If you take volunteer work, you have a chance to _____.

    A) get promoted in your current job

    B) practice skills needed for your work

    C) become familiar with your workplace

    D) work with people from different areas

41. By saying "stretching your wings at work" (Para. 2), the author means "_____".

    A) reducing your work time

    B) getting pay raise more easily

    C) making full use of your abilities

    D) avoiding making similar mistakes

42. Volunteering can also offer you a chance to _____.

    A) gain experience in a new career

B) become an organization member

C) get professional certificates

D) be accepted by a big firm

43. The skills you gain from a sales position in volunteering can help you develop _____.

A) management skills   B) marketing skills

C) leadership skills   D) computer skills

44. The best title of the passage might be "_____".

A) Volunteering Being Encouraged

B) Volunteering：A Must in Social Life

C) Volunteering：Does Benefit Your Career

D) Volunteering to Improve Learning Abilities

Task 2

Notes：1. participant 参与者   2. register 登记，注册

45. How long does the Operation JumpStart short course last?

   A) Two days.   B) Three days.

   C) Four days.   D) Five days.

46. The purpose of the training course is to _____.

   A) offer a high-paid job to the participants

   B) help participants start their own business

   C) provide participants with financial assistance

   D) train participants to develop a computer program

47. You can register for the training course by _____.

   A) calling the guest speakers   B) visiting the institute

   C) writing an e-mail   D) sending a fax

Task 3

Memo

To: Vancouver Area Sales Personnel

From: Jacob Taxis, System Manager

Date: June 13, 2016

Re: New client online reporting system

According to our meeting on Wednesday, there have been big changes made to the current online reporting system. Its accuracy(准确性) has been improved. New usernames have been assigned; these are now available in your mail-boxes. Please note, the new online client reporting system will take effect on June 20, 2016. The new steps for completing the report are as follow:

1. Log in to the company website with your new username and password.

2. On the top left, click "Client Reporting".

3. Select "Add New Client".

4. Enter the client information.

5. When the information is complete, select "Register Client".

Thank you for your cooperation.

Jacob Taxis

J. B. Taxis, Inc.

(555)555-9087

Memo

To: Vancouver __48__
From: Jacob Taxis, System Manager
Subject: Changes made in the current client __49__
Accuracy of the system: Having been __50__
Starting date of the new system: __51__, 2016
How to log in: Using your new __52__

Task 4

A ---------- bullet train
B ---------- intercity high-speed rail
C ---------- non-stop train
D ---------- dedicated rail link
E ---------- business cabins
F ---------- first-class seats
G ---------- second-class seats
H ---------- protective fence
I ---------- passenger flow
J ---------- floating prices
K ---------- real-name purchase
L ---------- replacement ticket
M ---------- on-schedule rate
N ---------- occupancy rate
O ---------- passenger rail line
P ---------- run chart
Q ---------- vehicle type

Examples: (P) 运行图   (B) 城际高铁

53. ( ) 实名购票		( ) 一等座
54. ( ) 直达列车		( ) 浮动票价
55. ( ) 客流		( ) 补票
56. ( ) 正点率		( ) 防护栏
57. ( ) 车型		( ) 商务车厢

Task 5

March 5, 2015

To: damo@gmail.com

Subject: Proposal to do business

Dear Mr. Damon,

We would like to introduce ourselves as a company supplying raw materials to garment(服装) manufacturers. We would be interested in doing business with you. We have been manufacturing raw cotton materials for the last five years. We supply our raw materials to most popular garment manufacturing companies in this country. Your company also manufactures cotton garments for which you must be requiring a steady supply of cotton materials. We can assure you that we provide the best quality of materials and the price of our materials is reasonable.

It would be an honor doing business with you. It would be great if you could arrange a business meeting so that we can discuss this in detail. I attach a copy of our company profile.

Thank you.

Norman Creed Marketing Manager

CBH Manufacturers Limited.

58. What kind of material does CBH Manufacturers Limited supply?

   It supplies _____ to garment manufacturers.

59. How long has CBH Manufacturers Limited been in this field of business?

   For _____ years.

60. What promise has the writer made to Mr. Damon?

   To provide the _____ of materials at a reasonable price.

61. What suggestion does the writer make at the end of the e-mail?

   To arrange _____.

62. What document is attached to the e-mail?

   A copy of the writer's _____.

2016 年 12 月真题

Part Ⅲ Reading Comprehension (35 minutes)

Directions: *This part is to test your reading ability. There are 5 tasks for you to fulfill. You should read the reading materials carefully and do the tasks as you are instructed.*

Task 1

What can we E-medical (E-med) offer?

We offer advices with your own private online doctor by e-mail or phone. If we cannot sort out your problems in that manner, we can refer you to a specialist(专家) in the field you need for further investigations or examinations.

What if you cannot make a diagnosis(诊断) by e-mail?

When we receive your e-mail and the doctor feels that he needs to speak to you to discuss your problems, he will call you immediately and we can help you that way.

But if we feel it is necessary, we may ask you to have a video consultation to make a diagnosis or to treat you, or even refer you to a specialist.

What about medical investigations?

If you need further medical investigations to work towards a diagnosis, such as blood tests or scans(扫描), your E-med doctor can usually refer you to a hospital in London. Other medical investigations can also be arranged remotely. The result will be sent to your E-med doctor, who can then advise you on what to do next.

40. We can learn from the passage that E-med service provides medical advices _____.

　　A) through a doctor's visit　　　　　　B) at a community hospital

　　C) from a medical center　　　　　　　D) by e-mail or phone

41. If E-med service is unable to find out your problems, you will be _____.

　　A) sent to a community hospital　　　　B) asked to wait for a solution

　　C) referred to a specialist　　　　　　　D) given further advices

42. If necessary, the E-med doctor will ask you to _____.

　　A) pay him a personal visit　　　　　　B) have a video consultation

　　C) have an immediate operation　　　　D) pay for the service in advance

43. The E-med doctors will refer the patients to a hospital in London if _____.

　　A) medical investigations cannot be arranged

　　B) they think that further diagnosis is needed

　　C) patients insist on being sent to the hospital

　　D) patients are not satisfied with the diagnosis

44. Which of the following can be used as a title of the passage?

　　A) E-medical Service.　　　　　　　　B) Video Medical Consultation.

　　C) Traditional Medical Diagnosis.　　　　D) Remote Medical Investigation.

Task 2

Notes: 1. internship 实习   2. recommendation 推荐

45. What is advertised in the poster?

    A) A language training program.   B) A youth internship program.

    C) A summer camp program.   D) A volunteer program.

46. By joining the program, the applicants will _____.

    A) improve communication skills   B) obtain a chance to go abroad

    C) gain career experience   D) get a diploma

47. How many hours will the applicants work each week?

    A) 16 hours.   B) 18 hours.   C) 20 hours.   D) 24 hours.

Task 3

December 9, 2016

Dear Committee Members and Guests,

Welcome to the Energy Capital of the World—Houston, Texas! You are warmly invited to attend the Spring 2017 Meeting of the IEEE/PES Transformers Committee (变压器协会), to be held on March 7–11, 2017. It is the sincere pleasure of Tulstar Products, Inc. to be your host for the event.

The meeting will be held at the Omni Houston Hotel, located at Four Riverway,

Houston, Texas (www. omnihouston. com). The hotel is located on the west side of Houston, in the Uptown Post Oak area, about 10 minutes from downtown. The group rate for guest rooms at the Omni Houston Hotel is US $139 per night (single or double rooms), with rooms reserved under the group name " IEEE Transformers". Please contact the hotel directly for room reservations +713-871-8181 and mention our group name.

The Institute of Electrical and Electronics Engineers, Inc. (IEEE)

www. transformerscommittee. org

Invitation Letter

Date: December 9, 2016

To: ____48____ and guests

From: The Institute of Electrical and Electronics Engineers, Inc. (IEEE)

The meeting

Name: Spring 2017 Meeting of the IEEE/PES Transformers Committee

Time: ____49____, 2017

Host: Tulstar Products, Inc.

Location: ____50____ Hotel

Address: Four Riverway, Houston, Texas

Group room reservation

Group rate for guest rooms: ____51____ per night

Group name: ____52____

Contact telephone: +713-871-8181

Task 4

A ---------- Advertising Budget
B ---------- Advertising Cost
C ---------- Art Director
D ---------- Brand Loyalty
E ---------- Brand Manager
F ---------- Click Rate
G ---------- Commercial Advertising
H ---------- Consumer Behavior
I ---------- Customer Relation Management
J ---------- Digital Marketing
K ---------- Direct Mail
L ---------- Interactive Advertising

M ———————————— Advertising Manager
N ———————————— Local Advertising
O ———————————— Page View
P ———————————— Senior Copy Writer
Q ———————————— Target Audience

Examples：（J）数字营销　　　　　　（P）资深文案

53. （　）广告部经理		（　）品牌忠诚度
54. （　）目标受众		（　）消费者行为
55. （　）广告预算		（　）直接邮寄
56. （　）艺术指导		（　）客户关系管理
57. （　）品牌经理		（　）点击率

Task 5

March 5, 2015

Dear Sir,

I recently purchased a computer from your store. When I got it home, the computer was unable to connect to any network. So I installed the latest operating system on it and that still did not fix the problem.

I attempted to return it to your store. However, your staff refused to accept the return because it had the operating system installed on it. But no return policy can be found on the receipt, nor has anyone informed me that I cannot return the computer if I have installed an operating system.

Additionally, your staff at this store were very rude when refusing the return and refused to let me speak to the store manager.

I request you accept the return or refund the money back to me. A copy of the receipt is attached (including your stated terms and conditions for a return).

Sincerely,

Tony Brown

58. What problem did the writer find with the computer when he got it back home?
   It was unable to connect to _____.

59. What did the writer do to fix the computer's problem?
   He installed the latest _____.

60. Why does the writer think he has the right to return the computer?
   Because no such return policy can be found _____.

61. What did the writer complain about the staff?
   They were _____.

62. What is attached to the letter?
   A _____ of the receipt.

2017年6月真题

Part III Reading Comprehension (35 minutes)

Directions: *This part is to test your reading ability. There are 5 tasks for you to fulfill. You should read the reading materials carefully and do the tasks as you are instructed.*

Task 1

Notice of Baggage Inspection(检查)

To protect you and your fellow passengers, the Transportation Security Administration (TSA) is required by law to inspect all checked baggage. As part of this process, some bags are opened and inspected. Your bag was among those selected for inspection.

During the inspection, your bag and its contents may have been searched for prohibited(违禁的) items. After the inspection was completed, the contents were returned to your bag.

If the TSA security officer was unable to open your bag for inspection because it was locked, the officer may have been forced to break the locks on your bag. TSA sincerely regrets having to do this. However, TSA is not responsible for damage to your locks resulting from this necessary security measures.

For packing tips and suggestions on how to secure your baggage during your next trip, please visit: www.tsa.gov.

We appreciate your understanding and cooperation. If you have questions, comments, or concerns, please feel free to contact the TSA Contact Center.

40. According to the passage, TSA is required to inspect your baggage _____.

    A) with your written permission   B) at the request of police
    C) by airlines   D) by law

41. According to the notice, the purpose of the inspection is to _____.

    A) find all overweight baggage   B) search for prohibited items
    C) charge customs duties   D) check damaged items

42. After the inspection, the contents in your bag would _____.

    A) be delivered to your address   B) be given to you in person
    C) be returned to your bag   D) be kept at the airport

43. If your bag is locked, the TSA security officer may have to _____.

    A) break the locks   B) hand it over to police
    C) give up the inspection   D) ask you to open the bag

44. If the locks of your bag are damaged because of the inspection, TSA will _____.

    A) pay for the damage   B) buy you a new lock

    C) not be responsible for it   D) not inspect it in your next trip

Task 2

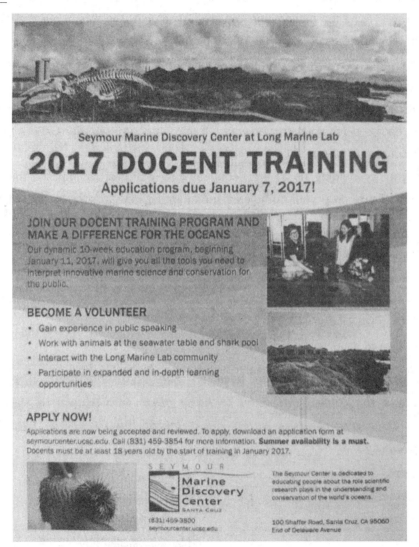

Notes: docent(博物馆等场所的)讲解员

45. How long does the docent training program last?

    A) Four weeks.   B) Six weeks.

    C) Eight weeks.   D) Ten weeks.

46. To apply for the program, you should _____.

    A) first download an application form   B) be good at working with animals

    C) be an experienced public speaker   D) first pay a visit to the lab

47. To attend the program, you must be at least _____.

A) 14 years old B) 16 years old
C) 18 years old D) 20 years old

Task 3

Thank you for selecting the Corvallis Clinic(诊所) for your recent healthcare needs. To continue delivering the highest possible level of service, we survey our patients to learn about their experiences at our clinic. The comments and suggestions you provide about your visit will help us evaluate(评价) our services and improve our care.

This survey takes only a few minutes to complete. Your comments and suggestions are very important to us, and they will be kept confidential(保密). A postage-paid reply envelope is enclosed for your convenience. If you have any questions about this survey, please call our Service Center at 541-754-1374.

Thank you for helping us as we continually try our best to improve the quality of medical care. Please drop your completed survey in the mail as soon as possible.

Patients' Survey

Survey conducted by: Corvallis Clinic

Aim of the survey: to deliver the highest possible level of service

Values of patients comments and suggestions:

1) helping to evaluate the clinic's __48__ ;

2) helping to improve the clinic's __49__

Promise by the clinic: comments and suggestions to be kept __50__

Enclosure: a __51__ reply envelope

Contact: to call Service Center at __52__

Task 4

A ———————————————— Warning equipment
B ———————————————— Accident management
C ———————————————— Protection measures
D ———————————————— Risk assessment
E ———————————————— Administrative controls
F ———————————————— Detection technique
G ———————————————— Failure analysis
H ———————————————— Responsible person
I ———————————————— Harmful substances
J ———————————————— Protection devices
K ———————————————— Accident statistics
L ———————————————— Safety standards

M —————————————— Accident prevention
N —————————————— Monitoring system
O —————————————— Special operation
P —————————————— Medical aid
Q —————————————— Emergency rescue

Examples：（Q）应急救援　　　　（D）风险评估

53. (　)事故统计	(　)检测技术
54. (　)报警设备	(　)医疗救护
55. (　)有害物质	(　)管理控制
56. (　)保护措施	(　)责任人
57. (　)特殊作业	(　)失效分析

Task 5

ITaP Instructional Lab Etiquette（守则）

* This lab is a study zone—please limit your noise. Cell phones and other electronic communication devices should be turned off while inside the lab.

* Group studying—limit group studying to non-busy times. Give chairs to others so they can use available computers.

* Log off from your computer—workstations left idle（空闲状态的）for more than 10 minutes will be reset to the log-in screen.

* Printouts are limited to 10-minute printing time—break large print jobs into smaller print jobs.

* Customer's forms or paper are not permitted in ITaP printers—this can damage the printers.

* Computers are available on a first-come-first-serve basis only during computer lab hours of operation and when no classes are scheduled in the room.

58. What should you do with your cell phones while you are inside the lab?

　　You should _____ your cell phones.

59. When can you do your group studying in the lab?

　　At _____ times.

60. Why should you break large print jobs into smaller ones?

　　Because printouts are limited to _____ printing time.

61. Why are the customer's forms or paper not permitted in ITaP printers?

　　They can _____.

62. When can you use the computers in the lab?

　　During the lab hours of _____ with no classes scheduled.

2017年12月真题

Part III Reading Comprehension (35 minutes)

Directions: *This part is to test your reading ability. There are 5 tasks for you to fulfill. You should read the reading materials carefully and do the tasks as you are instructed.*

Task 1

Starting a business is exciting and frightening. To add the excitement and ease the fear, you should get prepared from the beginning.

Set both your short-term and long-term goals. After you have created your goals, make sure you have a plan for your business that will guide you along the way.

There are a number of legal considerations when you start a business. For example, you need to decide on the structure of your business, register(注册) a business name, obtain necessary licenses and permits, and plan for business taxes.

Money is a major concern when you start a business, especially if you have to give up a well-paid job and if your business has considerable start-up expenses(费用). You can start your business while continuing to work full time, or you can work a part-time job until your business becomes established. You can also wait to start your business until you have saved enough money, and even apply for a bank loan when necessary.

40. According to the passage, one way to ease your fear while starting a business is to _____.

    A) look for partners   B) be prepared
    C) be creative   D) work hard

41. Before making your business plan, you are advised to _____.

    A) establish business relationships   B) consult experts in the industry
    C) set your own business goals   D) look for suitable employees

42. The third paragraph is mainly about _____.

    A) legal considerations   B) the business structure
    C) ways of borrowing money   D) the importance of a business name

43. According to the passage, the major concern for starting a business is _____.

    A) management   B) technology
    C) personnel   D) money

44. One way to overcome your difficulty in meeting business start-up expenses is to _____.

    A) look for a well-paid job   B) cut off operating costs
    C) apply for a bank loan   D) attract investors

Task 2

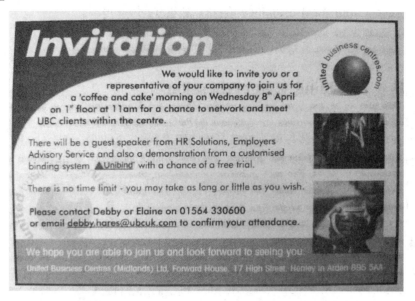

Notes: 1. representative 代表   2. customized binding system 定制的绑定系统
3. attendance 出席

45. The "coffee and cake" morning is to be held on _____.

   A) Monday   B) Wednesday   C) Thursday   D) Friday

46. Who will be invited to give a speech at the event?

   A) A representative of UBC clients.

   B) The president of Employers Advisory Service.

   C) A guest speaker from Employers Advisory Service.

   D) The chief engineer from United Business Centres Ltd.

47. You need to contact Debby or Elaine by phone or e-mail to _____.

   A) confirm your attendance   B) book the pick-up service

   C) ask for a registration form   D) get a free trial of the system

Task 3

Your life is in constant motion—do you have insurance that can keep you up? At age 33, get up to $250,000 of Group Term Life Insurance for just $8.54 a month. That may be just a bit of your monthly cell phone bill.

The American Society of Civil Engineers (ASCE) is offering Expedited (快速的) Insurance to its members for Group Term Life Insurance plans. You may be able to obtain coverage(保额) of up to $250,000 quicker than ever before!

This life insurance coverage is portable, so it stays with you even if you change jobs. As long as your policy is in force, you will have peace of mind knowing you have strengthened your financial position and helped fulfill your loved one's future needs.

Visit *asceinsurance.com/group-term* to apply for coverage today. If you have any questions, contact your local insurance agency at 800-846-3582.

Expedited Insurance
The plan:
1) premium(保费): $8.54 a month for people at age __48__
2) coverage: up to __49__
3) offered to: __50__ of ASCE for Group Term Life Insurance plans
Advantage: portable as long as the policy is __51__
Application: visit *asceinsurance.com/group-term*
Contact: local __52__

Task 4

A ———————————————————— Country of Citizenship
B ———————————————————— Passport Number
C ———————————————————— Country of Origin
D ———————————————————— Destination Country
E ———————————————————— City Where You Boarded
F ———————————————————— City Where Visa Was Issued
G ———————————————————— Date of Issue
H ———————————————————— Date of Birth
I ———————————————————— Accompanying Number
J ———————————————————— Official Use Only
K ———————————————————— Business Visa
L ———————————————————— Tourist Visa
M ———————————————————— Arrival Lobby
N ———————————————————— Departure Lobby
O ———————————————————— Boarding Gate
P ———————————————————— Boarding Card
Q ———————————————————— Visa Type

Examples: (J) 官方填写   (I) 同行人数

53. (	)护照号码	(	)登机口
54. (	)目的地国家	(	)签证签发地
55. (	)登机牌	(	)签证种类
56. (	)登机城市	(	)出生日期
57. (	)抵达大厅	(	)旅行签证

Task 5

Grounds Maintenance Workers

What Grounds Maintenance(维护) Workers Do

Grounds maintenance workers ensure that the grounds of house, businesses and parks are attractive, orderly, and healthy in order to provide a pleasant outdoor environment.

Work Environment

Many grounds maintenance jobs are seasonal, available mainly in the spring, summer, and fall. Most of the work is done outdoors in all weather conditions.

How to Become a Grounds Maintenance Worker

Most grounds maintenance workers need no formal education and are trained on the job.

Training

A short period of on-the-job training is usually enough to teach new hires the skills they need, which often include how to plant and maintain areas and how to use some tools and other equipment.

Pay

The hourly wage for grounds maintenance workers was $12.90 in May 2016.

58. What job is offered in the advertisement?

    _____.

59. What is the responsibility of the job?

    To provide a pleasant _____.

60. What is the working environment of the job?

    The work is mostly done outdoors in _____.

61. What kind of training will be provided?

    A short period of _____ training.

62. What was the hourly wage for grounds maintenance workers in May 2016?

    $_____.

2018 年 6 月真题

Part III Reading Comprehension(35 minutes)

Directions: *This part is to test your reading ability. There are 5 tasks for you to fulfill. You should read the reading materials carefully and do the tasks as you are instructed.*

Task 1

Your home is the place you feel safe and secure. We understand the importance of your home and the things in it and can help you if something unexpected should happen. Our Home Solutions insurance offers buildings, contents or combined buildings and contents cover.

In an emergency

Call the 24-hour Emergency Homeline. We'll arrange for a repairman to carry out repairs, out of usual business hours. As long as the policy covers the damage, you don't need to pay for the repairs.

Lost keys

We'll pay for the full cost of replacing locks on external(外部的) doors if you lose your keys, if they are stolen or if the lock is accidentally damaged.

Important events

We automatically increase your valuables(贵重物品) limit by $3,000 at certain special times, such as your wedding or a festival.

Alternative accommodation(住处)

We'll find somewhere for you and your pets to live if your home as been damaged by an insured event and you can't live there. With our buildings insurance we will pay up to $30,000 for alternative accommodation, and up to $20,000 with contents insurance.

40. According to the insurance company, by buying Home Solutions, you can get help _____.

    A) when your vehicle breaks down on your way to work

    B) when something unexpected happens to your home

    C) when anyone in your family gets hurt or sick

    D) when you want to move to a new house

41. When you call the Emergency Homeline, _____.

    A) a repairman will be sent to do the repairs

    B) they will pay you the repairing cost first

    C) you have to send a photo of the damage

    D) you will be told to wait for a doctor

42. If you lose your keys to the external doors, the insurance company will _____.

    A) pay for the cost of replacing locks   B) deliver new locks to your home

    C) tell you where to buy new locks   D) refuse to pay for new locks

43. According to the passage, in a festival your valuables limit will be _____.

    A) reduced to a certain degree   B) re-checked within a week

    C) automatically increased   D) doubled upon request

44. What is the company likely to do if your home is damaged by an insured event?

    A) It will pay you more than 50,000.

B) It will help you build a new house.

C) It will decrease your valuables limit.

D) It will find somewhere for you to live.

Task 2

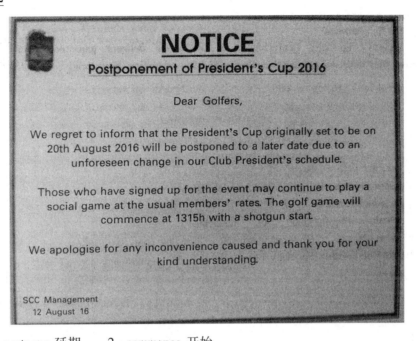

Notes: 1. postpone 延期   2. commence 开始

45. The notice is to inform the golfers of _____.

  A) the application for Club membership   B) the postponement of President's Cup

  C) the final result of President's Cup   D) the activities of Club President

46. The change of the game date is due to _____.

  A) a lack of funding   B) the absence of some golfers

  C) the terrible weather conditions   D) a change in President's schedule

47. According to the notice, the social game will start _____.

  A) in the morning   B) on August 30

  C) at 13:15   D) next week

Task 3

At Prime Medicine LLC, we have only one purpose—we help people to get the medicine they need to feel better and live well.

Our pharmacy(药店) experts are working hard to make your medicine cheaper, and your experience easier. Here are the ways of delivering our services.

Order your long-term medicine from PrimeMail. Receive up to a 90-day supply of your medicine anywhere in the U. S.

Retail pharmacy

Prime offers a large national network of pharmacies—over 66,000. Just bring your prescription(药方) and member ID to a network pharmacy. (If you use a pharmacy that is not in your network, you might need to pay more.)

Specialty(特种药) **pharmacy**

Prime Therapeutics Specialty Pharmacy is a full-service delivery pharmacy. Our experienced professionals and staff focus on specialty medicines and the conditions they treat.

Prime

a medicine company

Aim:

1) to help you get your medicine

2) to make your medicine __48__ and your experience easier

Ways of getting your medicine:

1) from PrimeMail, ordering your __49__ medicine

2) from a large national __50__ of pharmacies: bringing your prescription and __51__

3) from Prime Therapeutics Specialty Pharmacy, a __52__ pharmacy, for specialty medicines

---

Task 4

A	School Zone
B	Vendors Prohibited
C	Pass on Left
D	Don't Step On
E	Keep Away for Safety
F	Service Area
G	Administrative Area
H	Watch Your Hand
I	Please Don't Leave Valuables Unattended
J	Maintenance in Progress
K	Out of Service
L	Stand on Right
M	Break Glass in Emergency
N	Don't Touch
O	Keep Clear of the Door
P	Don't Exceed Speed Limit
Q	Icy Road

Examples：（E）注意安全，请勿靠近　　　　（B）禁止摆摊

53.（　）当心夹手	（　）请勿踩踏
54.（　）服务区	（　）勿靠车门
55.（　）严禁超速	（　）正在检修
56.（　）前方学校	（　）靠右站立
57.（　）路面结冰	（　）紧急情况击碎玻璃

Task 5

Please Contact us to Arrange a Safety Inspection.

Address：246 N. High St. , Columbus, Ohio 43215.

Columbia Gas must perform a safety inspection at the address above.

We are required by federal law to inspect your service line and meter setting. Please call us at 1-800-344-4077, Monday through Friday, 7:00 am—7:00 pm.

If you have already arranged an inspection, there is no reason to call. Please ignore this letter. Please understand, communications will continue until the inspection has been completed.

This important safety inspection is part of our promise to provide safe and reliable service to our customers.

We will make every effort to do the work at a date and time that is convenient to you.

If this inspection is not performed, we cannot continue your service. Please call us today to set up an inspection.

Thank you for your attention to this letter.

58. What is the gas company required to do by federal law?

　　To inspect the letter receiver's _____ and meter setting.

59. In what case can the letter receiver ignore this letter?

　　If he/she has already _____.

60. How long will the communications last?

　　Communications will continue until _____ has been completed.

61. What has the gas company promised to do?

　　To provide _____ service to its customers.

62. In what case will the gas company stop its service for its customers?

　　If the inspection _____.

2018年12月真题

Part III Reading Comprehension (35 minutes)

Directions: *This part is to test your reading ability. There are 5 tasks for you to fulfill. You should read the reading materials carefully and do the tasks as you are instructed.*

Task 1

PowerShow.com is a leading presentation/slideshows(展示与放映幻灯片) sharing website. Whether your application is business, how-to, education, medicine, school, sales, marketing, online training or just for fun, PowerShow.com is a great resource. And, best of all, most of its cool features are free and easy to use.

You can use PowerShow.com to find and download sample PowerPoint presentations on just about any topic you can imagine, so you can learn how to improve your own slides and presentations for free.

For a small fee you can get the industry's best online privacy(网络隐私) or publicly promote your presentations and slide shows with top rankings(排名). But aside from that, it's FREE. We'll even change your presentations and slide shows into the Flash, including 2D and 3D effects, music or other audio. All for free. Most of the presentations and slideshows on PowerShow.com are free to view; many are even free to download. Check out PowerShow.com today—for FREE. There is truly something for everyone!

40. According to the first paragraph, PowerShow.com is a website which _____.
    A) offers advertising spaces
    B) provides training courses
    C) shares slideshows
    D) sells APPs

41. Most of PowerShow.com's features are _____.
    A) convenient to develop
    B) expensive to buy
    C) difficult to log in
    D) easy to use

42. By using PowerShow.com, you can learn to _____.
    A) make your presentations better
    B) create your personal website
    C) develop your own software
    D) conduct an online survey

43. If you want to get the industry's best online privacy, you need to _____.
    A) sign a contract
    B) pay a small fee
    C) ask for permission
    D) register a new account

44. Which of the following could be the title of the passage?
    A) Introduction to PowerShow Website.
    B) Developing Presentation Skills.
    C) Setting up a Personal Website.
    D) Future of PowerShow.com.

Task 2

PUBLIC ANNOUNCEMENT:

We would like to take this opportunity to thank our friends and customers for their loyal patronage for the past four years.

At this time and after careful consideration, we have decided to close our retail store in order to expand our wholesale business. The Vinjerud Family, however, does plan to open in a more convenient location in the future.

If you have a gift card, please contact Olivia Costa at 508.910.2100 or olivia@oceans-fleet.com between the hours of 9:30 a.m. and 1:30 p.m. to make an appointment to be reimbursed for the full remaining value.

Again, we sincerely appreciate all the support we have received.

Sincerely,
The Management

Notes: 1. patronage 惠顾   2. reimburse 偿还

45. This announcement is to inform the public about _____.

    A) the awards and prize winners   B) the closing of a retail store

    C) the seasonal sales   D) the new arrivals

46. In the future, the Vinjerud Family intends to start its business _____.

    A) on a similar scale   B) with more employees

    C) under better management   D) in a more convenient place

47. What are people asked to do if they have a gift card?

    A) Contact the store for the remaining value.

    B) Shop in any other retail stores in the town.

    C) Exchange for gifts in the store.

    D) Keep it for future use.

Task 3

A sure way to grow your business is to get people excited about your products or services. Postcards, posters (海报), and brochures (小册子) are easy and effective ways to get the news out about sales, events and other promotions.

Postcards with discount information is a great way to attract customers to return. You can mail them out, add them to your packaging, leave them on your counter for customers to take and share.

Posters are eye-catching and easily seen. Show them outside to attract passersby (过路人), and hang them inside your store to guide and inform customers. Use bold, bright messaging and images to gain most attention.

Brochures allow you to present more detailed information about your business. Use photos and clear messaging to tell potential customers everything you want them to know. These products have plenty of room for pricing, service lists and menus, too.

Ways to Grow Your Business

Postcards with discount information:
 * why: attract customers to __48__
 * how: 1) mail them out
   2) add them to __49__
   3) leave them on the counter

Posters:
 * why: eye-catching and __50__
 * how: 1) show them outside to attract people
   2) hang them inside the store
   3) use bold, bright messaging and images

Brochures:
 * why: offer more __51__ about the business
 * how: use __52__ and clear messaging

Task 4

A ———————————— avoid loose clothing
B ———————————— install safety guards
C ———————————— keep workplace clean
D ———————————— know evacuation routes
E ———————————— know how to lift heavy loads
F ———————————— know machine operating procedure
G ———————————— never reach into running machines
H ———————————— place trash in proper containers
I ———————————— report any unsafe conditions
J ———————————— shut down machines when not in use
K ———————————— store chemicals correctly
L ———————————— store your tools after use
M ———————————— turn off machines in between jobs
N ———————————— wash hands
O ———————————— wear protective uniform
P ———————————— wear safety glasses
Q ———————————— use two-handed operations

Examples:(D) 熟悉疏散路线　　　　(F) 掌握机器操作程序

53. (　) 保持工作区域清洁　　(　) 工作间隙关闭机器
54. (　) 正确储存化学品　　　(　) 戴上防护眼镜
55. (　) 机器不用时请关闭　　(　) 任何不安全状况须报告
56. (　) 勿穿宽松服装　　　　(　) 穿好防护制服
57. (　) 使用双手操作　　　　(　) 了解如何提升重物

Task 5

Have your insurance card ready when you go to the doctor or to pick up a prescription (处方). You card will have basic information on it, including the insurance provider, the policy number, and the expiration(到期) date.

Knowing your policy benefits can make a huge difference, especially if you are involved in a medical emergency. Before getting insurance, you will find out about what and how much your insurance covers. You can find this information on your insurance provider's website.

Also, stay updated! Make sure you are aware of any changes in your insurance benefits.

Where to Start

Look into finding a doctor that you can go to regularly for your check-ups and illness. Having one doctor who knows about many aspects of your health ensures you get the best care.

If your college has a clinic(诊所), that may be a good place to start. If this isn't a good choice for you, look into nearby clinics in the area. Be careful to check what insurance plans they accept. This is important because health care can be expensive.

58. What should you do before going to a doctor?

    You should have your _____ ready.

59. What information can be found on your insurance card?

    The insurance provider, _____, and the expiration date.

60. Where can you find the information about what your insurance covers?

    On your _____.

61. Why should you always stay updated?

    To be aware of _____ in the insurance benefits.

62. Why is it important to check what insurance plans the clinics accept?

    Because health care can be _____.

2019 年 6 月真题

Part Ⅲ Reading Comprehension (35 minutes)

Directions: *This part is to test your reading ability. There are 5 tasks for you to fulfill. You should read the reading materials carefully and do the tasks as you are instructed.*

Task 1

Does it seem like hotel costs just go up and up? It's true that they rise each year. Rates for rooms in 2019 are over 15% more than 2018. Here are some tips to help you make the best decision.

Look for extras.

The more services your rate includes, the more you can save your money. Make sure you use the facilities you will actually need, or you'll spend more than you need to. Common extras that can save you a lot are free breakfast, free WI-FI, and kids eat free. So take advantage of them during your stay.

Stay in hotels right outside the city center.

If the costs for transportation won't be high, you can frequently get a good deal this way. You could also look into staying in the university district of city. Hotels are more affordable(廉价的), cheap eating places are plentiful(充足的) and public transportation is convenient.

Go out to eat.

Though room service sounds really great, prices for food on the hotel menu can be twice as much you would pay for the same food at a restaurant.

40. What is TURE of hotels according to the first paragraph?

   A) More hotels are to be built soon.　　B) Hotel costs increase year by year.

   C) Hotels are in great demand today.　　D) Hotel costs rise over 15% each year.

41. One piece of advice to hotel guests is _____.

   A) to use all the hotel entertainment equipment

   B) to take your family members along with you

   C) to take advantage of the common extras included in the rate

   D) to enjoy as many facilities provided by the hotel as possible

42. One advantage of staying in the university districts is _____.

   A) the friendly environment　　B) more entertainment activities

   C) easy access to the university library　　D) the convenient public transportation

43. Why are you advised to go out to eat when you are staying at a hotel?

   A) Food served in hotels is too expensive.

   B) Restaurants offer better services.

   C) Food in a restaurant is really great.

   D) Room service has limited food varieties.

44. The passage is mainly about how to _____.

   A) best enjoy room service in a hotel

   B) save money while staying in a hotel

   C) choose a hotel in a university district

   D) make use of common extras in a hotel

Task 2

Notes: 1. bid 投标   2. bonded 有担保的

45. What kind of service is provided by the company?

   A) Equipment rental.　　　　　　B) Machine repairing.

   C) Software designing.　　　　　D) Construction clean-up.

46. What should you do if you want to invite the company to bid for your project?

   A) Call Mike Jones.

   B) Visit the company's manager.

   C) Post your invitation for bid online.

   D) Send a bid form to Jones Clean-up Services.

47. What guarantee does Jones Cleaning Service promise in the poster?

   A) The latest design.　　　　　　B) The lowest price.

   C) 100 percent satisfaction.　　　D) The use of green materials.

Task 3

Attention, Residents!

Norris & Stevens is pleased to offer residents the ability to pay online via PayLease! PayLease is a leading payment processing company in the property management industry. Residents will enjoy the following benefits:

- Online payments via credit card or electronic check.
- One time payments at your convenience.
- Automatic payments to pay rent.
- Call center for support.

- Secure and easy to use payment system.

Here is how to get started:
- Please visit *PayLease. com.*
- Click on "Pay Rent Online" to register（注册）.
- You will need your Skyline account number to register.
- Once registered, you can process a one-time payment or set up automatic pay.

If you should have any questions regarding you balance or your account with Norris & Stevents, please contact your property manager. If you should have any questions regarding PayLease, please contact（联系）PayLease Support at 1-866-734-5322.

Thank you for using PayLease!

```
                    Norris & Stevens' New Service
Paying online via PayLease, a leading   48   company
Benefits of using PayLease: 1) paying online via   49   and electronic check
                           2) convenient
                           3) automatic rent payments
                           4) call center for   50
                           5) secure and easy
Registration: visiting   51   and clicking on "Pay Rent Online"
Contact: 1) your property manager
         2) PayLease Support at   52
```

Task 4

A	cost of quality
B	quality level
C	quality control
D	quality management
E	supply chain
F	quality assurance
G	major defect
H	inspection certificate
I	check list
J	quality engineering
K	sample size
L	inspection cost
M	rejection number
N	laboratory testing

O —————————————————— quality inspector
P —————————————————— consumer safety
Q —————————————————— appearance check

Examples：（G）主要缺陷　　　　　（M）退货数量

53. （　）质量控制	（　）消费者安全
54. （　）检验证书	（　）质量工程
55. （　）质量等级	（　）检验成本
56. （　）质检员	（　）供应链
57. （　）样本大小	（　）外观检查

Task 5

Return Policy：

We want you to be 100% satisfied with your purchase.

If for any reason you are not satisfied, you may return your product within 30 days of your purchase. All returned items must be in new condition as it is received, including the original box, packaging and accessories(附件). Missing or damaged accessories will result in additional fees.

Replacements of Defective(有缺陷的) **or Damaged Items**：

If you have received a defective (including missing, broken, non-functioning) or damaged item, please contact us within 1 week so that we may solve the issue and send you the replacement under our cost. For damaged products, pictures are required. If for any reason, pictures cannot be provided as proof of damages, items must be shipped back to us(prepaid postage is not covered by us).

Please email us at *sales@greennatrualsolar.com* to request a RMA number and return instruction before return.

58. When can you return the product if you are not satisfied with the purchase?
    Within _____ of your purchase.

59. What is required of your product if you want to return it?
    All its required items must be _____ as it is received.

60. What would happen to you if any accessories were found missing in your returned item?
    You will have to pay _____.

61. What is required of damaged products when they are returned?
    For the damaged products, _____ are required.

62. What should you do before returning the product?
    Ask for a RMA number and _____ before return.

2019 年 12 月真题

Part III Reading Comprehension (35 minutes)

Directions: *This part is to test your reading ability. There are 5 tasks for you to fulfill. You should read the reading materials carefully and do the tasks as you are instructed.*

Task 1

Starting a business takes time and energy—not to mention funding. So it helps if you're enthusiastic about what you do. Some business owners like Ms. Walton, have managed to turn their hobby into a business.

Ms. Walton is a former personal trainer and the founder and owner of a travel agency for runners of various adventure(冒险) races. She describes running a business as "a big job" and says there have been lots of difficulties to overcome along the way.

A challenge for new companies is marketing, as business owners often need to create a website and develop a brand strategy(策略) for the company. As she explains, being present at these events attracts the attention of the public to their business and enables the brand to reach its target market.

She adds that her relationship with her banker has supported her through <u>the ups and downs</u> of running her company. A banker can help with small business financing, your business banking requirements and also advise on ways to expand your business.

40. According to the first paragraph, to start a business, you should be _____.
    A) healthy   B) wealthy
    C) efficient   D) enthusiastic

41. Why does Ms. Walton say running a business is "a big job"?
    A) You have to take part in adventure races.
    B) You have many difficulties to overcome.
    C) You must travel a lot at home and abroad.
    D) You need to work on weekends frequently.

42. One thing business owners often need to do for marketing is _____.
    A) to hire a team of experts   B) to expand overseas market
    C) to build up a brand strategy   D) to find a location downtown

43. The expression "the ups and downs" in Para. 4 means "_____".
    A) present and past situations   B) good and bad experiences
    C) chances and challenges   D) happy and sad feelings

44. According to the passage, a banker can help small business in _____.

   A) financing   B) advertising

   C) hiring personnel   D) training their staff

Task 2

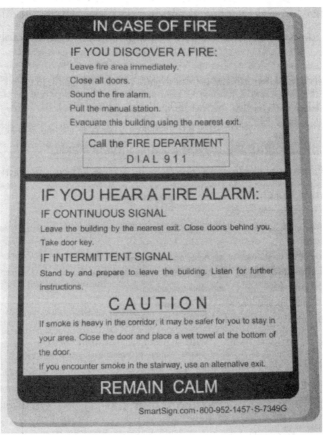

Notes: 1. evacuate 撤离   2. intermittent 间歇的   3. corridor 走廊

45. If you discover a fire, you are advised to _____.

   A) call your best friend   B) check the area carefully

   C) help the people in the area   D) leave the area immediately

46. What should you do if you hear a continuous fire alarm?

   A) Leave the building by the closest exit.

   B) Listen for further instructions.

   C) Stand by and get prepared.

   D) Wait for firefighters' help.

47. If smoke is heavy in the corridor, you are advised to _____.

   A) open the door at once   B) stay in your area

   C) lie on the floor   D) run downstairs

Task 3

BIZSHOT is Asia's most exciting deep tech startup(初创企业) competition to select top 100 global startups. BIZSHOT 2020 will be held from 11 to 13 March, 2020 in Tianjin. Startups of all fields and backgrounds are invited to BIZSHOT 2020. Please submit(提交) your most innovative(创新的) technical and business ideas! Keep in mind that we are not only looking for ideas. Your submission requires at least a workable product with a practical solution.

Your submission will be reviewed by more than 160 industry experts and decision-makers including major investors and companies. The Top 100 Global Startups will be selected to meet first class experts in their fields. This will be an excellent opportunity to display your startup in front of the biggest players in your fields!

Are you ready for the challenge? Sign up now, and then click on the "Participate" button to submit your material!

BIZSHOT 2020

Aim: to select top 100 __48__

Date: from __49__ March, 2020

Place: Tianjin

Businesses invited: startups of all fields and backgrounds

Submission required: at least __50__ with a practical solution

Reviewers: over 160 __51__ and decision-makers

Way to submit: clicking on the __52__ button

Task 4

A —— Chain store
B —— Consumer behavior
C —— Consumer satisfaction
D —— Direct selling
E —— Market demand
F —— Market research
G —— Target market
H —— Brand image
I —— Promotion methods
J —— Telephone sales
K —— Direct costs
L —— Product quality
M —— Purchase decision

N -- Added value
O -- After-sales service
P -- Brand management
Q -- Customer loyalty

Examples：（C）消费者满意度　　　　　（Q）消费者忠诚度

53.（　）促销方法	（　）市场需求
54.（　）市场调研	（　）售后服务
55.（　）直接成本	（　）消费者行为
56.（　）品牌形象	（　）购买决策
57.（　）目标市场	（　）品牌管理

Task 5

If you ever need help saving money on car insurance, contact your local GEICO office. You'll get the great rates from GEICO. And they'll help make sure you receive all the discounts and special benefits you deserve.

Your local GEICO office can help you find coverage（保险范围）for almost anything you own. We offer coverage for your motorcycle, ATV, boat or RV.

GEICO has been saving people money for more than 75 years and is the second-largest personal auto insurance in the country, insuring over 21 million drivers.

You can go to *www.geico.com* to report a claim, schedule an appointment, even view your estimate（估算）and photos of the damage. And when you take your car to a GEICO-approved shop, the claim repairs are guaranteed for as long as you own your vehicle.

58. Why are you advised to contact your local GEICO office?

　　It will help you save money on _____.

59. How can GEICO help you save money?

　　It helps you receive _____ and special benefits you deserve.

60. How long has GEICO been in operation?

　　For more than _____.

61. How many drivers have been insured by GEICO?

　　More than _____.

62. How can you report your claim?

　　By visiting _____.

第五章
英译汉

第一节 题型综述

高等学校英语应用能力考试 B 级测试的第四部分为英译汉(Translation—English to Chinese),该部分共有 5 题,占总分的 15%,测试时间为 25 分钟。所译材料为句子和段落,包括一般性内容(约占 60%)和应用性内容(约占 40%);所涉及的词汇限于《基本要求》中"词汇表"B 级范围。

英译汉部分要求掌握的技能包括两部分:一是理解英语;二是进行汉语表达。在翻译过程中,考生既要忠实于原文,又要正确完整地表达原文意思,行文要顺畅、连贯,符合汉语表达习惯,做到言简意赅。

该部分共设两种题型。其中 63–66 题是句子翻译,都是多项选择题,题目中给出一个句子,然后下面有三个选项,要求考生从选项中选择最恰当的一项;这种翻译句子都不太长,一般不超过 20 个字,而且句子中基本没有超纲词汇,句子结构也比较简单,一般都是简单句、并列句或主从复合句。这部分题的评分标准有点特别:按照等级分为最好答案、较好答案和较差答案,相应的分数是 2 分、1 分和 0 分,共 8 分。第 67 题是一篇段落翻译,文章一般都不超过 80 词,超纲生词不多于 2 个,句子不超过 6 个,多为简单句、并列句或主从复合句,总分为 7 分。

第二节 考点归纳

第一部分的题型为句子翻译,以选择题形式出现,要求考生从三个正确程度不等的选项中选择与给出的英语句子最一致的汉语译文。句子翻译考查的项目大多为语法结构,如虚拟语气及其各种变体、真实条件句、强调句、关系从句、并列结构、倒装、否定和转折等。此外,考查的还有动词短语、名词短语、介词短语、词类转换、多义词等。

根据高等学校英语应用能力考试 B 级的历年真题,2015—2019 年句子翻译常考的句型结构见表 5.1。

表 5.1　2015—2019 年句子翻译常考句型结构

句型	时间									
	2015-6	2015-12	2016-6	2016-12	2017-6	2017-12	2018-6	2018-12	2019-6	2019-12
简单句	4	3	1	1	2	1	1	1	0	2
并列句	0	0	2	1	0	1	1	0	1	0
复合句	0	1	1	2	2	2	2	3	3	2

注:数字表示考查的次数。

第二部分的题型为段落翻译,以主观题的形式出现,要求考生将一段 60～70 词的短文译成流畅的汉语。翻译题中所涉及的文章题材除了科普、人物、政治、商贸、文化等一般题材,还包括业务信函、传真、电子邮件、商场告示、申请、启事、广告、酒店预订、产品或厂家介绍、产品维护及使用说明等应用文类题材。

根据高等学校英语应用能力考试 B 级的历年真题,2015—2019 年段落翻译的相关参数见表 5.2。

表 5.2　2015—2019 年段落翻译的相关参数

时间	参数					
	字数	句子总数	超纲词数	简单句的句数	并列句的句数	复合句的句数
2015-6	58	3	0	1	0	2
2015-12	67	5	0	3	1	1
2016-6	70	5	0	4	1	0
2016-12	65	6	0	4	1	1
2017-6	62	5	1	1	1	3
2017-12	59	6	1	6	0	0
2018-6	66	5	1	4	0	1
2018-12	69	4	1	1	0	2
2019-6	67	4	0	2	1	1
2019-12	74	4	0	1	0	3

从表 5.2 可以看出,2015—2019 年段落翻译的平均字数为 65.7 个,句子总数最少 3 句,最多 6 句,超纲词偶尔出现,句型以简单句为主,复合句次之,并列句出现的概率最低,整体难度不高。

此外,2015—2019 年段落翻译的常考题材见表 5.3。

表 5.3 2015—2019 年段落翻译的常考题材

时间	题材								
	广告	旅游服务	公司介绍	施工通告	项目介绍	邮寄须知	酒店预订	理财服务	其他
2015-6			√						
2015-12	√								
2016-6									√
2016-12				√					
2017-6						√			
2017-12						√			
2018-6								√	
2018-12		√							
2019-6	√								
2019-12							√		

从表 5.3 可知,2015—2019 年所考的段落翻译题材几乎没有重复,各种题材均有出现,其中广告出现 2 次,其他题材只出现 1 次。由此,考生需要熟悉各种题材,尤其是在词汇方面,平时应加强对相关材料的阅读和词汇的积累。

第三节 技巧点拨

翻译过程包括两个阶段:正确理解和充分表达。考生做英译汉试题时,应先通读全文,把握全文的主旨、内容;在语义上弄清全句的整体意思和每个单词的意思,分析清楚句子结构,找出各分句之间的关系;从内容和语言两方面来考虑译文,将译文与原文进行对照,判断译文是否忠实于原文、通顺易懂和符合汉语规范。

一、词的译法

1. 词义的选择

英语中一词多义的现象十分普遍,而且英汉词典中给出的汉语解释未必全面,未必与英文的意思完全对等,这就带来两方面的问题:一是需要根据该多义词在其语言环境中的词类、搭配关系甚至单复数形式来确定其基本意思;二是,在"忠实"的原则下,如果词典上的释义显得不"通顺",那么为了"忠实"与"通顺"的统一,必须立足于原意,对其加以适当的引申。如:

Now things are different. 现在情况不一样了。

things 最常见的意思是"事务",但在这里翻译成"情况"比较合适。

2．词类的转化

英汉两种语言属于不同的语系,因此在词汇或语法方面都有很大的差别。在翻译实践中,很多情况需要进行词类转换,即把原文语言中的某一词类转化成汉语的另一种词类。

(1) 名词变动词

英语中有大量具有动作意义的名词和动词派生出来的名词可以被译成汉语动词。如：

This book is a **reflection** of Chinese society in the 1930s. 这本书反映了 20 世纪 30 年代的中国社会。

(2) 形容词变动词

英语中某些表示状态、知觉、情感、态度、感受、感觉等意义,在句子作表语的形容词,通常可被译成汉语动词。如：

I am **anxious** about her health. 我为她的健康担忧。

(3) 介词变动词

英语中的介词或介词短语在许多情况下可以被译成汉语动词,尤其是作表语或状语时。如：

Many laboratories are developing medicines **against** AIDS. 许多实验室正在研制治疗艾滋病的药物。

(4) 副词变动词

英语中有些作表语的副词或复合宾语中的副词,往往可被译成汉语动词。如：

The test was not **over** yet. 实验还没结束。

(5) 副词变名词

英语中有些副词,在句中作状语,译成汉语时可根据具体情况转换成汉语名词。如：

She is **physically** weak but mentally sound. 她体质差,但头脑健全。

(6) 动词变名词

英语中某些感觉动词,如 look、sound、taste、think 等,译成汉语时,可被转换成名词。如：

Western people **think** differently from Chinese People. 西方人与中国人的思维方式不同。

(7) 名词变副词

出于语法结构和修辞的需要,英语的名词可被译为汉语的形容词或副词。如：

The girl in the seat is studying the old woman beside her with **interest.** 那个坐着的女孩好奇地打量着她身边的老妇人。

3．词的增减

英汉两种语言由于语法结构的差异、修辞手法的不同,在翻译过程中常常出现词量增补或减少的现象。如：

It is acknowledged it is a good way to climb mountain in hot days. 大家赞同,在炎热的季节爬山常是人们避暑的好方法。(增词)

The earth moves round **the** sun. 地球绕着太阳转。(减词)

4．否定词与含否定意义的词的译法

(1) 正义反译

在翻译实践中,为了使译文忠实而合乎语法习惯地传达原文的意思,须把原文中的肯定说法变成译文中的否定说法。如:

deny 否决,否定→不给予

miss 错过→没赶上,没听到/看到或没听/看懂

(2) 反义正译

有时为了表达的需要,须将原文中的否定说法变成译文中的肯定说法。如:

no less than 简直就是

no less...than 和……一样

(3) 否定词的转移

在英语中,把否定词从原来应在的位置转移到句子的谓语动词前。如:

I didn't come to trade pins. 我来可不是为了买卖奥运会纪念品。

二、被动语态的译法

使用被动语态是科技文章的主要特点之一。在汉语中,我们可用"被""让""把""遭""换""使""由""受到""为……所"等词来表示被动。汉语中被动语态的使用频率比英语要低得多。因此,在遇到被动语态时,翻译应遵循汉语的习惯,如果译成被动语态不通,则译成主动语态。

1．保留被动语

在采用此说法时,往往在译文中使用"加以""经过""用……来""为"等词来体现原文中的被动含义。如:

How well the predictions will be validated by later performances depends on ... 这些预测在多大程度上为后来的表现所证实,取决于……

2．将被动改为主动

将英语原文中的主语译为宾语,同时增补泛指性的词语(如人们、大家等)作主语。如:

It is believed that... 有人认为或人们相信……

It is told that... 有人曾说过……

三、长句的译法

1．长句的分析

① 找出全句的主语、谓语和宾语,从整体上把握句子的结构;

② 找出句中所有的谓语结构、非谓语动词、介词短语和从句的引导词;

③ 分析从句和短语的功能;

④ 分析词、短语和从句之间的相互关系;

⑤ 注意插入语等其他成分;
⑥ 注意分析句子中是否有固定词组或固定搭配。

2. 长句的翻译

（1）顺译法

顺译法,即顺着英文原有的顺序翻译,条件是英语句子的内容与叙述方式同汉语习惯基本一致。如：

In this chapter, we shall take a closer look at the structure of a few particularly interesting atoms and molecules in order to see how they are fitted to the use man makes of them. 在本章中,我们将更仔细地研究几个特别有趣的原子和分子的结构,看看怎样使它们便于为人类所利用。

（2）逆译法

逆译法,即不再遵照英文原有的顺序,甚至完全逆着原有顺序翻译,如果英文的表达次序和汉语的表达习惯不同甚至相反的话。如：

It therefore becomes more and more important that, if students are not to waste their opportunities, there will have to be much more detailed information about courses and more advice. 因此,如果要使学生充分利用他们(上大学)的机会,就得为他们提供大量关于课程的更为详尽的信息,做更多的指导。这个显得越来越重要了。

（3）分译法

如果句子中的从句与主句的关系不是很密切,可以将它们与主句分割开来,使译文变成好几个短句。这与英汉两种语言表达较复杂的意思的习惯是一致的:前者偏向于使用含有多重层次的主从复合句或并列复合句,而后者往往崇尚"言简意赅"。如：

Television, it is often said, keeps one informed about current events, allow one to follow the latest developments in science and politics. 人们常说,通过电视可以了解时事,掌握科学和政治的最新动态。

（4）综合法

仔细分析,或按照时间的先后,或按照逻辑顺序,顺逆翻译结合,主次分明地对全句进行综合处理,以便把英语原文翻译成通顺忠实的汉语句子。如：

People were afraid to leave their houses, for although the police had been ordered to stand by in case of emergency, they were just as confused and helpless as anybody else. 尽管警察已接到命令,要做好准备以应付紧急情况,但人们不敢出门,因为警察也和其他人一样不知所措和无能为力。

四、各种从句的译法

1. 定语从句

译法一,译成含"的"字结构的定语,放在先行词之前。如：

The people who worked for him lived in mortal fear of him. 在他手下工作的人对他怕

得要死。

译法二,采用"分译法",将较长的定语从句独立出去,并将先行词重复一次。如:

I told the story to John, who told it to his brother. 我把这件事告诉了约翰,约翰又告诉了他的弟弟。

译法三,译成状语从句。如:

I don't know the reason why (for which) he didn't come to the meeting yesterday morning. 我不知道为什么他没有参加昨天上午的会议。

2. **名词性从句**

(1) 主语从句

如果主语从句和后面的成分都不长,则按顺序在一句话里完成;如果主语很长,而其他成分很短,则可采用逆译法;倘若二者长度相当且都较长,则采用分译法。如:

It's certain that she will succeed. 她会成功是肯定的。

(2) 表语从句

通常用顺译法。如:

The reason he did not come is that he is ill. 他没来的原因是他病了。

(3) 宾语从句

如果宾语从句较长,且是第一层次的从句,句子往往在主句谓语动词和宾语从句之间断开。如:

She promised us that she would give us more help later on. 她答应以后给我们更多的帮助。

(4) 同位语从句

采用类似于定语从句的译法——处理成含"的"字结构的定语,其同位语则成为该定语修饰的对象;或采用分译法,先译同位语,再补充同位语从句的内容。如:

The news that we are invited to the conference is very encouraging. 我们被邀请去参加会议的消息令人鼓舞。

3. **状语从句**

(1) when 引导的时间状语从句

when 引导的时间状语从句与主句之间有逗号隔开,说明主句已经是一个完整的句子,从句与主句关系松散,只是一种语气很弱的补充。如:

When she comes, I shall tell her to wait for you. 她来的时候我会告诉她等你的。

(2) so...that...引导的结果状语从句

一般不译成"如此……以至于……"。如:

The wind was so strong that we could hardly move forward. 风刮得那么大,我们简直寸步难行。

第四节 实战演练

2015年6月真题

Part Ⅳ　Translation—English into Chinese（25 minutes）

Directions： *This part, numbered 63 to 67, is to test your ability to translate English into Chinese. Each of the four sentences (No. 63 to No. 66) is followed by three choices of suggested translation marked A), B), and C). Make the best choice and write the corresponding letter on the Answer Sheet with a single line through the center. And then write your translation of the paragraph (No. 67) in the corresponding space on the Translation/Composition Sheet.*

63. The VIP customer can take advantage of discounted room rates on a "first-come, first-served" basis.

　　A）贵宾可以根据"先来先得"的原则，享受折扣房价的优惠。

　　B）本酒店按照"先来后到"的顺序安排贵宾入住并确定房价。

　　C）根据"先来后到"的原则，先来的客人可选择房价折扣率。

64. As the world's largest retailer, Walmart naturally wants to provide its customers with a wide range of products.

　　A）作为全球最大的超市，沃尔玛当然会向不同消费者提供不同的产品。

　　B）作为全球最大的零售商，沃尔玛自然要为它的消费者提供众多产品。

　　C）作为一家全球最大的跨国公司，沃尔玛在全球范围内销售大量商品。

65. *Cars.com* offers easy-to-understand information to help you decide what car to buy and how much to pay.

　　A）*Cars.com* 提供的信息容易理解，能帮你决定该买什么车和花多少钱。

　　B）*Cars.com* 列出的信息都很容易获取，并且告诉你要花多少钱买汽车。

　　C）*Cars.com* 销售的汽车都很容易驾驶，而且允许购车者办理分期付款。

66. According to a recent survey, there is demand for medical assistants in different areas of medicine.

　　A）各地区统计报告表明，许多地方的医院都急需补充医疗设备。

　　B）调查清楚表明，在许多不同的医药领域，都需要有医药助理。

　　C）根据最近的一项调查，不同的医学领域对医辅人员都有需求。

67. As an international company, ABC group has been in business for over 50 years. Finding a job within the company can lead you to new heights in your career, as there is room to be promoted to higher positions. These jobs can be the perfect fit for you if you are looking for a job within a growing company.

2015年12月真题

Part Ⅳ Translation—English into Chinese (25 minutes)

63. Before developing their new project, the management team had thoroughly examined the organization's current situation.

    A) 在开发新的项目之前,管理团队全面审视了该机构的现状。
    B) 管理团队要先研究策略,才能清楚地了解公司产品的情况。
    C) 要研发新的产品,管理团队须仔细地摸清公司原先的状况。

64. Our goal is to help business owners and professionals to master the art of effective communication.

    A) 我们公司近期的目标是希望能找到具有沟通能力的专业人员。
    B) 我们的宗旨是帮助企业主以及专业人士掌握有效交流的艺术。
    C) 我们的目的是帮助公司老板与专家熟悉情况,提高沟通效率。

65. With over 60,000 products available, we are able to provide you with the top brand names on the market.

    A) 我们能为你们提供市场上各种品牌,已拥有超过六万多商品。
    B) 我们将继续为你们提供各种产品,争取总量能达到六万多种。
    C) 我们拥有六万多个产品,可以向你们提供市场上的顶级品牌。

66. The training course is designed for managers who want to increase their confidence and understand different marketing styles.

    A) 本培训课程是为那些需要提高自信和了解不同营销风格的经理们而设计的。
    B) 本培训课程的目的是为提高员工自信心,使他们了解不同的市场销售手段。
    C) 本培训课程由经理设计,使员工掌握各种营销手段,用以提高他们的能力。

67. We repair computers of all brands. We provide you with professional advice, saving you both time and money in the long run. Our team understands technology well enough to make most computer systems work better. Bring your computer in for a Free Check-Up, and we will recommend the most efficient way to solve your problems. We will only charge money if we can provide you with results!

2016年6月真题

Part Ⅳ　Translation—English into Chinese（25 minutes）

63. You can try booking a flight by using your smartphone, but most airlines aren't that advanced yet.

   A）你可以用智能手机预选座位,但大多数航空公司还未能提供这种服务。

   B）你可以尝试用智能手机订机票,但是大多数航空公司还没有这么先进。

   C）你可以在飞行过程中使用智能手机,但是大多数航班都不允许这么做。

64. Candidates must meet all of the following basic qualifications and send an application for this position by email.

   A）求职者先要参加面试,达到所有的基本要求,才有可能上岗。

   B）求职者必须具备下列所有的基本任职资格,并电邮求职申请。

   C）求职者须了解所有岗位的资历要求,并且邮寄一份求职申请。

65. The new center will allow them to have a worldwide distribution network to supply products to customers.

   A）这个新设的中心将使他们拥有一个全球分销网络,向客户提供产品。

   B）欢迎客户到我们中心来参观,了解和体验我们最新的全球营销网络。

   C）为了能及时向客户提供产品,我们在这里新建了一个全球营销网络。

66. To learn another language is more than just learning words and grammar, which involves learning about another culture.

   A）要学好另一种语言,应多背单词并掌握语法规则,还要精通文化知识。

   B）学习另一种语言就是多掌握单词和语法,并且多多参与文化交流活动。

   C）学习另一种语言不仅仅是学习单词和语法,还涉及学习另一种文化。

67. 　　Remember, living green really does make our life different! It is a healthy choice both for us and for our planet. In the long run, small changes we make in our life will have a great impact on the planet. As the old saying goes, no one can do everything, but everyone can do something!

   　　With the idea of living green every single day, our Green Year is getting started.

2016年12月真题

Part IV Translation—English into Chinese (25 minutes)

63. To serve our club members better, we continually seek opportunities to open more clubs around the world.

    A) 为了提高俱乐部成员的整体素养,我们一直以各种不同的方式为大家提供免费的培训。

    B) 为了更好地为我们的俱乐部会员服务,我们不断寻找机会在世界各地开设更多的俱乐部。

    C) 为了使我们的俱乐部成员享受更好的服务,我们继续寻求机会与世界各地的俱乐部合作。

64. Changing jobs frequently gives you a lot of different experiences in different environments, which shows you can adapt quickly.

    A) 频繁更换工作使你在不同环境下具有众多的经验,这就表明你能很快地适应。

    B) 不同的工作让你学会更快地适应环境,积累的不同经验也会带给你更多机遇。

    C) 经常换工作让你体验在不同环境中的许多工作感受,从而学会迅速适应环境。

65. I am grateful for all the arrangement for this visit, and I enjoyed everything of it.

    A) 我对你们这次的安排深表谢意,你们组织的所有活动我都参加。

    B) 这次访问我们收获颇丰,我学到了你们的丰富经验,印象深刻。

    C) 非常感谢你们对这次访问的所有安排,每一项安排我都很满意。

66. If you include a photo in your application while not asked for, an employer can assume you rely on your looks.

    A) 求职信通常需要附一张照片,老板会因为看到过你的照片而对你产生印象。

    B) 虽然未要求在求职函中附照片,但你还是附了照片,老板会认为你可靠。

    C) 虽没要求,如果你还是在求职信中附了照片,雇主会认为你想靠颜值取胜。

67.   The road construction will start on Monday, January 9th, 2017. It is expected to last one month. The area between 7th Street and 9th Street will be completely closed.

      We apologize for any inconvenience this may cause you, but the construction work is to make the roads safer. Thank you for your understanding.

      If you have any questions regarding the construction, please call at (650) 903-6311.

2017年6月真题

Part Ⅳ Translation—English into Chinese (25 minutes)

63. The healthcare and social assistant sector will account for almost a third of the job growth from 2012 to 2022.

    A) 从2012年至2022年,从事医疗保健工作的员工将占社会救助业的三分之一。

    B) 从2012年至2022年,医疗保健和社会救助业几乎将占就业增长的三分之一。

    C) 从2012年至2022年,医疗保健和社会救助业将会占到三分之一的就业岗位。

64. Regardless of your line of work, sending business invitations will certainly be something you will face from time to time.

    A) 无论你从事哪个行业,发业务邀请函必然是你时不时要遇到的事情。

    B) 只要你从事这个业务,就摆脱不了需要经常去处理商务函电等事项。

    C) 不管从事的是哪一个行当,你经常要做的一件事情就是收发邀请函。

65. Our company makes a special effort to establish good communication and cooperative relationships between management and labor.

    A) 本公司重视与管理层和服务人员的沟通,建立了良好的合作关系。

    B) 本公司为已与我们建立良好贸易合作关系的客户提供特殊的服务。

    C) 本公司特别致力于建立管理层与员工之间良好的沟通与合作关系。

66. If you need any help in starting a business, our team will be right here for you.

    A) 如果你需要创业,我们团队就可以在此给你提供帮助。

    B) 你在创业中如需任何帮助,我们团队会随时为你提供。

    C) 如果你创业失败,我们团队将会帮助你重新制订计划。

67.   Many items may be dangerous goods and could cause serious accidents when mailed. It is your responsibility to ensure that your parcel does not contain any dangerous goods. With your cooperation, accidents can be prevented. You could be held responsible if an accident occurred. If you wish to know whether you can mail a certain item, please call Customer Service at 1-800-267-1177.

2017年12月真题

Part Ⅳ Translation—English into Chinese (25 minutes)

63. Having trust in each other is very important because doing business requires good interpersonal relationships.

A) 有了信誉才有助于搞好与别人的关系,也有助于企业的发展。

B) 彼此之间的信任非常重要,因为做生意需要良好的人际关系。

C) 建立良好的人际关系至关重要,因为做生意必须要相互信任。

64. I am sorry I won't be able to attend the business meeting scheduled for next Friday.

A) 我无法出席拟于下星期五举行的业务会议,深表歉意。

B) 不巧得很,我没有时间,下周五我已经安排了生意谈判。

C) 不好意思,我实在来不及参加下周五进行的业务会谈。

65. To show our goodwill, we would like to offer you a 5% discount on your next order with us.

A) 为表现我们的善意,我们对贵方这次订货可以给予5%的优惠。

B) 为体现我们的诚意,贵方下次订货时,我们愿意给你5%的折扣。

C) 为促进商品销售,我们决定即日起对本公司所有产品让利5%。

66. I am writing to complain about the unfair treatment that I received in your restaurant last Friday.

A) 就你们餐馆低劣的服务质量,我上周五已致信消协反映。

B) 我在贵餐馆受到了不礼貌的待遇,我上周五已写信投诉。

C) 我写此信是投诉上星期五在贵餐厅受到的不公平的待遇。

67.　　Some people may find it difficult to visit this park due to old age. Now, our project provides free services for these people. We have trained volunteers to work as drivers. They are familiar with the park's history. And this wonderful project is supported by donation(捐赠)from the community. We ask you to give your support to this project.

2018 年 6 月真题

Part Ⅳ　Translation—English into Chinese（25 minutes）

63. We deal with a lot of foreign customers and are considered to be one of their most reliable agents.

A) 我们同许多国外客户打过交道,被一致认为是国内外首屈一指的代理商。

B) 我们与国外许多客户保持联系,而且我们为他们寻找国内最好的代理商。

C) 我们与许多外国客户有业务往来,并被认为是他们最可靠的代理商之一。

64. Anything you want to know can be found in seconds if you use the right keywords to search for it.

A) 如果你使用正确的关键词,就可以即刻搜索到你想知道的任何事物。

B) 你搜索的关键词得准确,这样才能很快地找到你所想要的数据。

C) 你先要知道使用关键词搜索的方法,才能从事你所做的研究工作。

65. We have all been so impressed with your abilities and potential that we are pleased to offer you a position.

   A）我们面试过的所有求职者中,你的能力最强,潜力最大。

   B）我们都对你的能力和潜力印象深刻,乐于为你提供职位。

   C）我们很欣赏你的能力和潜质,很高兴能有机会和你共事。

66. The aim of our website is to control or reduce noise at work without stopping people from enjoying music.

   A）本网站的方针是不断阻止或减少噪声,同时又能够使人们欣赏音乐。

   B）本网站的目的是控制或减小工作中的噪声,却不妨碍人们欣赏音乐。

   C）本网站的优势是用播放人们喜爱的音乐的方式,来缓解和抵消压力。

67.   If you're ready to take your next step in life, we can offer help to make the most of your money. You can have an informal meeting with your account manager(客户经理). The account manager will help you to find out a way to make your money work better. We'll also help you arrange your credit cards and loans. To book an appointment, call 0345-000-888.

2018 年 12 月真题

Part Ⅳ Translation—English into Chinese（25 minutes）

63. Before setting up the business, they conducted a market survey about production, sales and after-sales service.

   A）如果要创业,他们得有一笔启动资金,并且要有销售渠道。

   B）在创业前,他们对生产、销售和售后服务进行了市场调研。

   C）在开展业务前,他们对该产品的售后服务进行了市场调查。

64. Many Americans understand the life-saving value of the seat belt—the national use rate of it is at 90.1%.

   A）许多美国人懂得安全带的救生价值,全国安全带的使用率达到90.1%。

   B）许多美国人习惯于使用安全带,系安全带可以减少死亡率达到90.1%。

   C）许多美国人知道开车必须系安全带,90.1%的人都自觉遵守这一规则。

65. We are building a network of business experts who are ready to help you when you need it.

   A）我们正在筹建一个商业专家系统,他们可以向公众随时提供专业指导和帮助。

   B）我们正在创办一个专家信息库,急需一些能够随时提供帮助的专家给予指导。

   C）我们正在建立一个商务专家网络,当你需要帮助的时候,他们很乐于帮助你。

66. As our products have a good reputation both at home and abroad, their demand is

increasing year by year.

A) 我们的产品在国内外享有良好的声誉,所以其需求量正在逐年增加。

B) 由于我们的产品质量非常好,它们在国内外的需求量一年超过一年。

C) 因为国内外对我们产品的需求量很大,所以我们每年都扩大生产。

67. We hope that you found the tips on this page helpful and can put them to use on your next vacation. Whether you plan to fly or drive, use our travel comparison tool for all your transportation and hotel needs. Please visit us again and sign up for our newsletter(业务通讯)to keep getting the best deals and travel tips. By comparing hotel prices, you can save up to 70%.

2019 年 6 月真题

Part IV　Translation—English into Chinese（25 minutes）

63. This online business training site not only provides an introduction to its online program, but also offers business information.

A) 此在线商务培训网站不但介绍了线上活动的内容,另外还提供联系方式。

B) 该在线商业培训网站不仅提供其在线项目的内容介绍,还提供商业信息。

C) 参加本期网上业务的培训,你不但能学会如何编程,还能获得就业信息。

64. If you had checked the engine more carefully you would have found out what was missing.

A) 假如你当时能更仔细地检查一下发动机,你就会发现少了什么东西。

B) 一旦你对发动机有了兴趣,你就可自己动手拆开看看它的构造原理。

C) 如果你对照了发动机的基本工作原理,你就会知道它缺少什么部件。

65. According to this contract, if your job doesn't meet your expectation, you have the right to end your contract with notice.

A) 据本合同条款规定,如果你对工作感到不满意,你有权随时提出修改合同的建议。

B) 本合同的条款规定了你工作的职责、权利和福利待遇以及对违反合同的惩罚。

C) 根据本合同,如果你的工作不符合你的期望,你有权终止合同,无须提前告知。

66. All guests are required to carry their original passport and room card when they leave the ship.

A) 所有的游客在登船时应该主动出示身份证。

B) 所有旅客在离船时须携带护照原件和房卡。

C) 所有客人在离船前要仔细核对护照和房号。

67. Our center was founded in 1999 in Beijing. One of its goals is to develop computer

materials and to teach business owners how to use computer technologies in their business activities. It offers training programs on a variety of business topics based on demand. If you are interested in the business training on any of the following topics, please contact us at 701-223-0707 or email to *info@trainingnd.com*.

2019 年 12 月真题

Part Ⅳ　Translation—English into Chinese（25 minutes）

63. Before you start, make sure you have a clear idea of why you are starting a company.
    A) 在创业前,你务必做好规划,牢记自己创业的目的。
    B) 在创业前,你一定要清楚自己为何要创办一家公司。
    C) 在创业前,你要想好自己的公司是否需要银行贷款。

64. Becoming a volunteer allows individuals to give back and learn something about themselves in the process.
    A) 成为一名志愿者可以使个人在这个过程中给予回报并对自己有些了解。
    B) 要变为志愿者就必须让人们在学习中和付出时逐渐提高自己的精神境界。
    C) 要成为一名志愿者需要让自己在这个过程中付出并且要学习到一些东西。

65. When setting up a new business, you should pay careful attention to designing your company's organizational structure.
    A) 当新业务建设的时候,你们要仔细考虑公司机构的职能。
    B) 设置一家新的企业时,你要关心你公司组织体系的设计。
    C) 成立一家新企业,您应该特别仔细设计公司的组织结构。

66. Retired people may feel lonely for being away from their former work and colleagues.
    A) 退休的人虽然摆脱了繁忙的工作,却常常喜欢找老同事聊天。
    B) 退休的人由于离开他们过去的工作和同事,可能会感到孤独。
    C) 退休的人会觉得难以适应,因为失去了熟练的工作和老同事。

67. After you have selected your ideal hotel, you can book it on our website. You will be asked to provide some basic information about yourself for the booking: whether you are staying as a family or by yourself, and how long you will stay. You can confirm your booking by calling the hotel directly. For those who are looking for a meeting room, please call the hotel directly and speak to the front desk.

第六章

写作/汉译英

第一节 题型综述

高等学校英语应用能力考试 B 级测试的第五部分为"写作/汉译英"(Writing/Translation—Chinese into English),占总分的15%,测试时间为25分钟,要求考生在规定时间内根据所给提示完成不少于80词的英语短文写作。本部分测试考生运用所学词汇和语法套写应用性短文、填写英文表格或翻译简短的应用性文字的能力,涉及的体裁主要有通知、便条、留言、海报、备忘录、简短信函、简历、申请信等。

本部分的测试目的是考查学生的英语书面表达能力,要求词句基本正确,无重大语法错误,格式基本恰当,表达清楚。以下是写作部分的评分标准,可以作为参考。

第一,按综合方式评分,从格式、内容和语言三方面全面衡量,只给一个分数(整数),即总体印象分。综合评分依据文章内容的完整性、语言表达的准确性(语法、用词等)和语篇的流畅性来判定。

第二,分数一般分为如下 5 个等级:

★ 14 分:格式正确,内容完整,表达清楚;语言上仅有个别小错。

★ 11 分:格式基本正确,内容较完整,表达尚清楚;语言错误不多,可以有个别句子结构上的错误。

★ 8 分:格式基本正确,内容大体完整,表达可勉强理解;有较多的语言错误,包括一些严重错误。

★ 5 分:格式勉强正确,内容不完整,但是没有离题,表达有较大困难;语言错误多,其中较多是严重错误。

★ 2 分:格式不正确,内容表达不清楚;语言支离破碎,仅有个别句子尚正确。

第三,在以上几个等级的基础上,可以根据作文的总体情况酌情加减 1 分。如果不按提示写作文或语言表达完全无法理解,应给零分。

第四,评分要防止趋中倾向。

第二节 考点归纳

高等学校英语应用能力考试 B 级每年考查的作文类型各不相同,但是均为常见的题材,如通知、留言、备忘录、电子邮件、简历、海报、报告、各类信函、申请信等,其中申请信出现的频率较高,一般都以表格的形式体现,难度较低,要求考生熟悉常见应用文的格式,能够用英文填写应用文的基本要素,掌握一定的词汇、句型和语法知识并加以运用,具备写作的基本技能。2015—2019 年写作真题的题材情况见表 6.1。

表 6.1 2015—2019 年写作真题的题材汇总

时间	题材									
	备忘录	请假申请表	求职申请表	加班申请表	意见反馈表	考察报告	通知	志愿者申请表	电话留言	电话采访
2015-6	√									
2015-12		√								
2016-6			√							
2016-12				√						
2017-6					√					
2017-12						√				
2018-6							√			
2018-12								√		
2019-6									√	
2019-12										√

第三节 技巧点拨

高等学校英语应用能力考试 B 级的写作部分以应用文为主,考生需要熟悉英语应用文的写作体裁、写作格式和规范,掌握相应的写作方法。下面将对常见的英语应用文逐一进行分析和讲解。

一、书信(Letter)

1. 书信格式

英文书信通常由 6 个部分组成:信头(heading),包括寄信人的地址和日期;信内地址

(inside address),指收信人的地址;称呼(salutation);正文(body);结束语(complimentary close);签名(signature)。

在B级考试中,由于篇幅所限,考生只需要在书信中撰写日期、称呼、正文、结束语和签名几个部分。

(1) 日期

日期是考生容易失分的部分,英文日期的撰写需要注意以下几点。

第一,年份要完全写出,不能简写。

第二,月份用英文,不要用数字代替。一般用公认的缩写形式,但是 May、June、July 这几个月份由于拼写较短,不可缩写。

第三,写日期时,可用基数词 1,2,3,4,5,…,28,29,30,31 等,也可用序数词 1st,2nd,3rd,4th,5th,…,28th,29th,30th,31st 等,建议用基数词,简单明了,不容易出错。

日期通常有四种写法:Dec. 21,2020;21 Dec.,2020;21st Dec., 2020;Dec. 21st,2020。

(2) 称呼

称呼与左边线对齐,在称呼后,英国人常用逗号,美国人则常用冒号。在私人信件中可以直呼收信人的名字,但在公务信件中要写收信人的姓。大部分信件在称呼前加"Dear"。如:Dear Professor/Prof. Bergen;Dear Dr. Johnson。

对不相识的人可按性别称呼,如:Dear Sir,Dear Madam,Dear Ladies;如果不知收信人的性别则可用"Dear Sir or Madam"。

(3) 正文

书信正文通常直接说明写信人的身份及写信的目的,然后提出写信人的想法或要求,并加以必要的解释或说明。陈述目的时,写作应直截了当,意思明确,层次清楚,言简意赅。正文的写作格式有以下两种:

一是英式结构:缩进式结构,即每一段的第一行都向里缩进 4~8 个字符,且所有段落的缩进距离保持一致;称呼顶格写,落款则在中间偏右的位置。

二是美式结构:齐头式结构,即所有段落的第一行都顶格写,段与段之间空一行,称呼、落款等也都顶格写。

(4) 结束语

结束语写在签名上面一行,第一个字母要大写,套语结尾后面要加逗号。

常用的结尾套语有 Truly yours、Yours truly、Respectfully yours、Yours respectfully、Faithfully yours、Yours faithfully、Sincerely yours、Yours sincerely、Yours 等。

私人信件中,发信人常用的结尾套语有 Sincerely yours、Lovely yours、Your lovely、Your loving son/daughter 等。

2. 邀请信(Invitation Letter)

邀请信有正式和非正式之分,正式邀请信一般属于公函类,私人邀请信一般属于非正式文体。邀请信一般分为三个部分。

(1) 首段

开门见山说明写作目的。

(2) 主体段

① 具体交代邀请原因;

② 撰写邀请内容:活动内容、时间、地点、日期、参加人员、注意细节等;

③ 提出有关要求和希望。

(3) 尾段

① 再次盛情邀请;

② 希望收到对方回复。

参考模板

> Dear ×××,
>
>   There will be a(内容) at/ in(地点) on(时间). We would be honored to have you there with us.
>
>   The occasion will start at(具体时间). This will be followed by a(进一步的安排). At around(时间),(另一个安排).
>
>   I really hope you can make it. If you need further information, please contact me at(联系方式)before(通知的最后期限).
>
> Yours sincerely,
×××

3. 投诉信(Letter of Complaint)

投诉信主要是指日常生活中人们因产品质量或对服务不满等原因而撰写的,以求问题得到解决的信函,其主要内容包括三个部分。

(1) 首段

① 自我介绍;

② 引出投诉内容;

③ 表明目的、要求。

(2) 主体段

① 详细说明情况,中肯提出问题;

② 提出改进建议,表明希望如何解决;

③ 提出警告,强调如果问题不解决所带来的后果。

(3) 尾段

① 对有关人员的努力表示感谢;

② 希望尽快得到满意答复。

参考模板

> Dear ×××,
>   I am(自我介绍). I feel bad to trouble you but I am afraid I have to make a complaint about(投诉的具体事件).
>   The reason for my dissatisfaction is(总体介绍). In the first place, (投诉的第一个方面). In addition, (投诉的第二个方面). Under these circumstances, I find it(带来的负面影响).
>   I appreciate it very much if you could(建议和请求), preferably(进一步的要求), and I would like to have this matter settled by(解决的最后期限).
>   Thank you for your consideration and I will be looking forward to your reply.
>   Yours sincerely,
>   ×××

4. 感谢信（Letter of Thanks）

感谢信是用来对馈赠礼物或曾经得到某人的关怀、照顾表示感谢的信函，在西方国家用得比较普遍。感谢信在格式上没有很严格的要求，与普通信件的格式相同，主要是要写得真挚，表达诚挚的感激之情，不能给人一种草率的印象。

由于感谢的对象、原因和内容不同，感谢信的内容也会有所区别。例如，对朋友赠送礼物表示感谢的信，一定要提到所赠的礼物以及自己对礼物的喜爱之情。一封感谢信通常包括感谢的原因、内容以及诚挚的感激之情。

（1）首段
简述写信的目的。
（2）主体段
致谢并详述所收到的礼物或得到的帮助。
（3）尾段
① 再次表示感谢；
② 表达希望回报对方的愿望。

参考模板

> Dear ×××,
>   I am writing to extend my sincere gratitude for(感谢的原因). If it had not been for your assistance in(对方给予的具体帮助), I fear that I would have been(若没有对方帮助的后果). Everyone agrees that it was you who(给出细节). Again, I would like to express my warm thanks to you! Please accept my gratitude.
>   Yours sincerely,
>   ×××

5. 道歉信（Letter of Apology）

道歉信是指因某人的过失或疏忽做错事，给别人带来麻烦或损失，写信给对方赔礼道歉时写的信件。道歉信的内容一般包括：表示歉意，说明道歉的缘由和出现差错的原因，提出弥补措施，请求原谅。

（1）首段
表示歉意。

（2）主体段

① 说明具体原因；

② 提出补救办法。

（3）尾段

① 再次致歉；

② 表明希望得到理解。

参考模板

> Dear ×××,
> 　　I'm writing to make an apology to you for(过失或错误). Last time, I(出错原因). To make up my fault, I will(补救措施). I sincerely hope you can understand my situation and accept my apology. Once again, I am sorry for any inconvenience caused.
> 　　　　　　　　　　　　　　　　　　　　　　　　　　　　　　Yours,
> 　　　　　　　　　　　　　　　　　　　　　　　　　　　　　　×××

6. 申请信（Letter of Application）

申请信的种类很多，常见的有求职申请、留学申请、加入某组织的申请等。无论哪一种申请信，一般都包括：申请原因，具备的资格条件，恳请申请单位考虑自己的申请，表示感谢和期盼回复。申请信开篇应点明主题，语言简练；接着说明做此申请的原因，即自己所具备的申请条件，这一部分须重点明确、论述充分；最后请求回复并表示感谢时，应采用礼貌、诚恳的措辞。

（1）首段

① 进行自我介绍；

② 说明写信目的。

（2）主体段

① 详述有关背景资料：资历、教育经历、工作经历、兴趣爱好等；

② 询问具体内容。

（3）尾段

① 期盼回复；

② 表示感谢。

参考模板

> Dear ×××,
> 　　I am extremely pleased to see(广告) for the position(职位). And I'm writing to apply for(职位). I am confident that I am suitable for(职位). On the one hand,(原因), on the other hand,(原因).
> 　　I shall be much honored if you offer me the opportunity to(尝试). I am looking forward to your reply at your earliest convenience.
> 　　Best regards.
> 　　　　　　　　　　　　　　　　　　　　　　　　　　　　　Yours sincerely,
> 　　　　　　　　　　　　　　　　　　　　　　　　　　　　　×××

7．祝贺信（Letter of Congratulation）

英语祝贺信可用于不同的场合，如订婚、结婚、生子、晋升、毕业、考试成功或出国留学等。祝贺信可长可短，用词必须真诚自然、亲切有礼，表达出真挚的喜悦之情。

（1）首段

表达听到喜讯的心情。

（2）主体段

对喜讯进行积极评价。

（3）尾段

表达衷心的祝贺之情。

参考模板

> Dear ×××,
>   I am much delighted to learn that（喜讯）. This is a special and happy moment for you and I am very proud of your achievement.
>   Firstly,（评价1）. Secondly,（评价2）. Finally,（评价3）.
>   Please accept my most sincere congratulations!
>   Best wishes.
>
>   　　　　　　　　　　　　　　　　　　　　　　　　　　　Yours faithfully,
>   　　　　　　　　　　　　　　　　　　　　　　　　　　　　　　×××

二、备忘录（Memo）

备忘录也称公务便条，是一种非正式的公文函件，通常用于公司、团体内部快速、有效地传递关于人事任免、会议通知、公司政策等方面的信息，是公司内部最常见的一种书面交流方式。备忘录具有简洁短小、结构清晰、阅读方便、传递迅速的特点，一般由标题、收件人、发件人、日期、主题和正文几个部分组成。

参考范文

> **Memo**
> - To：Managers of all the departments
> - From：John Green (The Sales Manager)
> - Date：June 16th, 2020
> - Subject：Discussion on the sales plan of the 3rd quarter in 2020
>
>   Our department has made the sales plan of the 3rd quarter in 2020. To discuss the plan, a meeting will be held in the Conference Room of our corporation at 1:00 p.m. on June 19th, 2020. It is hoped that managers of all the departments will come to the meeting.
>   If anyone cannot attend it, please notify the secretary of the Sales Department in advance.

三、通知（Notice）

英文通知的格式与中文通知的格式大体相同，由标题、正文、落款（或时间）三部分组成。标题写在正文上方正中的部位，常以"Notice"作标题。正文要求写明具体事项，以便告知相关人员。落款即发出通知的单位和时间,写在正文右下角。

参考范文

> **Notice**
>
> All the members of the Students' Union are requested to meet in the department conference room on Sunday, March 15, at 7:30 p. m., to discuss the plan of the sports meet.
>
> Students' Union
March 13, 2020

四、电子邮件(E-mail)

电子邮件具有传统邮件无法比拟的优势,它传递速度快,成本低,传送的信息内容丰富、形式多样。电子邮件一般包括以下内容:发件人(From)、收信人(To)、抄送(Cc)、主题(Subject)、日期(Date)和正文(Body)。其中,抄送是指在"Cc"一栏中输入其他人的电子邮件地址,这样就可以将一封邮件同时发给多人。主题的作用是便于读信人即刻了解所收信件的主要内容。因此,主题要简洁明了。正文部分由称谓、正文和落款署名三个部分组成。

参考范文

> From:yumeilin@163.com
> To:Education@Calstate.L.A.
> Subject:Application
> Date:Aug. 28, 2020
> Dear Sirs,
>   My name is Lin Yumei. I graduated from Jinan University in 2018, majoring in chemistry with a B. S. degree. After my graduation, I've been teaching Chemistry in a high school.
>   With a view to get some advanced studies, I am writing to you to apply for admission to your university to pursue my M. S. degree. I am also applying for a scholarship or a teaching assistantship that will enable me to come to your university sooner.
>   Hoping to be favored with an early reply.
>
> Yours,
Lin Yumei

五、便条和留言条(Note & Message)

便条和留言条都是一种间接的书信,内容比较简短,大多是因为无法直接通知或者咨询而采取的一种传递信息的方式,用以表达临时的咨询、留言、通知、要求等。常见的格式一般包括日期、称呼、正文、署名等。

① 日期一般只需写某日上午或下午;
② 称呼比较随意,可直呼其名,如:John, Dear Ann, Liu Ying,等等;
③ 正文部分尽量通俗化、简单明了;
④ 署名部分一般写上留言人的姓名,如果十分熟悉可以只写姓或名;

⑤ 便条和留言条无须邮寄，因此不须说明留条人的地址。

便条参考范文

Sick Leave

April 4, 2020

Ms. Smith,

　　Owing to a severe headache, I shall be unable to attend English class today. I enclose a medical certificate from the doctor.

　　Hoping you will excuse my non-attendance.

Yours respectfully,
Li Mei

留言条参考范文

Telephone Message

June 12

Mr. Green,

　　Mr. Johnson of IMB Co. called to tell you that he will leave for Beijing on business tomorrow. He wishes to put off the appointment he made with you for tomorrow until next week. He will contact you as soon as he is back on weekend.

Catherine

六、简历(Resume)

个人简历是求职者向招聘单位发送的一份简要介绍,是必不可少的求职材料之一。如今,求职者往往通过网络寻找工作,一份良好的个人简历对于获得面试机会至关重要。个人简历可以是表格的形式,也可以是其他形式。简历要写得简洁精练,切忌拖泥带水。

简历通常包括以下几个方面的内容:

① 基本信息(Personal Data)

② 求职意向/求职目标(Objective)

③ 教育背景(Education Background)

④ 工作经历(Work Experience)

⑤ 奖励和荣誉(Awards & Honors)

⑥ 兴趣爱好(Hobbies)

参考范文

Resume

* Steve Lee

Tel：010-××××××××

Email：*stevelee@jxue.com*

Add：No.29 Beisanhuan Road, Xicheng District, Beijing

* Objective

  software engineer

* Education

  1997.9 – 2000.6 Dept. of Automation, Graduate School of Tsinghua University, M.E.

  1993.9 – 1997.7 Dept. of Automation, Beijing Institute of Technology, B.E.

* Computer Abilities

  Skilled in the use of MS

* English Skills

  Have a good command of both spoken and written English. Passed CET-6.

* Scholarships and Awards

  1999.3 First-class Scholarship for Graduates

  1998.11 Metal Machining Practice Award

  1997.4 Academic Progress Award

* Qualifications

  General business knowledge relating to financial, healthcare

  Have a passion for the Internet, and an abundance of common sense

---

第四节　实战演练

2015年6月真题

Part V　Writing (25 minutes)

Directions: *This part is to test your ability to do practical writing. You are required to complete a memo according to the following information given in Chinese. Remember to do your writing on the Translation/Composition Sheet.*

说明：根据所给信息完成以下备忘录。

送达：全体员工

发自：经理

主要内容：关于奖金

发件日期:2015 年 6 月 14 日

内容:

公司去年取得很大业绩。每位员工下月将收到奖金 $500,与下月工资一起发放。希望大家继续努力工作,为公司发展做出新的贡献。祝愿公司明年取得更大成绩。

签名:Joan Blackburn

Words for reference:奖金 bonus   业绩 achievement   做贡献 make contributions

---

MEMO

Date:(1)＿＿＿＿＿＿

From:(2)＿＿＿＿＿＿

To:(3)＿＿＿＿＿＿

Re:(4)＿＿＿＿＿＿

Message:

＿＿

＿＿

＿＿

＿＿

Signature:(5)＿＿＿＿＿＿

2015 年 12 月真题

Part V   Writing(25 minutes)

说明:假定你是李俊,请根据下列内容填写请假申请表。

姓名:李俊

员工号:120485

所在部门:市场部(Marketing Department)

请假类别:病假(Sick Leave)

拟请假日期:2016 年 1 月 10 日 – 24 日

请假理由:

在过去数周本人身体一直不适。由于本人在外地出差,无法及时就医。出差回来后,根据医生建议,须住院检查并治疗。请假时间为 2 周。

Leave Request Form

Employee Information

Name：(1)_____

Employee Number：(2)_____

Department：(3)_____

Leave Type：(4)_____

Starting Date：(5)_____   Resumption Date：January 25th, 2016

Reason for Leave：

_____

_____

_____

_____

Signature of Applicant：*Li Jun*

2016年6月真题

Part V　Writing（25 minutes）

说明：假设你是东方职业技术学院的学生李明，即将毕业，想应聘 ABC 公司销售员的职位，请根据以下内容完成求职申请表。

1. 填表日期：2016年6月19日
2. 家庭住址：南京市新华路50号
3. 家庭电话：020-123＊＊678
4. 手机号码：150＊＊＊＊6789
5. 电子邮箱：*liming123@163.com*
6. 期望月薪：约3 000元
7. 能力与爱好：

我能熟练使用计算机，并具有较强的英语口语能力。我还有较强的沟通能力与团队合作精神。我爱好阅读、运动与旅游。我愿意加班与出差。

Employment Application		
Personal Details		
Date of Application：	(1) _____	
Name of Applicant：	(2) _____	
Address：	50 Xinhua Road, Nanjing	
Personal Contact		
Home telephone：	020-123＊＊678	
Mobile：	(3) _____	
E-mail Address：	(4) _____	
Applied Position：	(5) _____	
Expected Salary：	About 3,000 *yuan*	
Education Background		
2013 – 2016	Dongfang Professional Technical College	
Skills & Hobbies：		

（注：最后部分写成段落。）

2016 年 12 月真题

Part V Writing (25 minutes)

说明：假定你是人力资源部的员工李建新，请根据下列内容填写一份加班申请表。

申请日期：2017 年 3 月 1 日

部门：人力资源部(Human Resources Department)

加班时间：2017 年 3 月 5 日 9:00 a.m.—5:00 p.m.

总加班时间：不超过 8 小时

加班原因：公司最近需要招聘各类员工。人力资源部一周前登了招聘广告，并已收到很多求职信(application letter)。为了协助各部门安排面试，本人需要在周六加班一天，了解应聘人员情况，并安排面试。

```
                        Overtime Request Form
Request Date: (1) _____
Employee's name: (2) _____
Department: (3) _____
Date of Overtime: March 5, 2017
Overtime Needed: from (4) _____ to 5:00 p.m.
Total Overtime: not to exceed (5) _____ hours
Reasons for Overtime Required:
_____
_____
_____
_____
```

2017年6月真题

Part V Writing (25 minutes)

说明:假定你是张建林,根据所给内容填写下列顾客意见反馈表。

顾客姓名:张建林

顾客邮址:zhangj1999@163.com

抵达日期:2017年6月15日

抵达时间:上午11:30

内容:

酒店员工非常友好,提供了良好的服务,尤其是一位名叫John Chen的员工。

酒店的房间干净整洁,餐厅的食物美味可口,住店的体验很不错。

但是酒店离市中心较远,建议酒店增设从酒店到地铁站的班车(shuttle bus),为客人提供方便。

Guest Experience Card

We value your feedback

Name：(1) _____

E-mail address：(2) _____

Date of visit：(3) _____

Time of visit：(4) _____

Did our Team Members exceed your expectations?   Yes

If yes, please provide their names：(5) _____

Comments：

_____

_____

_____

_____

_____

_____

Thank you for choosing our hotel.

If you would like to talk to us about your experience today,

please contact the Guest Services Department at 1-888-601-1616.

2017年12月真题

Part V　Writing (25 minutes)

说明：请根据所给信息，完成下列现场考察报告。

写报告人：李俊杰

接受报告人：王晓林

送交报告日期：2017年12月24日

考察地点：JUK 工厂

考察时间：自2017年12月4日至2017年12月8日

参加考察人员：李俊杰及其团队成员

内容要点：为了了解水污染问题，我们去 JUK 工厂参观一周。我们了解了污染的主要来源。工程师们向我们介绍了几种废水处理的方法。这次参观对我们的研究工作很有帮助。

Words for reference：废水处理 waste water treatment

Field Trip Report

Report to: Mr./Mrs. (1) _____

Report from: Mr./Mrs. (2) _____

Date: (3) _____

Trip destination: (4) _____

Trip period: from December 4, 2017 to (5) _____

Participants: Li Junjie & His team members

Summary

_____
_____
_____
_____
_____
_____

2018 年 6 月真题

Part V   Writing

说明:假设你是总经理秘书 Tom Brown 先生,发一份通知给各部门经理。

主题:讨论下半年销售计划

时间:2018 年 6 月 18 日

抄送(CC):John Smith 先生

主要内容:

市场部已制订了公司下半年的销售计划,现发给你们,见附件。总经理办公室将于 6 月 20 日下午 2 点在公司会议室召开会议,讨论该计划,并听取各部门的意见。请各部门经理参加会议。如无法到会,请提前告知总经理办公室。

Words for reference:

市场部 Marketing Department

附件 attachment

总经理办公室 General Manager's Office

Memo

To: (1) _____

From: (2) _____

Date: (3) _____

CC: (4) _____

Subject: (5) _____

2018 年 12 月真题

Part V　Writing

说明:假设你是陈大明,你想参加 Reading Together 志愿者组织,根据下列内容填写一份志愿者申请表。

手机号码:177＊＊＊＊8956

电子邮箱:chendm999@163.com

出生日期:1998 年 12 月 15 日

就读学校:东方技术学院

所在系部:计算机系

所学专业:计算机技术

申请原因:

1. 对阅读很感兴趣;

2. 希望用自己所学的知识帮助乡村儿童;

3. 通过志愿者活动认识更多喜欢阅读的朋友;

4. 提高自己的阅读与沟通能力。

Volunteer Application Form

Thank you for your interest in volunteering with Reading Together.

Personal Details

Name：(1) _____   ☐ Mr. ☐ Mrs. ☐ Ms.

Mobile：(2) _____

E-mail：(3) _____

Birth Date：(4) _____

College Information

College Name：Dongfang Technical College

Major：Computer Technology   Department：(5) _____

Describe why you are interested in working as a volunteer with us.

_____
_____
_____
_____

2019 年 6 月真题

Part V Writing

说明：

假设你是办公室秘书王晓虹。你接到约翰·史密斯(John Smith)先生的来电,他的电话号码为 021-77542＊＊1,传真号码为 021-7754＊＊43,你接电话的时间是 6 月 20 日上午 9 点。史密斯先生要你转告安·泰勒(Ann Taylor)女士以下内容：

1. 你所需要的资料都已准备好了,请告诉史密斯先生需要打印多少份、他什么时间派人去取。

2. 他们公司打算举办一个培训班,想邀请你做一个有关电子商务的发言。

Important Message

For：(1) _____

From：(2) _____

Time：9 a.m.   Date：(3) _____

Tel No.：021-77542＊＊1   Fax：(4) _____

| Please call ☐ | Returned your call ■ |
| Will call again ☐ | Urgent ■ |

Message:
_____
_____
_____

Taken by: (5) _____

2019年12月真题

Part V Writing

说明:假定你是ABC-1品牌手机的经销商李华,最近对一位客户做了一次电话采访。请根据所给内容填写表格。

客户姓名:John Smith

客户电话:12333311190

客户电邮:JohnS@126.com

调查日期:2019年12月15日

采访人:李华

反馈意见:

1. 他很喜欢使用ABC-1手机;
2. 他认为ABC-1手机价格太高,希望能便宜一些;
3. ABC-1手机的用户主要是老年人,因此他希望屏幕再大一些;
4. 他希望改善售后服务。

Customer Interview

Date: (1) _____

Information about the customer

Name: (2) _____

Telephone: (3) _____

E-mail address: (4) _____

Feedback(反馈意见):
_____
_____
_____

Interviewer: (5) Li Hua

附录一 听力原文

2015年6月真题

Section A

1. How is everything going, Peter?
2. May I have your name, please?
3. Do you like to chat in English online?
4. Would you please sign your name here, sir?
5. Do you often travel on business?
6. Can you put me through to the manager's office?
7. Shall we arrange a meeting sometime next week?

Section B

8. W: Tom, why were you late for the interview?

   M: I missed the bus.

   Q: Why was Tom late?

9. W: How do you like to pay for the computer?

   M: By credit card, please.

   Q: How will the man pay for the computer?

10. W: We are really impressed by your work experience.

    M: Thank you very much.

    Q: What impresses the woman deeply?

11. M: Mary, why isn't Linda working here now?

    W: She retired last week.

    Q: What can we learn about Linda from the conversation?

12. M: Excuse me. Where can I learn more about your company?

    W: From our website.

    Q: Where can the man get more information about the company?

13. M: Good morning. I have an appointment with Dr. Green at 10:30.

    W: Please wait a moment. He is with another patient.

    Q: Where does this conversation most probably take place?

14. W: I'm afraid we can't have the meeting today, as John isn't here.

    M: I see. Let's have it tomorrow.

Q: When will they have the meeting?

Section C

Conversation 1

W: Good morning. May I help you?

M: Yes. I'd like to see a doctor, please.

W: Are you a new patient here?

M: Yes. This is my first time here.

W: I see. What's your trouble?

M: I've caught a bad cold.

Q15. What does the man want to do?

Q16. What's the matter with the man?

Conversation 2

W: Good afternoon. Park Industries.

M: Hello! May I speak to Mr. Black, please?

W: I'm sorry. He is not in. Can I take a message?

M: Yes. I'm John Brown. Please tell him our meeting will be held on Friday at 3:30.

W: Friday, at 3:30.

M: And would you ask him to call me this afternoon?

W: What's your phone number, please?

M: It's 358-4058.

W: OK. I'll pass the message to Mr. Black.

Q17. Whom does the man want to speak to?

Q18. When will they have the meeting?

Q19. What will the woman do for the man?

Section D

Good afternoon, ladies and gentlemen. Thank you very much for coming to our conference this afternoon. I'm Henry Johnson, the sales manager of Smart Toys. Now I'd like to introduce you to a completely new idea of toy manufacture. Firstly, I'll talk about the market research which led to the development of this product. Then I'll explain the production and our sales plan. Finally, I'll make some suggestions so that you can make this product a success. We are confident this new product will sell well in the American market. At the end of my speech, we'll have a question-and-answer section.

2015 年 12 月真题

Section A

1. Hello, Mr. Smith! How is your journey?

2. Can I take your name, please?

3. Do you live on campus?

4. Who will attend the conference?

5. How is everything with you, Linda?

6. Jennet, may I have a word with you, please?

7. Shall we discuss our plan this afternoon?

Section B

8. M: Helen, why did you give up the job?

   W: It was too boring.

   Q: Why did Helen give up the job?

9. W: What can I do for you, sir?

   M: I am looking for sports shoes, size 7.

   Q: What does the man want to buy?

10. W: Mike, what's the matter with you?

    M: I am not feeling well. I've caught a bad cold.

    Q: What can we learn about the man?

11. W: Hello, GBS Company.

    M: I'm calling to ask about the after-sales service.

    Q: What is the man asking about?

12. M: I often stay up late online.

    W: Better not. It's no good for your health.

    Q: What does the woman think of staying up late online?

13. M: Jane, how is your new job?

    W: Great. They offer a good salary.

    Q: What can we learn about the woman's new job?

14. M: Hi, Jane, how are things with you?

    W: Oh, I am now working on a new project.

    Q: What's the woman doing now?

Section C

Conversation 1

M: Excuse me, I've booked a room in your hotel for two nights.

W: Your name, please?

M: John Carson.

W: Let me have a check. Yes, Mr. Carson. Your room is ready.

M: And where can I park my car?

W: In our parking lot, just behind the building.

Q15. How long will the man stay at the hotel?

Q16. Where is the parking lot?

Conversation 2

W: Hi, Tom. Can I have a talk with you?

M: Sure. Take a seat.

W: Well, I really think I should have a pay raise.

M: How long have you been working here?

W: Five years. And I've now taken on more responsibilities.

M: I see. I'll discuss it with the managers first.

Q17. What does the woman ask for?

Q18. How many years has the woman been working in the company?

Q19. What will the man probably do next?

Section D

Have you ever thought what keeps people happy in their work? We've recently carried out a survey. Of course, salary is important. Apart from salary, what else makes people happy with their jobs? Now please look at the chart. You can see the biggest factor is the opportunities to learn and grow. It represents 28 percent of the people we asked. And 20 percent of the people say the ability to achieve their goal is important. Our survey also shows that another two important factors are a good working relationship with co-workers and a good working condition.

2016年6月真题

Section A

1. How is everything going?

2. Did you go to the lecture yesterday?

3. What do you think about our new design?

4. May I have your passport please?

5. Mr. White, would you please fill out this application form?

6. Can I have a copy of your report?

7. Do you want business class or economy class?

Section B

8. M: How was your holiday, Maria?

   W: Oh, wonderful! I had a great time on the beach.

   Q: What are the speakers talking about?

9. W: Would you spare me some time to discuss my marketing plan?

   M: Sorry. I'm busy at the moment. How about this afternoon?

   Q: When will the two speakers discuss the plan?

10. M: Hello! I want to rent an apartment.

    W: What kind of apartment are you interested in?

    Q: What does the man want to do?

11. W: Why were you late for the meeting this morning?

    M: My car broke down on the way.

    Q: What happened to the man this morning?

12. M: I don't know how to use this new software.

    W: Why not ask Jack to help you?

    Q: What will the man probably do?

13. W: Dou you know Mr. Johnson has been promoted?

    M: Yes. He is now our new manager.

    Q: What can we learn about Mr. Johnson?

14. M: I want to start a business, but where can I get the money?

    W: You can apply for a bank loan.

    Q: What did the woman advise the man to do?

Section C

Conversation 1

M: Excuse me, madam.

W: Is there a problem, officer?

M: You ran the red light, madam.

W: No, officer. I was making a right turn.

M: Didn't you see the sign "No Turn" on red?

W: Oh, sorry. I didn't see it.

M: Your license, please.

W: Here you are.

Q15. Why did the officer stop the woman?

Q16. What did the officer ask the woman to show?

Conversation 2

W: Hi, Bob! Are you looking for a new job?

M: Yeah. I just had an interview with ABC company yesterday.

W: Oh, ABC company? It's an IT company. What position are you applying for?

M: Sales manager.

W: How was your interview?

M: I think I did well. They say they'll tell me the result next Monday.

W: I guess you'll have a good chance to get the job.

M: I hope so. The interview seems to appreciate my background.

W: Well, good luck then.

Q17. What position is the man applying for?

Q18. What type of company is ABC company?

Q19. When will Bob get the result of the interview?

Section D

Ladies and gentlemen, good afternoon. First of all, let me express our thanks to you for coming to the opening ceremony of our new branch office.

This branch is the 25th office we have set up so far. We are very happy that we have finally opened a branch in this city. This branch, we believe, will help improve the local economy. And our company will in turn benefit from doing business here. We promise that we will provide the best service to our customers. And, of course, we will need your support and cooperation.

2016 年 12 月真题

Section A

1. Can I speak to your department manager?

2. Do you know Mr. Green, the chief engineer?

3. How can I start the machine?

4. Do you enjoy travelling on business?

5. How long have you been in the new position?

6. Where did you get the information?

7. What do you think of your boss?

Section B

8. W: Do you know what day is April 22?

   M: It's Earth Day.

   Q: What day is April 22?

9. W: Do you have telephone banking services?

   M: Yes, of course.

   Q: What is the woman asking about?

10. W: Where should I sign my name?

    M: At the bottom of the page.

    Q: What does the woman want to know?

11. M: Where can I learn more about your training program?

    W: From our website.

    Q: How can the man get more information?

12. W: How does our new product sell in the market?

    M: It sells well.

附录一 听力原文

Q: What are the two speakers talking about?

13. M: When can we get our orders?

    W: You will receive them within three days.

    Q: What is the man asking about?

14. W: When did you start your company?

    M: In 1998. Now it has over 350 employees.

    Q: What do we know about the company from the dialogue?

Section C

Conversation 1

W: You seem quite busy these days.

M: Yes. We're doing a market survey.

W: Really? What's it about?

M: About people's attitudes toward online shopping.

W: What results have you got?

M: Most young people prefer shopping online.

W: How about old people?

M: Some old people also like online shopping.

Q15. What is the man doing these days?

Q16. What can we learn about online shopping from the conversation?

Conversation 2

M: Hi, Jenny. I found a summer job.

W: That's fine.

M: I will be working at Disney Land.

W: Wow! Sounds great.

M: How about you, Jenny?

W: I've got an offer as a tour guide.

M: But a tour guide has to work long hours.

W: That's why I haven't made up my mind yet.

Q17. What do we learn about the man?

Q18. What job is offered to the woman?

Q19. Why hasn't the woman made up her mind to accept this job?

Section D

Good evening, ladies and gentlemen!

First of all, I'd like to express a sincere welcome to you all, the new comers of our company. As you know, our company is one of the top 50 companies in the country and has a history of more than 100 years. I think you must be proud of being a member of such a great company. But we cannot depend on tradition alone. We need new employees with new knowledge and creative ideas. I would like to welcome you once again, and from today, let's begin to work together.

2017年6月真题

Section A

1. Can I help you, Madam?
2. May I have your name, please?
3. Would you like a cup of coffee?
4. Shall we meet on Friday?
5. Excuse me, are you John Smith from England?
6. Are you interested in this training course?
7. Would you like to attend the sales meeting?

Section B

8. M: This building looks quite old.
   W: It was built about 150 years ago.
   Q: When was the building built?

9. W: Are you satisfied with your job?
   M: Yes. The boss is nice and the pay is good.
   Q: What does the man think of his job?

10. W: Does your city have a large population?
    M: Yes, about three million people.
    Q: What does the woman ask about the city?

11. M: Have you ever been to Shenzhen?
    W: Yes, many times. It is a very modern city.
    Q: What does the woman think of the city?

12. M: Are you planning to study abroad?
    W: I wish I could. But I haven't got enough money.
    Q: What problem does the woman have?

13. M: Excuse me, how can I apply for a membership card?
    W: Please fill in this form first.
    Q: What will the man probably do first?

14. M: Hi, Jane. What's wrong with you?
    W: I've got a headache.
    Q: What can we learn about the woman?

Section C

Conversation 1

W: Good morning.

M: Good morning. I want to rent an apartment.

W: What kind apartment do you want?

M: A two-bedroom one.

W: Where do you want it to be?

M: Near my office in the downtown.

W: Yes. We have several apartments available.

Q15. What kind of apartment does the man want to rent?

Q16. Where does the man want the apartment to be?

Conversation 2

W: Good morning.

M: Good morning.

W: Why are you interested in this job?

M: I want to have more opportunities.

W: Good. How long have you been working at your current position?

M: For five years.

W: What do you expect to be in a few years?

M: I hope I can become a skilled engineer.

Q17. Why does the man apply for the job?

Q18. How long has the man been working at his current position?

Q19. What does the man expect to be in the near future?

Section D

First of all, on behalf of all the people from our company, I would like to say "Thank you for inviting us to such a wonderful party". I think the music is lovely, the food and wine are very nice, and the people here are all very kind. Also we've enjoyed meeting and talking to you, sharing the comfortable time together. We have really enjoyed ourselves. I hope we will be able to maintain the good relationship and make next year another great one together. Thank you again for the party. We've really had a great time.

2017年12月真题

Section A

1. Excuse me. Where is the Information Center?

2. Can you show me how to use this machine?

3. How was your flight, Mr. Smith?

4. It's a new model. Do you want to try it?

5. Would you sign your name here, please?

6. What do you think about our holiday plan?

7. This T-shirt is a little too small. Can I have a larger size?

Section B

8. W: Why do you look so worried?

   M: I have a job interview this afternoon.

   Q: What is the man worried about?

9. W: Mr. Smith. Here is the new price list.

   M: Thank you. That's what I need.

   Q: What does the woman give to the man?

10. M: Shall we tell John about what's going on?

    W: Yes, of course. I'll call him right now.

    Q: What will the woman do?

11. W: We need to use the meeting room this Friday.

    M: Well, I'm sorry, it has been booked.

    Q: Why can't the woman use the meeting room?

12. W: Sam, how was your presentation?

    M: I have no idea. I was so nervous.

    Q: How did the man feel of making his presentation?

13. W: Jack, you are looking for a new job, aren't you?

    M: Yeah. I've got a job offer.

    Q: What can we learn about the man?

14. M: Have you got the driving license?

    W: Not yet. I've just passed the road test.

    Q: What can we learn from the conversation?

Section C

Conversation 1

W: Hello, Mr. Brown, it's Linda.

M: Hello, Linda.

W: I'm calling to ask whether you've decided to place an order of our products.

M: Not yet.

W: Our products are of high quality. You won't be disappointed.

M: Umm, but we still have to think about the price.

W: We always offer good discounts.

Q15. Why does the woman call the man?

Q16. What does the woman say about their products?

Conversation 2

W: Mr. Wang, what's wrong with your car?

M: It wouldn't start this morning.

W: Did you check the battery?

M: Yeah, it was dead again.

W: Perhaps you have to buy a new battery.

M: But I bought it only last month. It's still new.

W: What are you going to do then?

M: I'll return it to the store.

Q17. What happened to the man's car?

Q18. What does the man say about the battery?

Q19. What will the man do with the battery?

Section D

I am Mike Wang, a real estate agent. I manage to sell this home in just 15 days. I would love to help you buy or sell. Properties in this area are in high demand. If you have considered selling your home, I would love to speak with you and help you in any way possible. If you are currently renting a home and would like to buy one, give me a call. Home ownership has many advantages over renting and is not as difficult as many people think. Call me today and let me help you make the right decision.

2018年6月真题

Section A

1. May I take your order now?

2. Hi, John, how was your trip to Paris?

3. Could I book a double room for next Friday?

4. May I come in and have a talk with you?

5. Could I make an appointment with Doctor Green?

6. Tom, could you give me the report?

7. Mr. Brown, can you fill in this form now?

Section B

8. M: How shall we go to the city center?

   W: Let's walk there. It's not far from here.

   Q: How will the two speakers go to the city center?

9. M: When can you have the design ready, Mary?

   W: Will tomorrow morning be okay?

Q: What are the two speakers talking about?

10. W: Have you got any work experience?

    M: Yes, I have been a programmer for two years.

    Q: What can we learn about the man?

11. M: Is your job difficult?

    W: Yes, it's hard to deal with angry customers.

    Q: What is the difficult part of the woman's job?

12. M: You are here on holiday, aren't you?

    W: No, I'm here on business.

    Q: Why does the woman come here?

13. W: What's wrong with your car?

    M: The front window was broken.

    Q: What happened to the man's car?

14. W: I'm trying to look for a new job, any tips?

    M: Why not attend a job fair?

    Q: What does the man advise the woman to do?

Section C

Conversation 1

M: Good morning, can I help you?

W: Morning, sir. I need to report a case.

M: What is it about?

W: My handbag was stolen.

M: When did you find it was stolen?

W: Ten minutes ago.

M: What's in your handbag?

W: My passport.

Q15. Why did the woman make the phone call?

Q16. What was in the woman's handbag?

Conversation 2

M: What's wrong with you?

W: It's my stomach. It's killing me here.

M: How long have you got this pain?

W: Since this morning.

M: Have you ever had stomach pain before?

W: No.

M: I think we have to get you to the emergency room right away.

W: OK.

Q17. What is the woman's problem?

Q18. When did the woman begin to have this illness?

Q19. What is the doctor going to do for the patient?

Section D

Volunteers are our heart and soul. Please come and help us build homes for local low-income families. There is no experience needed and we supply the safety training. Just volunteer for a day. It's fun, rewarding and you can learn some new skills! If building isn't your thing, come and volunteer for one of our events or at our offices. You must be at least 14 years of age to volunteer and those 15 years and under must come with a parent.

Come and sign up now to volunteer your time.

2018 年 12 月真题

Section A

1. How are things going in your company?

2. Can I help you with your luggage?

3. Will you join us in the new project?

4. How is your work these days?

5. Do you mind if I ask you a question?

6. Would you help me check my report?

7. May I say a few words about the new plan?

Section B

8. M: Hello, Linda. Why are you so busy these days?

   W: I am preparing for the New Year's Party.

   Q: What is Linda busy with?

9. W: Where did you learn about our job position?

   M: From your website.

   Q: Where did the man get the information of the job position?

10. W: Who's going to give a lecture at tomorrow's meeting?

    M: Doctor Johnson, a professor from the community college.

    Q: Who will give the lecture tomorrow?

11. M: I'm calling to talk with your manager.

    W: Sorry, he's meeting with a customer.

    Q: What is the manager doing now?

12. W: Tom, you were late for the meeting. Are you okay?

    M: Sorry, I just forgot the meeting time.

Q: Why was Tom late for the meeting?

13. W: Oh, my god! The traffic is too slow.

    M: I think there must be a traffic accident ahead.

    Q: What probably has happened on the road?

14. W: Are you going to accept the job?

    M: Yes, it's good for me.

    Q: What does the man think of the job?

Section C

Conversation 1

W: Hey, Steve. How's everything with you?

M: Good. I'm now working on a project.

W: Did you watch yesterday's football match?

M: No, I didn't.

W: How about going to watch tomorrow's match? It's the weekend.

M: That sounds great.

W: I'll give you a call to let you know the time.

M: Okay. I'll see you tomorrow.

W: See you.

Q15. What has the man been doing these days?

Q16. What are the two speakers going to do tomorrow?

Conversation 2

M: Hello, John Smith speaking.

W: Good morning, Mr. Smith. This is ABC Company. We've decided to offer you the position of Project Manager.

M: I'm very excited to hear the news. When will I start the work?

W: How about next Wednesday, July 1st?

M: No problem.

W: Do you know how to get to our company?

M: Yes, I know. I can take subway Line 2. Am I right?

W: Yes, you get off at Nanjing Road Station.

M: Thank you.

W: My pleasure. Look forward to working with you.

Q17. What job position is offered to Mr. Smith?

Q18. When will Mr. Smith start his work?

Q19. How will Mr. Smith go to the company?

Section D

When I need gas for my car, I pull into a gas station right around the corner from my house and use my gas card. Years ago, full-service gas stations were very common. However, things have changed. Now, most gas stations are self-service centers. Personally, I usually fill the car up with gas every time I stop. I generally pay in cash, but more and more gas stations accept credit cards. As gas prices are on the rise, I'm now thinking about buying a more fuel-efficient vehicle or just taking the bus to work.

2019年6月真题

Section A

1. Are you here on holiday?

2. Excuse me, is this seat taken?

3. Mr. Wang, could you tell Mary to call me back, please?

4. May I help you with your luggage?

5. Could I make an appointment with your manager?

6. What do you think of the weather here?

7. Would you like to come to our business party?

Section B

8. M: Do you have a job right now?

   W: Yes, I am a nurse in a local hospital.

   Q: What is the woman's job?

9. M: I'm surprised Mary sold her house.

   W: She had to pay for her debt.

   Q: Why did Mary sell her house?

10. W: What are we going to discuss at tomorrow's meeting?

    M: Our sales plan for next year.

    Q: What will they discuss at tomorrow's meeting?

11. M: Dr. Peterson's office. How may I help you?

    W: I'd like to make an appointment with the doctor.

    Q: What does the woman want to do?

12. W: Would you please tell us a little bit about your work?

    M: Sure. I've been working as a salesperson for three years.

    Q: What are the two speakers most probably doing now?

13. W: How did you get your job?

    M: I searched the Internet and found the job online.

    Q: Where did the man find his job?

14. M: Get down. You're on the wrong way.

    W: Sir, I'm sorry. I didn't see the sign.

Q: Why does the man ask the woman to get down?

Section C

Conversation 1

W: ABC Company. How may I help you?

M: Hello. This is John Smith of Tel Trading Company. Is it possible to make a change to our order?

W: And what kind of change do you want to make?

M: Well, we ordered 180 computers, but now we only need 100.

W: What's your order number?

M: HCP10098.

W: Just a moment, please ... Oh, I'm sorry, but they've already been delivered.

Q15. Why does the man call the woman?

Q16. How many computers does the man want now?

Conversation 2

M: May I have a look at this pair of sun glasses?

W: Sure, here you are.

M: How much does it cost?

W: It's 300 dollars.

M: Oh, it's a bit too expensive.

W: We can offer you a discount since you're our regular customer.

M: So how much exactly should I pay you?

W: 240 dollars.

M: How about 200?

W: Alright.

Q17. What does the man want to buy?

Q18. Why does the woman offer the man a discount?

Q19. How much does the man pay in the end?

Section D

Thank you very much for meeting with me yesterday about our project. I really appreciate your help. And we'll take your suggestions into consideration when we make a plan for the next year. It was helpful to have someone like you who has had experience with similar projects. I appreciate your taking the time out of your busy schedule to speak with me. I'll be sure to send you a follow-up when this project is completed. Please let me know if I can return the favor and when.

2019 年 12 月真题

Section A

1. Do you like the design of the new product?
2. Would you sign your name here, please?
3. Could I have your business card, please?
4. Would you help me type the paper?
5. Excuse me, where is the nearest subway station?
6. Can I help you with your luggage?
7. How would you like to pay, Sir?

Section B

8. W: Excuse me, how can I book a meeting room?

   M: You can book it online or in person.

   Q: What does the woman want to book?

9. W: Why are you looking so excited?

   M: I've got a job offer.

   Q: What can we learn about the man?

10. M: I couldn't find John yesterday afternoon. Where was he?

    W: Oh, he went to the airport to see off a customer.

    Q: Why did John go to the airport yesterday afternoon?

11. M: Your office looks quite new.

    W: Yes, we just moved here last month. The old one was too crowded.

    Q: What can we learn about the woman's old office?

12. W: Do you like your new job?

    M: Yes. The pay is good and the people in my department are friendly.

    Q: What does the man think of the people in his department?

13. W: Doctor Johnson's office. May I help you?

    M: I'd like to make an appointment to see the Doctor.

    Q: What does the man want to do?

14. M: Has Bill returned from Nanjing?

    W: No, not yet. He is going to meet our new clients there tomorrow.

    Q: What is Bill going to do tomorrow?

Section C

Conversation 1

M: Do you know Mr. Smith will give a lecture next Wednesday?

W: Yes. It's about the use of big data in marketing.

M: An interesting topic.

W: Yes. I'll attend the lecture. Are you going?

M: I'd like to, but I am leaving for New York on business next Tuesday.

W: What a pity!

Q15. What is Mr. Smith's lecture about?

Q16. Why is the man unable to attend the lecture?

Conversation 2

W: Mr. Smith, what's wrong with your smart phone?

M: It wouldn't give sound when phone calls come in.

W: Have you checked its sound system?

M: Yes. The sound system is OK.

W: When did you buy this smart phone?

M: Three days ago.

W: In that case, you can return it to us or change it for a new one.

M: I want to change it for a new one.

W: OK. Have you brought the receipt with you?

M: Yes, here you are.

Q17. What has happened to the man's smart phone?

Q18. When did the man buy the smart phone?

Q19. What does the woman ask the man to show?

Section D

I should say that teaching English in China is a real job, and the schools expect you to be professional and you have to work hard. If you don't meet their requirements, it is easy to get fired. But with a little effort and the right attitude, it will be a very good experience where you will learn a lot about China and yourself! I am so happy that I took this opportunity when I had it, and the memories will be with me for the rest of my life.

附录二 答案与解析

听力理解

2015年6月真题

Section A

1. 【答案】C

【解析】本题测试考生对句型"How is ..."的理解和应答能力。题目问"彼得,一切都好吗",选项C"很好。谢谢"符合题意,因此答案为C。

2. 【答案】A

【解析】本题测试考生对请求句型"Can I ..."的理解和应答能力。题目问"请问您叫什么名字",选项A"我叫约翰·史密斯"符合题意,因此答案为A。

3. 【答案】B

【解析】本题测试考生对一般疑问句的理解和应答能力。题目问"你喜欢用英语在网上聊天吗",选项B"是的,当然"是对一般疑问句的肯定回答,且符合题意,因此答案为B。

4. 【答案】A

【解析】本题测试考生对请求句型"Would you please ..."的理解和应答能力。题目问"先生,请您在这里签名好吗",选项A"好的"符合题意,因此答案为A。

5. 【答案】D

【解析】本题测试考生对一般疑问句的理解和应答能力。题目问"你经常出差吗",选项D"是的,一个月一次"符合题意,因此答案为D。

6. 【答案】C

【解析】本题测试考生对请求句型"Can you ..."的理解和应答能力。题目问"请帮我转到经理办公室好吗",选项C"当然"符合题意,因此答案为C。

7. 【答案】D

【解析】本题测试考生对请求句型"Shall we ..."的理解和应答能力。题目问"我们下星期安排时间开会好吗",选项D"没问题"符合题意,因此答案为D。

Section B

8. 【答案】A

【解析】本题测试考生理解细节的能力。女士问"汤姆,你面试为什么迟到了",男士回答"我错过了公共汽车",问题是"汤姆为什么迟到",因此答案为A。

9. 【答案】D

【解析】本题测试考生理解细节的能力。女士问"你想怎样支付这台电脑的费用",男士回答"用信用卡",问题是"这位男士如何支付这台电脑的费用",因此答案为D。

10. 【答案】D

【解析】本题测试考生理解细节的能力。女士说"你的工作经验给我们留下了深刻的印象",问题是"什么给女士留下了深刻的印象",因此答案为D。

11. 【答案】C

【解析】本题测试考生理解细节的能力。男士问"玛丽,为什么琳达现在不在这里工作",女士回答"她上周退休了",问题是"从对话中我们可以了解到关于琳达的什么信息",因此答案为C。

12. 【答案】B

【解析】本题测试考生理解细节的能力。男士问"我从哪里可以更多地了解贵公司",女士回答"从我们的网站",问题是"男士从哪里可以得到更多关于公司的信息",因此答案为B。

13. 【答案】A

【解析】本题测试考生的推断能力。男士说"早上好,我和格林医生约好10:30见面",女士回答"请稍等,他正在看另一个病人",问题是"这段对话最有可能发生在哪里",因此答案为A。

14. 【答案】C

【解析】本题测试考生理解细节的能力。女士说"因为约翰不在,恐怕我们今天不能开会了",男士回答"我明白了。那就明天吧",问题是"他们将在什么时候开会",因此答案为C。

Section C

15. 【答案】C

【解析】本题测试考生理解细节的能力。对话中女士问"早上好,有什么可以帮您吗",男士回答"我想看医生",因此答案为C。

16. 【答案】A

【解析】本题测试考生理解细节的能力。对话中女士问"你哪儿不舒服",男士回答"我得了重感冒",因此答案为A。

17. 【答案】D

【解析】本题测试考生理解细节的能力。对话中男士说"请让布莱克先生听电话",因此答案为D。

18. 【答案】A

【解析】本题测试考生理解细节的能力。对话中男士说"请告诉他我们的会议将在周五3:30举行",因此答案为A。

19. 【答案】D

【解析】本题测试考生理解细节的能力。对话结束时女士说"我会把口信传给布莱克先生",因此答案为 D。

Section D

20.【答案】manager

【解析】根据空格前后的单词和听到的录音,可知此处应填入名词 manager。

21.【答案】new idea

【解析】本题空格前有不定冠词 a,后面是介词 of,根据听到的录音,可知此处应填入名词短语 new idea。

22.【答案】development

【解析】根据本题空格前后的单词和听到的录音,可知此处应填入名词 development。

23.【答案】success

【解析】本题空格前有动词 make,根据搭配和听到的录音,可知此处应填入名词 success。

24.【答案】American market

【解析】本题空格处须填地点状语,根据听到的录音,可知此处应填入 American market。

2015 年 12 月真题

Section A

1.【答案】A

【解析】本题测试考生对句型"How is ..."的理解和应答能力。题目问"你好,史密斯先生,你旅途如何",选项 A"很棒"符合题意,因此答案为 A。

2.【答案】D

【解析】本题测试考生对请求句型"Can I ..."的理解和应答能力。题目问"请问您叫什么名字",选项 D"我叫约翰·史密斯"符合题意,因此答案为 D。

3.【答案】B

【解析】本题测试考生对一般疑问句的理解和应答能力。题目问"你住在校园里吗",选项 B"是的,我住校园里"是对一般疑问句的肯定回答,且符合题意,因此答案为 B。

4.【答案】D

【解析】本题测试考生对特殊疑问句的理解和应答能力。题目问"谁会参加会议",选项 D"部门经理"符合题意,因此答案为 D。

5.【答案】C

【解析】本题测试考生对句型"How is ..."的理解和应答能力。题目问"琳达,你一切都好吗",选项 C"不错"符合题意,因此答案为 C。

6.【答案】A

【解析】本题测试考生对请求句型"May I ..."的理解和应答能力。题目问"詹妮特,我可以和你谈谈吗",选项 A"当然"符合题意,因此答案为 A。

7.【答案】B

【解析】本题测试考生对请求句型"Shall we ..."的理解和应答能力。题目问"今天下午我们讨论一下计划好吗",选项 B"没问题"符合题意,因此答案为 B。

Section B

8.【答案】B

【解析】本题测试考生理解细节的能力。男士问"海伦,你为什么放弃这个工作",女士回答"太无聊了",问题是"为什么海伦放弃这个工作",因此答案为 B。

9.【答案】A

【解析】本题测试考生理解细节的能力。女士问"我可以为你做什么吗",男士回答"我在找 7 号的运动鞋",问题是"男士想买什么",因此答案为 A。

10.【答案】B

【解析】本题测试考生理解细节的能力。女士说"迈克,你怎么了",男士回答"我感觉不舒服。我得了重感冒",因此答案为 B。

11.【答案】C

【解析】本题测试考生理解细节的能力。男士说"我打电话想咨询一下售后服务的情况",问题是"男士在咨询什么",因此答案为 C。

12.【答案】D

【解析】本题测试考生理解细节的能力。男士说"我经常上网玩到很晚",女士说"最好不要。这对你的健康没有好处",问题是"女士对熬夜上网有什么看法",因此答案为 D。

13.【答案】C

【解析】本题测试考生的推断能力。男士问"简,你的新工作怎么样",女士回答"太好了。他们给的薪水不错",问题是"关于女士的新工作,我们能了解到什么",因此答案为 C。

14.【答案】B

【解析】本题测试考生理解细节的能力。男士问"简,你好吗",女士回答"我正在做一个新项目",问题是"女士现在在做什么",因此答案为 B。

Section C

15.【答案】B

【解析】本题测试考生理解细节的能力。根据对话,男士说"我已经在你们旅馆订了两个晚上的房间",因此答案为 B。

16.【答案】A

【解析】本题测试考生理解细节的能力。对话中男士问"哪里可以停车",女士回答"在我们的停车场,就在这栋楼后面",因此答案为 A。

17.【答案】B

【解析】本题测试考生理解细节的能力。对话中女士说"我真的认为我应该加薪",因此答案为 B。

18.【答案】C

【解析】本题测试考生理解细节的能力。对话中男士问"你在这里工作几年了",女士回答"五年",因此答案为 C。

附录二 答案与解析

19. 【答案】D

【解析】本题测试考生理解细节的能力。对话结束时男士说"我明白了,我先和人事经理商量一下"。因此答案为 D。

Section D

20. 【答案】carried out

【解析】本题空格前有现在完成时态的助动词 have,空格后是 a survey,根据搭配和听到的录音,可知此处应填入 carried out。

21. 【答案】biggest

【解析】本题空格前有动词 see,空格后是名词 factor,根据听到的录音,可知此处应填入 biggest。

22. 【答案】28

【解析】本题空格后是 percent,根据听到的录音,可知此处应填入数字"28"。

23. 【答案】the ability

【解析】本题空格后是介词 to,根据搭配和听到的录音,可知此处应填入 the ability。

24. 【答案】working condition

【解析】本题空格前有并列词 and,后面应填入并列成分,根据听到的录音,可知此处应填入 working condition。

2016 年 6 月真题

Section A

1. 【答案】D

【解析】本题测试考生对句型"How is … going?"的理解和应答能力。题目问"一切可好",选项 D"不错"符合题意,因此答案为 D。

2. 【答案】A

【解析】本题测试考生对一般疑问句的理解和应答能力。题目问"你昨天去听讲座了吗",选项 A"没有"是对一般疑问句的否定回答,且符合题意,因此答案为 A。

3. 【答案】B

【解析】本题测试考生对评价句型"What do you think about …"的理解和应答能力。题目问"你觉得我们的新设计怎么样",选项 B"很好"符合题意,因此答案为 B。

4. 【答案】C

【解析】本题测试考生对请求句型"May I …"的理解和应答能力。题目问"请出示您的护照好吗",选项 C"给你"符合题意,因此答案为 C。

5. 【答案】B

【解析】本题测试考生对请求句型"Would you please …"的理解和应答能力。题目问"怀特先生,您填一下这张申请表好吗",选项 B"好的"是对请求的肯定回答,且符合题意,因此答案为 B。

165

6. 【答案】A

【解析】本题测试考生对请求句型"Can I …"的理解和应答能力。题目问"能给我一份你的报告吗",选项A"当然可以"符合题意,因此答案为A。

7. 【答案】D

【解析】本题测试考生对选择疑问句"… or …"的理解和应答能力。题目问"您要公务舱还是经济舱",选项D"经济舱"符合题意,因此答案为D。

Section B

8. 【答案】C

【解析】本题测试考生理解细节的能力。男士问"玛丽亚,假期过得怎么样",女士回答"太棒了！我在海滩上玩得很开心",问题是"两个人在谈论什么",因此答案为C。

9. 【答案】A

【解析】本题测试考生理解细节的能力。女士问"您能给我一些时间讨论一下我的营销计划吗",男士回答"对不起。我现在正忙。今天下午怎么样",问题是"两人将在何时谈论这个计划",因此答案为A。

10. 【答案】D

【解析】本题测试考生理解细节的能力。男士说"你好！我想租一套公寓",女士回答"你对什么样的公寓感兴趣",问题是"男士想要做什么",因此答案为D。

11. 【答案】C

【解析】本题测试考生理解细节的能力。女士问"今天早上你为什么开会迟到了",男士回答"我的车在路上抛锚了",问题是"今天早上男士发生了什么",因此答案为C。

12. 【答案】B

【解析】本题测试考生的推断能力。男士说"我不知道如何使用这个新软件",女士回答"为什么不让杰克帮你呢",问题是"男士可能要做什么",因此答案为B。

13. 【答案】A

【解析】本题测试考生的推断能力。女士问"你知道约翰逊先生被提升了吗",男士回答"是的。他现在是我们的新经理",问题是"关于约翰逊先生我们能了解到什么",因此答案为A。

14. 【答案】D

【解析】本题测试考生理解细节的能力。男士问"我想创业,但是到哪里去弄钱呢",女士回答"你可以向银行申请贷款",问题是"女士建议男士做什么",因此答案为D。

Section C

15. 【答案】C

【解析】本题测试考生理解细节的能力。根据对话,女士问"有什么问题吗,警官",男士回答"女士,您闯红灯了",因此答案为C。

16. 【答案】D

【解析】本题测试考生理解细节的能力。问题是"警官让这位女士出示什么",对话中男士说"请出示你的驾照",因此答案为 D。

17.【答案】B

【解析】本题测试考生理解细节的能力。对话中女士问"你申请的是什么职位",男士回答"销售经理",因此答案为 B。

18.【答案】C

【解析】本题测试考生理解细节的能力。对话中女士说"哦,ABC 公司吗?这是一家 IT 公司",因此答案为 C。

19.【答案】A

【解析】本题测试考生理解细节的能力。对话中男士说"他们说下星期一会告诉我结果",因此答案为 A。

Section D

20.【答案】express our thanks

【解析】本题考查固定搭配 express one's thanks,空格前有动词 let,后面应填动词原形,根据听到的录音,可知此处应填入 express our thanks。

21.【答案】set up

【解析】本题空格前是现在完成时态的助动词 have,根据听到的录音,可知此处应填入 set up。

22.【答案】improve

【解析】本题空格前是动词 help,后面应填入动词原形,根据听到的录音,可知此处应填入 improve。

23.【答案】best service

【解析】本题空格前是动词 provide,后面应填入宾语成分,根据搭配和听到的录音,可知此处应填入 best service。

24.【答案】support

【解析】本题空格前有动词 need,后面应填入宾语成分,根据听到的录音,可知此处应填入 support。

2016 年 12 月真题

Section A

1.【答案】A

【解析】本题测试考生对请求句型"Can I …"的理解和应答能力。题目问"我可以和你们的部门经理谈谈吗",选项 A"抱歉,他不在"符合题意,因此答案为 A。

2.【答案】C

【解析】本题测试考生对一般疑问句的理解和应答能力。题目问"你认识总工程师格林先生吗",选项 C"我不认识"是对一般疑问句的否定回答,且符合题意,因此答案为 C。

3.【答案】D

【解析】本题测试考生对特殊疑问句的理解和应答能力。题目问"我怎样启动这台机器",选项D"按这里的按钮"符合题意,因此答案为D。

4. 【答案】B

【解析】本题测试考生对一般疑问句的理解和应答能力。题目问"你喜欢出差吗",选项B"是的,我喜欢"是对一般疑问句的肯定回答,且符合题意,因此答案为B。

5. 【答案】C

【解析】本题测试考生对特殊疑问句"How long …"的理解和应答能力。题目问"你在新岗位上工作多久了",选项C"只有一个星期"符合题意,因此答案为C。

6. 【答案】A

【解析】本题测试考生对地点句型"Where …"的理解和应答能力。题目问"你从哪里得到这个消息的",选项A"在网上"符合题意,因此答案为A。

7. 【答案】D

【解析】本题测试考生对评价句型"What do you think of …"的理解和应答能力。题目问"你觉得你的老板怎么样",选项D"他人很好"符合题意,因此答案为D。

Section B

8. 【答案】A

【解析】本题测试考生理解细节的能力。女士问"你知道4月22日是什么日子吗",男士回答"地球日",问题是"4月22日是什么日子",因此答案为A。

9. 【答案】C

【解析】本题测试考生理解细节的能力。女士问"你们有电话银行服务吗?",男士回答"当然有",问题是"女士在咨询什么",因此答案为C。

10. 【答案】B

【解析】本题测试考生理解细节的能力。女士问"我应该在哪里签名",男士回答"在这一页的底部",问题是"女士想知道什么",因此答案为B。

11. 【答案】D

【解析】本题测试考生理解细节的能力。男士问"我从哪里可以更多地了解你们的培训计划",女士回答"从我们的网站",问题是"男士如何获得更多信息",因此答案为D。

12. 【答案】C

【解析】本题测试考生的推断能力。女士问"我们的新产品在市场上卖得怎么样",男士回答"卖得很好",问题是"两个人在谈论什么",因此答案为C。

13. 【答案】A

【解析】本题测试考生理解细节的能力。男士问"我们什么时候能拿到订单",女士回答"你将在三天之内收到",问题是"男士在问什么",因此答案为A。

14. 【答案】B

【解析】本题测试考生理解细节的能力。女士问"你什么时候创办的公司",男士回答"1998年。现在它有350多名员工",问题是"从对话中我们对公司有什么了解",因此答案为B。

Section C

15.【答案】C

【解析】本题测试考生理解细节的能力。根据对话,女士说"你最近似乎很忙",男士回答"是的,我们在做一项市场调查",因此答案为 C。

16.【答案】D

【解析】本题测试考生的推断能力。问题是"从对话中我们可以了解到关于网上购物的什么信息",对话中男士说"大多数年轻人喜欢在网上购物",因此答案为 D。

17.【答案】A

【解析】本题测试考生的推断能力。问题是"关于这位男士我们能了解到什么",对话中男士说"嗨,珍妮,我找到了一份暑期工作",因此答案为 A。

18.【答案】B

【解析】本题测试考生理解细节的能力。问题是"给这位女士提供了什么工作",对话中女士说"我得到了一份当导游的工作",因此答案为 B。

19.【答案】D

【解析】本题测试考生的推断能力。对话中男士说"但是导游必须长时间工作",女士说"这就是我为什么还没有下定决心的原因",因此答案为 D。

Section D

20.【答案】express

【解析】本题空格前是介词 to,后面应填入动词原形,根据听到的录音,可知此处应填入动词 express。

21.【答案】be proud of

【解析】本题空格前是情态动词 must,后面应填,动词原形,根据听到的录音,可知此处应填入 be proud of。

22.【答案】depend on

【解析】本题空格前是情态动词 cannot,后面应填入动词原形,根据听到的录音,可知此处应填入 depend on。

23.【答案】ideas

【解析】本题空格前是形容词 creative,后面应填入名词成分,根据听到的录音,可知此处应填入 ideas。

24.【答案】once again

【解析】本题空格前的句子成分完整,后面应填入副词等修饰成分,根据听到的录音,可知此处应填入 once again。

2017 年 6 月真题

Section A

1.【答案】D

【解析】本题测试考生对请求句型"Can I …"的理解和应答能力。题目问"需要帮忙吗，夫人"，选项 D"不用，谢谢"符合题意，因此答案为 D。

2.【答案】B

【解析】本题测试考生对请求句型"May I …"的理解和应答能力。题目问"请问您叫什么名字"，选项 B"约翰·史密斯"符合题意，因此答案为 B。

3.【答案】C

【解析】本题测试考生对邀请句型"Would you like …"的理解和应答能力。题目问"你想喝杯咖啡吗"，选项 C"好的"符合题意，因此答案为 C。

4.【答案】A

【解析】本题测试考生对请求句型"Shall we …"的理解和应答能力。题目问"我们星期五见面好吗"，选项 A"恐怕不行"是对请求的否定回答，且符合题意，因此答案为 A。

5.【答案】B

【解析】本题测试考生对一般疑问句的理解和应答能力。题目问"对不起，你是从英国来的约翰·史密斯吗"，选项 B"是的，我是"符合题意，因此答案为 B。

6.【答案】D

【解析】本题测试考生对一般疑问句的理解和应答能力。题目问"你对这个培训课程感兴趣吗"，选项 D"是的，当然"符合题意，因此答案为 D。

7.【答案】C

【解析】本题测试考生对请求句型"Would you like …"的理解和应答能力。题目问"你愿意参加销售会议吗"，选项 C"当然，我愿意"是对请求的肯定回答，且符合题意，因此答案为 C。

Section B

8.【答案】A

【解析】本题测试考生理解细节的能力。男士说"这座建筑看起来很旧"，女士回答"是的，它是大约 150 年前建造的"，问题是"建筑物是何时建造的"，因此答案为 A。

9.【答案】D

【解析】本题测试考生的推断能力。女士问"你对你的工作满意吗"，男士回答"老板很好，薪水也不错"，问题是"男士认为他的工作如何"，因此答案为 D。

10.【答案】C

【解析】本题测试考生理解细节的能力。女士问"你的城市人口多吗"，男士回答"是的，大约 300 万人口"，问题是"女士询问城市的什么情况"，因此答案为 C。

11.【答案】A

【解析】本题测试考生理解细节的能力。男士问"你去过深圳吗"，女士回答"是的，很多次。它是一座很现代化的都市"，问题是"女士认为这个城市如何"，因此答案为 A。

12.【答案】C

【解析】本题测试考生理解细节的能力。男士问"你想出国留学吗"，女士回答"希望可以,但是我没有足够的钱",问题是"这位女士有什么问题",因此答案为 C。

13.【答案】B

【解析】本题测试考生理解细节的能力。男士问"我怎么才能申请会员卡",女士回答"请先填这张表",问题是"男士很有可能先做什么",因此答案为 B。

14.【答案】D

【解析】本题测试考生理解细节的能力。男士问"你怎么了",女士回答"我头疼",问题是"关于女士,我们能了解到什么",因此答案为 D。

Section C

15.【答案】B

【解析】本题测试考生理解细节的能力。对话中女士问"你想要什么样的公寓",男士回答"有两间卧室的公寓",因此答案为 B。

16.【答案】C

【解析】本题测试考生的推断能力。对话中女士问"你想租哪里的公寓",男士回答"在市中心我的办公室附近",因此答案为 C。

17.【答案】A

【解析】本题测试考生理解细节的能力。对话中女士问"你为什么对这个工作感兴趣",男士回答"我想得到更多的机会",因此答案为 A。

18.【答案】B

【解析】本题测试考生理解细节的能力。对话中女士问"你在现在的职位上工作多久了",男士回答"五年",因此答案为 B。

19.【答案】C

【解析】本题测试考生理解细节的能力。对话中女士问"几年后你想做什么",男士回答"我希望能够成为一名熟练的工程师",因此答案为 C。

Section D

20.【答案】inviting

【解析】本题考查固定搭配 thank sb. for (doing sth.),根据听到的录音,可知此处应填入动名词 inviting。

21.【答案】lovely

【解析】本题空格前是系动词 be,后面应填入成分作表语,根据听到的录音和句意,可知此处应填入形容词 lovely。

22.【答案】talking to

【解析】本题空格前有动词 enjoy,后面应填入动词-ing 形式,根据听到的录音,可知此处应填入 talking to。

23.【答案】good relationship

【解析】本题空格前有动词 maintain,后面应填入成分作宾语,根据听到的录音,可知此处应填入 good relationship。

24. 【答案】a great time

【解析】本题考查固定搭配 have a great time，根据空格前的动词和听到的录音，可知此处应填入 a great time。

2017年12月真题

☐ Section A

1. 【答案】A

【解析】本题测试考生对地点句型"Where is …"的理解和应答能力。题目问"打扰了，请问问讯处在哪里"，选项 A"在那里"符合题意，因此答案为 A。

2. 【答案】C

【解析】本题测试考生对请求句型"Can you …"的理解和应答能力。题目问"你能教我如何使用这台机器吗"，选项 C"当然可以"是对请求的肯定回答，且符合题意，因此答案为 C。

3. 【答案】B

【解析】本题测试考生对句型"How is …"的理解和应答能力。题目问"史密斯先生，航班怎么样"，选项 B"很好"符合题意，因此答案为 B。

4. 【答案】D

【解析】本题测试考生对一般疑问句的回答。题目问"这是新款。您要不要试一试"，对一般疑问句一般作肯定或否定回答，选项 D"当然"是肯定回答，符合题意，因此答案为 D。

5. 【答案】C

【解析】本题测试考生对请求句型"Would you …"的理解和应答能力。题目问"你能在这里签字吗"，当对方以"Would you/Could you …"提出请求时，应给予肯定或否定回答，选项 C"好的"是对请求的肯定回答，且符合题意，因此答案为 C。

6. 【答案】B

【解析】本题测试考生对评价句型"What do you think about …"的理解和应答能力。题目问"你觉得我们的假期计划怎么样"，选项 B"很好"符合题意，因此答案为 B。

7. 【答案】A

【解析】本题测试考生对请求句型"Can I …"的理解和应答能力。题目问"这件t恤有点小，我可以换件大点的吗"，选项 A"当然"是对请求的肯定回答，且符合题意，因此答案为 A。

☐ Section B

8. 【答案】D

【解析】本题测试考生理解细节的能力。女士问"你为什么看起来很担心"，男士回答"我今天下午有一个面试"，问题是"男士在担心什么"，因此答案为 D。

9. 【答案】B

【解析】本题测试考生理解细节的能力。女士说"史密斯先生，这是新的价格单"，男士回答"这正是我想要的"，问题是"女士给了男士什么东西"，因此答案为 B。

10.【答案】A

【解析】本题测试考生理解细节的能力。男士说"我们把发生的事告诉约翰好吗",女士回答"好的,当然。我现在就给他打电话",问题是"女士将要做什么",因此答案为A。

11.【答案】B

【解析】本题测试考生理解细节的能力。女士说"这周五我们要用一下会议室",男士回答"对不起,会议室已经被预订了",问题是"女士为什么不能使用会议室",因此答案为B。

12.【答案】D

【解析】本题测试考生理解细节的能力。女士问"你的演讲如何",男士回答"我不知道。我很紧张",问题是"男士认为他的演讲如何",因此答案为D。

13.【答案】A

【解析】本题测试考生理解细节的能力。女士问"你在找新工作吗",男士回答"是的,我已经得到了一份工作邀请",问题是"关于男士,我们能了解到什么",因此答案为A。

14.【答案】C

【解析】本题测试考生的推断能力。男士问"你拿到驾照了吗",女士回答"没有,我只通过了路考",问题是"从对话中我们能了解到什么",因此答案为C。

▋Section C

15.【答案】B

【解析】本题测试考生理解细节的能力。对话中女士说"我打电话是想问你是否决定订购我们的产品",因此答案为B。

16.【答案】D

【解析】本题测试考生理解细节的能力。对话中女士说"我们的产品质量很高,你不会失望的",因此答案为D。

17.【答案】A

【解析】本题测试考生理解细节的能力。对话中女士问"王先生,你的车怎么了",男士回答"今天早上不能发动了",因此答案为A。

18.【答案】B

【解析】本题测试考生理解细节的能力。对话中女士说"也许你要买新电池了",男士回答"但是我上个月刚买了电池,还是新的",因此答案为B。

19.【答案】C

【解析】本题测试考生理解细节的能力。问题是"男士将如何处理这个电池",对话结束时男士说"我会把它退给商店",因此答案为C。

▋Section D

20.【答案】manage

【解析】本题空格前是主语,后面是介词to,根据动词搭配和听到的录音,可知此处应填入 manage。

21.【答案】in high demand

【解析】本题空格前是系动词be，后面应填入成分作表语，根据听到的录音，可知此处应填入in high demand。

22. 【答案】possible

【解析】本题空格前是短语in any way，后面应填入成分作补语，根据听到的录音，可知此处应填入possible。

23. 【答案】advantages

【解析】本题考查固定搭配have advantage over，根据听到的录音，可知此处应填入advantages。

24. 【答案】a right decision

【解析】本题空格前是动词make，后面应填入成分作宾语，根据固定搭配和听到的录音，可知此处应填入a right decision。

2018年6月真题

Section A

1. 【答案】A

【解析】本题测试考生对请求句型"May I …"的理解和应答能力。题目问"现在可以点菜了吗"，选项A"请吧"符合题意，因此答案为A。

2. 【答案】C

【解析】本题测试考生对句型"How is …"的理解和应答能力。题目问"嗨，约翰，你的巴黎之行怎么样"，选项C"太棒了"符合题意，因此答案为C。

3. 【答案】C

【解析】本题测试考生对请求句型"Could I …"的理解和应答能力。题目问"下星期五我能订一间双人房吗"，当对方以"Can I/May I/Could I …"提出请求时，应给予肯定或者否定回答，选项C"对不起，我们的房间都订满了"是对请求的否定回答，且符合题意，因此答案为C。

4. 【答案】B

【解析】本题测试考生对请求句型"May I …"的理解和应答能力。题目问"我可以进来和你谈谈吗"，当对方以"Can I/May I/Could you …"提出请求时，应给予肯定或者否定回答，选项B"请吧"是对请求的肯定回答，且符合题意，因此答案为B。

5. 【答案】A

【解析】本题测试考生对请求句型"Could I …"的理解和应答能力。题目问"我能和格林医生约个时间吗"，选项A"当然可以。星期五可以吗"是对请求的肯定回答，且符合题意，因此答案为A。

6. 【答案】D

【解析】本题测试考生对请求句型"Could you …"的理解和应答能力。题目问"汤姆，你能把报告给我吗"，选项D"好的。给你"是对请求的肯定回答，且符合题意，因此答案为D。

附录二 答案与解析

7.【答案】B

【解析】本题测试考生对请求句型"Can you ..."的理解和应答能力。题目问"布朗先生,您现在可以填一下这张表吗",选项B"好的"是对请求的肯定回答,且符合题意,因此答案为B。

📄 Section B

8.【答案】B

【解析】本题测试考生理解细节的能力。男士问"我们怎么去市中心",女士回答"我们步行过去。它离这儿不远",问题是"两位讲话者如何去市中心",因此答案为B。

9.【答案】C

【解析】本题测试考生的推断能力。男士问"玛丽,设计什么时候能准备好",女士回答"明天早上可以吗",问题是"这两个人在谈论什么",因此答案为C。

10.【答案】C

【解析】本题测试考生理解细节的能力。女士问"你有工作经验吗",男士回答"是的,我当了两年的程序员",问题是"关于这位男士,我们能了解到什么",因此答案为C。

11.【答案】A

【解析】本题测试考生理解细节的能力,男士问"你的工作有困难吗",女士回答"是的,对付愤怒的顾客很困难",问题是"女士的工作有什么困难",因此答案为A。

12.【答案】D

【解析】本题测试考生理解细节的能力。男士问"你是来度假的,对吗",女士回答"不,我是来出差的",问题是"女士为什么来这里",因此答案为D。

13.【答案】B

【解析】本题测试考生理解细节的能力。女士问"你的车怎么了",男士回答"前窗被打破了",因此答案为B。

14.【答案】A

【解析】本题测试考生理解细节的能力。女士问"我正在找一份新工作,有什么建议吗",男士回答"为什么不参加招聘会呢",问题是"男士建议女士做什么",因此答案为A。

📄 Section C

15.【答案】D

【解析】本题测试考生理解细节的能力。对话中女士说"早上好,先生,我想要报案",因此答案为D。

16.【答案】A

【解析】本题测试考生理解细节的能力。对话中男士问"你的手提包里有什么",女士回答"我的护照",因此答案为A。

17.【答案】C

【解析】本题测试考生理解细节的能力。对话中男士问"你怎么了",女士回答"是我的胃,难受得要命",因此答案为C。

18.【答案】A

【解析】本题测试考生理解细节的能力。对话中男士问"疼了多久了",女士回答"今天早上开始的",因此答案为 A。

19.【答案】D

【解析】本题测试考生理解细节的能力。对话结束时男士说"我想我们得马上送你去急诊室",因此答案为 D。

Section D

20.【答案】local

【解析】本题空格前是介词 for,后面是名词短语,根据听到的录音,可知此处应填入形容词 local。

21.【答案】safety training

【解析】本题空格前有及物动词 supply,后面应填入成分作宾语,根据听到的录音,可知此处应填入 safety training。

22.【答案】new skills

【解析】本题空格前有及物动词 learn,后面应填入成分作宾语,根据听到的录音,可知此处应填入 new skills。

23.【答案】at our offices

【解析】根据句意和听到的录音,可知此处应填入短语 at our offices。

24.【答案】at least

【解析】本题空格后是 14 years,根据听到的录音,可知此处应填入固定搭配 at least。

2018 年 12 月真题

Section A

1.【答案】A

【解析】本题测试考生对句型"How are things going?"的理解和应答能力。题目问"你们公司最近怎么样",选项 A"一切都好"符合题意,因此答案为 A。

2.【答案】C

【解析】本题测试考生对请求句型"Can I …"的理解和应答能力。题目问"我帮您拿行李好吗",当对方以"Can I/May I/Could you …"提出请求时,应给予肯定或者否定回答,选项 C"你真好"是对请求的肯定回答,且符合题意,因此答案为 C。

3.【答案】D

【解析】本题测试考生对请求句型"Will you …"的理解和应答能力。题目问"你愿意加入我们的新项目吗",当对方以"Will you/Could you …"提出请求时,应给予肯定或者否定回答,选项 D"我愿意"是对请求的肯定回答,且符合题意,因此答案为 D。

4.【答案】B

【解析】本题测试考生对句型"How is sth./sb. …"的理解和应答能力。题目问"你最近工作怎么样",选项B"很好"符合题意,因此答案为B。

5. 【答案】D

【解析】本题测试考生对请求句型"Do you mind …"的理解和应答能力。题目问"你介意我问你一个问题吗",选项D"请吧"是对请求的肯定回答,且符合题意,因此答案为D。

6. 【答案】A

【解析】本题测试考生对请求句型"Would you …"的理解和应答能力。题目问"你能帮我检查一下我的报告吗",当对方以"Would you/Could you …"提出请求时,应给予肯定或者否定回答,选项A"我的荣幸"是对请求的肯定回答,且符合题意,因此答案为A。

7. 【答案】B

【解析】本题测试考生对请求句型"May I …"的理解和应答能力。题目问"我可以就这个新计划说几句吗",当对方以"Can I/May I …"提出请求时,应给予肯定或者否定回答,选项B"请吧"是对请求的肯定回答,且符合题意,因此答案为B。

Section B

8. 【答案】B

【解析】本题测试考生理解细节的能力。男士问"你好,琳达。你这些天为什么这么忙",女士回答"我正在为新年晚会做准备",问题是"琳达在忙什么",因此答案为B。

9. 【答案】C

【解析】本题测试考生理解细节的能力。女士问"你从哪里知道我们的工作职位的",男士回答"从你们的网站",问题是"男士从哪里得到工作职位的信息",因此答案为C。

10. 【答案】A

【解析】本题测试考生理解细节的能力。女士问"明天的会议上谁做报告",男士回答"约翰逊博士,社区大学的教授",因此答案为A。

11. 【答案】D

【解析】本题测试考生理解细节的能力。男士说"我想和你们经理谈谈",女士说"对不起,他正在见一位客户",问题是"经理现在在做什么",因此答案为D。

12. 【答案】C

【解析】本题测试考生理解细节的能力。女士问"汤姆,你开会迟到了。你还好吗",男士回答"对不起,我刚刚忘了会议时间",问题是"汤姆开会为什么迟到",因此答案为C。

13. 【答案】B

【解析】本题测试考生理解细节的能力。女士说"哦,天哪!交通太拥堵了",男士说"我想前面一定发生了交通事故",问题是"路上可能发生了什么",因此答案为B。

14. 【答案】A

【解析】本题测试考生理解细节的能力。女士问"你会接受这份工作吗",男士回答"是的,对我有好处",问题是"男士认为这份工作怎么样",因此答案为A。

Section C

15. 【答案】D

【解析】本题测试考生理解细节的能力。对话中女士问"嗨,史蒂夫。你一切都好吗",男士回答"很好。我现在正在做一个项目",因此答案为 D。

16. 【答案】B

【解析】本题测试考生对建议句型"How about …"的理解和应答能力。问题是"说话的两个人明天要做什么",根据对话,女士提议"明天去看比赛怎么样?那是周末",因此答案为 B。

17. 【答案】C

【解析】本题测试考生理解细节的能力。问题是"为史密斯先生提供了什么工作",根据对话,女士说"这里是 ABC 公司。我们决定给你项目经理的职位",因此答案为 C。

18. 【答案】B

【解析】本题测试考生理解细节的能力。问题是"史密斯先生什么时候开始工作",根据对话,女士回答"下周三怎么样",因此答案为 B。

19. 【答案】D

【解析】本题测试考生理解细节的能力。问题是"史密斯先生如何去公司",根据对话,男士说"我可以乘地铁 2 号线",因此答案为 D。

Section D

20. 【答案】common

【解析】本题空格前有 be 动词,后面应填入成分作表语,根据听到的录音,可知此处应填入 common。

21. 【答案】usually

【解析】本题空格前是主语,后面是谓语动词,根据听到的录音,可知此处应填入副词 usually。

22. 【答案】pay in cash

【解析】本题空格前是副词,后面应填入动词原形,根据听到的录音,可知此处应填入 pay in cash。

23. 【答案】on the rise

【解析】本题空格前是系动词 be,后面应填入成分作表语,根据听到的录音,可知此处应填入 on the rise。

24. 【答案】taking the bus

【解析】本题空格前有"buying … or …",后面应填入并列成分,根据听到的录音,可知此处应填入 taking the bus。

2019 年 6 月真题

Section A

1. 【答案】D

【解析】本题测试考生对一般疑问句的回答。题目问"你在这儿度假吗",对一般疑问句一般作肯定或否定回答,选项 D"是的"为肯定回答,且符合题意,因此答案为 D。

2. 【答案】A

【解析】本题测试考生对一般疑问句的回答。题目问"对不起,这个位子有人坐吗",对一般疑问句一般作肯定或否定回答,选项 A"是的"为肯定回答,且符合题意,因此答案为 A。

3. 【答案】B

【解析】本题测试考生对请求句型"Could you …"的理解和应答能力。题目问"王先生,你能告诉玛丽给我回个电话吗",选项 B"当然可以"是对请求的肯定回答,且符合题意,因此答案为 B。

4. 【答案】C

【解析】本题测试考生对请求句型"May I …"的理解和应答能力。题目问"我帮您拿行李好吗",当对方以"Can I/May I …"提出请求时,应给予肯定或者否定回答,选项 C"不用了,谢谢"是对请求的否定回答,且符合题意,因此答案为 C。

5. 【答案】A

【解析】本题测试考生对请求句型"Could I …"的理解和应答能力。题目问"我可以和你们经理约个时间吗",当对方以"Can I/May I/Could I …"提出请求时,应给予肯定或者否定回答,选项 A"没问题"是对请求的肯定回答,且符合题意,因此答案为 A。

6. 【答案】C

【解析】本题测试考生对评价句型"What do you think of …"的理解和应答能力。题目问"你觉得这里的天气怎么样",回答特殊疑问句秉承"问什么,答什么"的原则即可。只有选项 C"非常好"可以表示对天气的评价,且符合题意,因此答案为 C。

7. 【答案】D

【解析】本题测试考生对邀请句型"Would you like …"的理解和应答能力。题目问"你愿意来参加我们的业务聚会吗",应该用"Yes, I'd love to."或"No, thanks."来回答,因此答案为 D。

Section B

8. 【答案】C

【解析】本题测试考生理解细节的能力。男士问"你现在有工作吗",女士回答"是的,我是当地医院的一名护士",因此答案为 C。

9. 【答案】B

【解析】本题测试考生理解细节的能力。男士说"玛丽把房子卖了,我感到很惊讶",女士说"她不得不偿还债务",问题是"玛丽为什么卖房子",因此答案为 B。

10. 【答案】C

【解析】本题测试考生理解细节的能力。be going to 相当于 will,表示将来。女士问"明天的会议讨论什么",男士回答"我们明年的销售计划",问题是"他们明天将在会议上讨论什么",因此答案为 C。

11. 【答案】A

【解析】本题测试考生理解细节的能力。would like 相当于 want，表示想要。女士说"我想要预约医生"，因此答案为 A。

12. 【答案】D

【解析】本题测试考生的推理能力。女士说"请您介绍一下您的工作情况好吗"，男士回答"当然。我做销售已经三年了"，由此可推知女士在对男士进行面试，因此答案为 D。

13. 【答案】A

【解析】本题测试考生理解细节的能力。女士问"你是怎么找到工作的"，男士回答"我上网搜索，在网上找到了工作"，因此答案为 A。

14. 【答案】D

【解析】本题测试考生理解细节的能力。男士说"下车。你走错路了"，女士说"对不起，先生。我没有看到标志"，因此答案为 D。

Section C

15. 【答案】D

【解析】本题测试考生理解细节的能力。对话中，男士向女士介绍完自己之后就提出了要求，问女士能否改变订单，因此答案为 D。

16. 【答案】C

【解析】本题测试考生理解细节的能力。对话中，男士回答女士说他现在只需要 100 台电脑，因此答案为 C。

17. 【答案】B

【解析】本题测试考生理解细节的能力。对话中，男士说"我能看一下这副太阳镜吗"，可知他想买太阳镜，因此答案为 B。

18. 【答案】A

【解析】本题测试考生理解细节的能力。since 表示"因为"。对话中女士说男士是老顾客，所以给他打折，因此答案为 A。

19. 【答案】C

【解析】本题测试考生理解细节的能力。对话中，女士给男士打折后价格为 240 美元，男士砍价说"200 美元怎么样"，女士表示同意，最后以 200 美元成交。因此答案为 C。

Section D

20. 【答案】make a plan

【解析】本题空格前有主语，后面缺少谓语和宾语，根据听到的录音，可知此处应填入 make a plan。

21. 【答案】helpful

【解析】本题空格前有系动词 be，后面应填入成分作表语，根据听到的录音，可知此处应填入 helpful。

22. 【答案】speak with

【解析】本题空格前是介词 to，后面应填入动词原形，根据听到的录音，可知此处应填入

speak with。

23.【答案】be sure

【解析】本题空格前有 will,后面应填入动词原形,根据听到的录音,可知此处应填入 be sure。

24.【答案】return

【解析】本题空格前是情态动词 can,后面应填入动词原形,根据听到的录音,可知此处应填入 return。

2019 年 12 月真题

Section A

1.【答案】A

【解析】本题测试考生对一般疑问句的回答。题目问"你喜欢新产品的设计吗",对一般疑问句一般作肯定或否定回答,选项 A"是的"为肯定回答,且符合题意,因此答案为 A。

2.【答案】C

【解析】本题测试考生对请求句型"Would you …"的理解和应答能力。题目问"请您在这里签名好吗",选项 C"好的"是对请求的肯定回答,且符合题意,因此答案为 C。

3.【答案】B

【解析】本题测试考生对请求句型"Could I …"的理解和应答能力。题目问"能给我一张您的名片吗",当对方以"Can I/May I/Could you …"提出请求时,应给予肯定或者否定回答,选项 B"给你"是对请求的肯定回答,且符合题意,因此答案为 B。

4.【答案】D

【解析】本题测试考生对请求句型"Would you …"的理解和应答能力。题目问"你能帮我打印那张纸吗",当对方以"Would you/Could you …"提出请求时,应给予肯定或者否定回答,选项 D"好的"是对请求的肯定回答,且符合题意,因此答案为 D。

5.【答案】C

【解析】本题测试考生对地点句型"Where …"的理解和应答能力。题目问"最近的地铁站在哪里",只有选项 C"沿着街道走"符合题意,因此答案为 C。

6.【答案】A

【解析】本题测试考生对请求句型"Can I …"的理解和应答能力。题目问"我帮您拿行李好吗",当对方以"Can I/May I …"提出请求时,应给予肯定或者否定回答,选项 A"好的"是肯定回答,且符合题意,因此答案为 A。

7.【答案】D

【解析】本题测试考生对方式句型"How would you like …"的理解和应答能力。题目问"先生,您想怎样付款",选项 D"用现金"符合题意,因此答案为 D。

Section B

8.【答案】C

【解析】本题测试考生理解细节的能力。女士问"我应该如何预订会议室",男士回答"可以在网上或亲自预订",问题是"女士想预订什么",因此答案为C。

9. 【答案】D

【解析】本题测试考生对推断句型"What can we learn about …"的理解和应答能力。女士问"你为什么看起来这么兴奋",男士回答"我得到一个工作机会",问题是"关于这位男士,我们能了解到什么",因此答案为D。

10. 【答案】B

【解析】本题测试考生理解细节的能力。男士说"昨天下午我没能找到约翰。他在哪里",女士回答"他去机场送客户了",问题是"约翰昨天下午为什么去机场",因此答案为B。

11. 【答案】A

【解析】本题测试考生对推断句型"What can we learn about …"的理解和应答能力。男士说"你的办公室看起来很新",女士回答"是的,我们上个月刚搬到这里。旧的那个太挤了",问题是"关于这位女士的旧办公室,我们能了解到什么",因此答案为A。

12. 【答案】B

【解析】本题测试考生理解细节的能力。女士问"你喜欢你的新工作吗",男士回答"是的,薪水不错,我们部门的人也很友好",问题是"这位男士认为他部门的人怎么样",因此答案为B。

13. 【答案】D

【解析】本题测试考生理解细节的能力。女士问"这是约翰逊大夫的办公室。我能帮你吗",男士回答"我想预约看医生",问题是"这位男士想做什么",因此答案为D。

14. 【答案】C

【解析】本题测试考生理解细节的能力。男士问"比尔从南京回来了吗",女士回答"不,还没有,他明天要去见我们的新客户",因此答案为C。

Section C

15. 【答案】B

【解析】本题测试考生理解细节的能力。对话中男士问"你知道史密斯先生下周三要做讲座吗",女士回答"讲座是关于大数据在营销中的应用",因此答案为B。

16. 【答案】A

【解析】本题测试考生理解细节的能力。问题是"男士为什么不能参加讲座",根据对话,男士回答女士"我很想去,但我下星期二要去纽约出差",因此答案为A。

17. 【答案】D

【解析】本题测试考生理解细节的能力。问题是"男士的智能手机怎么了",根据对话,男士说"当电话打进来时,它不会发出声音",因此答案为D。

18. 【答案】A

【解析】本题测试考生理解细节的能力。问题是"男士什么时候买的智能手机",根据对话,男士回答"三天前",因此答案为A。

附录二 答案与解析

19. 【答案】C

【解析】本题测试考生理解细节的能力。问题是"女士让男士出示什么",根据对话,女士问"你带收据了吗",因此答案为C。

Section D

20. 【答案】expect

【解析】本题空格前有主语,后面缺少谓语,根据听到的录音和后面的不定式 to be,可知此处应填入 expect。

21. 【答案】work hard

【解析】本题空格前有 have to,空格处应填入动词原形,根据听到的录音,可知此处应填入 work hard。

22. 【答案】a little effort

【解析】根据空格前的 with 和空格后的 and,可知空格处应填入名词短语,根据听到的录音,此处应填入 a little effort。

23. 【答案】learn a lot

【解析】本题空格前有助动词 will,空格处应填入动词原形,根据听到的录音,可知此处应填入 learn a lot。

24. 【答案】opportunity

【解析】本题空格前有动词 take,根据动词搭配和听到的录音,可知此处应填入 opportunity。

词汇与结构

2015 年 6 月真题

Section A

25. 【答案】C

【解析】句意为:我非常高兴地宣布,今年的销售目标已经提前完成了。完成销售量是过去设定的目标,从过去一直到"我"宣布的那一刻,"我们"一直在努力完成这个目标,因此,需要用现在完成时来表达这个过程,另外,"目标"与"完成"之间是动宾关系,"目标"位于句首作主语,"完成"相应地就要用被动语态。

26. 【答案】D

【解析】句意为:新的交通规则将从 2016 年元旦起生效。A 项意为"舒适的;舒服的";B 项意为"优秀的";C 项意为"具有挑战性的";D 项意为"生效的;起作用的"。根据题意,D 项正确。

27. 【答案】C

【解析】句意为:他在比赛中获得一等奖的消息迅速传遍整个校园。同位语从句紧随一些抽象名词,对其进行详细说明。这些抽象名词常见的有 announcement(通知)、fact(事实)、hope(希望)、idea(想法)、proposal(提议)、suggestion(建议)等。此题中同位语从句由 that 来引导,that 在从句中不充当任何成分,并且不能省略。

28.【答案】B

【解析】句意为:受雪暴影响,货物的配送推迟了。A 项意为"想出,得到(解决方法)";B 项意为"推迟";C 项意为"打开(设备)";D 项意为"吸收;理解;欺骗"。根据题意,B 项的意思贴切。

29.【答案】A

【解析】句意为:这个项目如果完成的话,将极大地改进这个社区的环境。project 和 finish 之间是动宾关系,project 既是主句的主语,又是从句的主语,finish 相应地要用被动形式,表达"计划的被完成"。

30.【答案】B

【解析】句意为:除非我们能从其他部门获得帮助,否则这项任务完成不了。句中主句和从句之间是一种表示否定的条件关系。unless 相当于 if ... not,表示"除非"。

31.【答案】A

【解析】句意为:维生素 B 可以让身体充分利用所摄入的食物。make full use of 表示"充分利用",是一个固定搭配。

32.【答案】C

【解析】句意为:要求这些建筑工人参加安全培训项目。participate in 为固定搭配,表示"参加,参与"。

33.【答案】B

【解析】句意为:我们会提前发送备忘录,这样大家都有充足的时间去做准备。A 项意为"以防,免得";B 项意为"因此,以便";C 项意为"好像,仿佛";D 项意为"自从;打……以后一直"。根据题意,主句、从句之间表示因果关系,B 项符合题旨。

34.【答案】A

【解析】句意为:祝贺你们去年以来所取得的巨大成绩。A 项意为"进步";B 项意为"措施";C 项意为"预约";D 项意为"意义"。根据题意,A 项的意思贴切。

Section B

35.【答案】to guess

【解析】句意为:难以猜测经理对设计会做何评论。"It is + *adj.* + to do sth."是固定搭配,it 作形式主语,真正的主语是后面的动词不定式。

36.【答案】be made

【解析】句意为:可通过您的活期或储蓄账户在线支付。make 与 payment 之间是动宾关系,payment 被前置,make 相应地要变成被动语态。

37.【答案】frequently

【解析】句意为:这类贷款常用于这个目的。副词在句中作状语,修饰谓语动词 use。

38.【答案】agreement

【解析】句意为:我们有可能跟那家公司达成长期协议。根据空格前的 a long-term 可以判断,空格处须填入名词 agreement。

39.【答案】more difficult

【解析】句意为:我得承认,形势要比我所认为的要难。根据 than 可以判断,空格处要填入比较级。difficult 是多音节形容词,其比较级为 more difficult。

2015 年 12 月真题

Section A

25.【答案】C

【解析】句意为:这家公司的一些员工被允许采取灵活的办公形式。A 项意为"拿走,取走";B 项意为"实现";C 项意为"允许";D 项意为"形成"。根据题意,公司允许员工采取灵活的办公形式,员工是被允许的,所以 allow 需要用被动语态。

26.【答案】A

【解析】句意为:由于我们的网站目前正在建设中,如需了解更多信息,请来电咨询。under 表示"在……过程中",可以跟 construction(建设)搭配,其他介词不能表达这个意思。

27.【答案】B

【解析】句意为:像往常一样,销售经理以上月的销售统计来开始他的报告。A 项意为"到现在为止";B 项意为"照例,像往常一样";C 项意为"迄今为止";D 项意为"至多"。根据题意,B 项的意思贴切。

28.【答案】D

【解析】句意为:我们真的很喜欢我们的工作环境,在这里可以坦诚而友好地进行职场上的沟通。非限定性定语从句修饰 working environment,修饰的是物,由 which 来引导。此外,介词后的引导词一般用 which。

29.【答案】B

【解析】句意为:公司会议提供了一个机会,大家在会上可以分享想法,讨论职场上出现的问题。A 项意为"达到,实现";B 项意为"分享";C 项意为"采取,采纳";D 项意为"带领"。根据题意,B 项的意思贴切。

30.【答案】C

【解析】句意为:自从新经理来后,市场部发生了巨大的变化。主句中用的是现在完成时,一般跟连词 since 搭配,表示自从过去某个时间直到说话的时候,某个行为或动作一直在进行。

31.【答案】D

【解析】句意为:他说只要我们不违反规则,他会继续支持我们。A 项意为"也,又";B 项意为"一……就";C 项意为"据……就";D 项意为"只要"。主句和从句之间是一种条件关系,D 项符合。

32.【答案】A

【解析】句意为:这所学校成立于1929年,为一位中国学者所建。A项意为"建立,成立";B项意为"放置";C项意为"想象,设想";D项意为"制造,做"。根据题意,A项相符。

33.【答案】C

【解析】句意为:我们达成了一项协议,就是我们应该在互联网相关的行业投资。that引导的同位语从句,对agreement进行详细说明和补充。

34.【答案】B

【解析】句意为:除了优质服务,在我们餐厅客人可以享用美味佳肴。A项意为"代替";B项意为"除了……之外";C项意为"负责";D项意为"万一"。根据题意,B项符合。

Section B

35.【答案】receiving

【解析】句意为:我们期待着尽早收到你们的回复。look forward to 表示"期待,盼望",后接动名词。

36.【答案】education

【解析】句意为:教育的主要目的是教学生独立思考。of后接名词组成介宾结构,educate的名词形式是education。

37.【答案】was completed

【解析】句意为:我被告知,他们的项目在上周按计划完成了。complete 与 project 之间是动宾关系,project被前置,complete相应地要变成被动语态,同时宾语从句中的时间状语 last week 提示谓语动词要用过去式。

38.【答案】generally

【解析】句意为:一般认为大约14%的新车会有电气方面的问题。副词在句中作状语,修饰谓语动词believe。

39.【答案】interesting

【解析】句意为:作为新入职人员,几乎公司里的一切对我来说都很有趣。interesting 表示"有趣的,有吸引力的",常作定语或表语,并且主语为事物;而interested表示"感兴趣的",常作表语,主语一般是人。

2016年6月真题

Section A

25.【答案】D

【解析】句意为:我换了个工作,要转到另外一个部门去。A项意为"收集,聚集";B项意为"邮寄";C项意为"掌握";D项意为"移动,改变"。根据题意,D项符合题旨要求。

26.【答案】A

【解析】句意为:我们正在招聘一位中文说得流利的秘书。定语从句修饰a secretary,表示人,要用who来引导,who在定语从句中作主语。

附录二 答案与解析

27.【答案】C

【解析】句意为:这个记录会帮你们的安全官员找到问题所在。A 项意为"提出(问题、建议);抚养";B 项意为"穿;戴";C 项意为"发现;查明";D 项意为"吸取;欺骗"。根据题意,C 项符合题旨要求。

28.【答案】C

【解析】句意为:你越专注于训练,结果就会越好。"the + 比较级……,the + 比较级……"表示"越……,越……"。

29.【答案】B

【解析】句意为:这个工作坊是为了解决我们在全球面临的挑战问题。cope with 是固定搭配,表示"解决"。

30.【答案】D

【解析】句意为:传统商店最近发现很难与网上商店竞争。A 项意为"争论,争吵";B 项意为"开始";C 项意为"遇见";D 项意为"竞争"。四个动词都可以跟 with 搭配,但根据题意,只有 D 项符合题旨要求。

31.【答案】B

【解析】句意为:根据报告,当地经济在那段时期经历了高速增长。A 项意为"练习,训练";B 项意为"经历,经受";C 项意为"控制";D 项意为"连接"。根据题意,B 项符合题旨要求。

32.【答案】A

【解析】句意为:除了中文版的网站,还提供英语版的。A 项意为"除了……之外";B 项意为"由于";C 项意为"代表";D 项意为"出于……目的"。根据题意,A 项符合题旨要求。

33.【答案】B

【解析】句意为:去年,我们公司采取了一些额外措施来保护顾客的个人信息。take measures 意为"采取措施",表示动宾关系。measures 被前置,take 要用被动语态。last year 提示要用过去时。

34.【答案】C

【解析】句意为:自从去年我们发布新产品以来,销售情况有了一些改善。现在完成时一般跟连词 since 一起使用,表示从过去某个时间一直延续到现在的动作或行为。

Section B

35.【答案】careful

【解析】句意为:过马路时要当心,要记住在英国他们靠左行驶。be 是连系动词,后面接形容词。care 的形容词有 careful 和 careless。根据题意,careful 符合题旨要求。

36.【答案】is/was designed

【解析】句意为:展览会上的这款新行李箱是由一家中国公司设计的。design 与 the new suitcase 之间是动宾关系,the new suitcase 被前置,design 相应地要变成被动语态。由于没有明确的时间提示,被动语态可以用一般现在时,也可以用一般过去时。

187

37. 【答案】efficiently

【解析】句意为:相关的信息可以帮助你有效地操作机器。efficiently 在句中作状语,修饰谓语动词 operate。

38. 【答案】discussion

【解析】句意为:这个项目仍在建设中,期望能找到一些实际的解决方案。under 为介词,后接名词组成介宾结构。

39. 【答案】will grow

【解析】句意为:根据报告,北美的健康市场在 2025 年将以 7.4% 的速度增长。根据 in 2025 可以判断,要用将来时。

2016 年 12 月真题

Section A

25. 【答案】A

【解析】句意为:互联网让农村学校的孩子们也可以了解世界上正在发生的事情。allow 表示"允许,准许",常用于"allow sb. to do sth."这一结构中。

26. 【答案】C

【解析】句意为:因为没有人来接管生意,这家杂货店倒闭了。A 项意为"建造;张贴";B 项意为"发出;放出";C 项意为"接收,接管";D 项意为"导致,引起"。根据题意,C 项符合题旨要求。

27. 【答案】B

【解析】句意为:首席执行官说,为糟糕的服务而道歉,什么时候都不晚。too 表示数量过多,程度过甚,因而导致某一特定结果没有或不能发生,常用于"too + adj. /adv. + to do sth."结构中。

28. 【答案】A

【解析】句意为:总统在会上详细地解释了他的提议。A 项意为"解释;解说";B 项意为"搜索";C 项意为"平衡";D 项意为"单词;话语"。根据题意,A 项符合题旨要求。

29. 【答案】D

【解析】句意为:去年我们部门的员工太忙,最后连休假都没去成。"so .... that ...."表示"如此……,以至于……"。so 后常接形容词或副词。

30. 【答案】A

【解析】句意为:他们下周的会谈预计会专门谈论业务管理的问题。focus on 为固定搭配,表示"关注,聚焦于"。

31. 【答案】C

【解析】句意为:目前公司没有空缺,也就不会聘用谁了。A 项意为"处理,解决";B 项意为"带领";C 项意为"录用,聘用";D 项意为"解雇;消除"。根据题意,C 项符合题旨要求。

32. 【答案】D

【解析】句意为:我想了解一下我们应该在什么时间和在什么地方交作业。A项意为"使延误,耽误";B项意为"开始(攀谈)";C项意为"拿掉,起飞";D项意为"上交"。根据题意,D项符合题旨要求。

33.【答案】B

【解析】句意为:我们刚开始考虑搬到加利福尼亚去,但最后决定还是不搬了。consider表示"考虑",后接动名词形式。

34.【答案】D

【解析】句意为:澳大利亚有它自己的文化身份,跟英国的差别很大。A项意为"忙碌的";B项意为"中心的,首要的";C项意为"有能力的";D项意为"文化的"。根据题意,D项符合题旨要求。

Section B

35.【答案】Surprisingly

【解析】句意为:令人惊奇的是,这个团队可以提前两周完成任务。surprisingly作状语,修饰整个句子。surprisingly位于句首,首字母要大写。

36.【答案】to assist

【解析】句意为:在整个过程中,我们公司的设计师很乐意给您提供协助。be ready to do sth.是固定搭配,表示"愿意的,乐意的"。

37.【答案】more effective

【解析】句意为:对我来说,他的解决方案似乎比我的更加有效。由than可以判断出,空格处须填比较级,effective是多音节形容词,其比较级要加more。

38.【答案】impression

【解析】句意为:你们改进服务的坚定决心给我们留下了深刻的印象。根据a deep可以判断出,空格处要填名词。

39.【答案】meeting

【解析】句意为:你们到我们这里来参观,我们很高兴。期待下周再见。look forward to表示"期待,盼望",后接动名词形式。

2017年6月真题

Section A

25.【答案】C

【解析】句意为:直到昨天,他们才决定重启商业会谈。"It was .... that ...."是强调句型。判断是否为强调句的一个方法是,观察去掉"It was .... that ...."之后,语法结构是否还完整。

26.【答案】A

【解析】句意为:我们得计算出在那个区域建立一座新医院的费用。A项意为"计算出,解出";B项意为"穿;戴";C项意为"(使)装满,(使)注满";D项意为"实施,执行"。根据题意,A项符合题旨要求。

27.【答案】B

【解析】句意为:我们得留意所有的活动来确保大家都能安全。keep an eye on 是固定搭配,表示"留意,密切注意"。

28.【答案】C

【解析】句意为:当地政府一直非常重视教育和职业培训。put/lay/place emphasis on sth. 是固定搭配,表示"强调,重视某事"。

29.【答案】D

【解析】句意为:在达到火车站前别拐错弯。A项意为"有";B项意为"奔跑";C项意为"保持";D项意为"到达"。根据题意,D项符合题旨要求。

30.【答案】B

【解析】句意为:只要能完成任务,班组并不介意在周末上班。mind 表示"介意",后接动词的-ing 形式。

31.【答案】A

【解析】句意为:我们是一个非营利企业,成员来自全国各地。成员是公司的一部分,两者之间存在一种领属关系,定语从句要用表示领属关系的 whose 来引导。

32.【答案】C

【解析】句意为:会议室太小,只能容纳下至多 20 人。A项意为"最终";B项意为"起初";C项意为"至多";D项意为"立即"。根据题意,C项符合题旨要求。

33.【答案】B

【解析】句意为:她给我们详细地解释了当地政府的新医保倡议。A项意为"印象";B项意为"解释";C项意为"教育";D项意为"交流"。根据题意,B项符合题旨要求。

34.【答案】D

【解析】句意为:琳达将在下个月月末结束她在一家合资企业的培训。将来完成时表示动作或行为从过去某个时间一直持续到将来某个时间,会在将来某个时间结束。by the end of next month 表示在下个月月末截止。

Section B

35.【答案】suggestion(s)

【解析】句意为:我们对你们在昨天会议上提出的建议印象深刻。由 the 可以判断出,空格处要填一个名词。

36.【答案】longer

【解析】句意为:查理在这座城市居住的时间越长,他就越喜欢这座城市。"the + 比较级……,the + 比较级……"表示同比例增长或减少,意为"越……,越……"。

37.【答案】helpful

【解析】句意为:如果你想了解跟你的领域相关的一些专业术语,你会发现这本书可能有帮助。be 动词为连系动词,后接形容词组成系表结构作谓语。

38.【答案】to smoke

【解析】句意为:根据新的规定,在公共场所不准抽烟。在 allow sb. to do sth. 结构中,动词不定式作宾语补足语,sb. 被置于句首后,动词不定式相应地作主语补足语。

39.【答案】was asked

【解析】句意为:在昨天的采访中,记者问了这位新总统一些棘手的问题。ask 后接双宾语,sb. 被置于句首后,ask 相应地要变成被动语态。另外,by 也提示空格处要填被动语态。

2017 年 12 月真题

Section A

25.【答案】C

【解析】句意为:我们把客户的投诉当作我们改进服务的一次机会。A 项意为"带来";B 项意为"收到";C 项意为"改进";D 项意为"获得"。根据题意,C 项符合题旨要求。

26.【答案】B

【解析】句意为:我们住在那家宾馆时使用了它的体育设施。A 项意为"尽管";B 项意为"当……的时候";C 项意为"直到";D 项意为"除非"。根据题意,从句表示一种时间关系,B 项符合题旨要求。

27.【答案】D

【解析】句意为:已经做出决定,在首席执行官退休后由李先生来接管公司。A 项意为"推迟";B 项意为"要求,呼吁";C 项意为"导致,引起";D 项意为"接收,接管"。根据题意,D 项符合题旨要求。

28.【答案】A

【解析】句意为:研究显示,有些学生在阅读英语长篇文章时会有困难。have difficulty/trouble (in) doing sth. 为固定搭配,表示"在……上有困难"。

29.【答案】D

【解析】句意为:如果你改变主意了,可以在周六前用这个号码给我打电话。主句是祈使句,If 引导的应是真实条件状语从句,其谓语动词用动词的一般现在时,表示一般或未来情形下的条件。

30.【答案】C

【解析】句意为:他拿到大学毕业证之后,就到那家公司去应聘。A 项意为"继续;进行";B 项意为"吸取;欺骗";C 项意为"申请";D 项意为"穿;戴"。根据题意,C 项符合题旨要求。

31.【答案】B

【解析】句意为:管理层得确保员工不会劳累过度。此句为强调句,强调主语 the management。

32.【答案】A

【解析】句意为:这个地区的大多数人认为他们应该发展重工业。A 项意为"发展";B 项意为"提供";C 项意为"拿走,取走";D 项意为"做"。根据题意,A 项符合题旨要求。

33.【答案】C

【解析】句意为:无论你是否我们的第一位买家,我们今天都会给你一个优惠的价格。A 项意为"无论什么",引导让步状语从句,在句中作主语或宾语;B 项意为"无论什么时候",引导让步状语从句,在句中作状语;C 项意为"是否",表示两种情况都真实;D 项意为"无论如何"。根据题意,C 项符合题旨要求。

34.【答案】D

【解析】句意为:我们的购买决定一般基于价格、发货日期和售后服务。on the basis of 为固定搭配,表示"基于……"。

Section B

35.【答案】to give

【解析】句意为:我答应在五个工作日之内给你一个答复。promise 表示"许诺,承诺",后常接 that 或 to do sth. 。

36.【答案】greatly

【解析】句意为:银行贷款极大地巩固了我们在这个工业领域里的金融地位。greatly 在句中作状语,修饰 strengthen。

37.【答案】viewing

【解析】句意为:摄影改变了我们看待世界的方式。of 是介词,后接名词或动名词。

38.【答案】production

【解析】句意为:那款新机器在 2022 年年末不可能投入生产。into 是介词,后接名词或动名词。

39.【答案】is required

【解析】句意为:任何申请到中国签证的人都要采集指纹。require sb. to do sth. 结构中的 require 后接复合宾语,sb. 被置于句首,require 相应地要用被动语态。该句说的是规定,是现在的一个状况,谓语动词要用现在时。

2018 年 6 月真题

Section A

25.【答案】D

【解析】句意为:让我们找些掌握电脑技术的人,为这个项目组成一个团队。A 项意为"查找,查阅";B 项意为"给……打电话";C 项意为"放弃";D 项意为"组成,构成"。根据题意,D 项符合题旨要求。

26.【答案】A

【解析】句意为:如果我是你,我会访问这家公司的网站去获取更多的详细信息。对现在情况的虚拟,从句使用过去时,主句的谓语动词要使用 would visit 的形式。

27.【答案】B

【解析】句意为:没有公司能承担得起顾客信心丧失的损失。A项意为"压力";B项意为"损失";C项意为"担心,担忧";D项意为"匆忙,急忙"。根据题意,B项符合题旨要求。

28.【答案】C

【解析】句意为:尽管她在中国工作了只两年的时间,但她可以说一口流利的中文。主句与从句之间表示一种转折的逻辑关系,C项表达了这种逻辑关系。

29.【答案】D

【解析】句意为:我们已经看了好几遍说明书,对我们要采取的所有步骤都熟悉。A项意为"类似的";B项意为"有用的";C项意为"有益的,有帮助的";D项意为"熟悉的"。be familiar with sth.是固定搭配,表示"对……熟悉"。

30.【答案】D

【解析】句意为:雇员喜欢跟随那些可以做出表率的领导工作。set an example是固定搭配,表示"树立榜样,以身作则"。

31.【答案】A

【解析】句意为:你需要时可以随时向我们寻求法律咨询。先行词any time表示时间,需要由when引导的定语从句来修饰。B项表示方式,C项表示地点,D项表示原因。

32.【答案】C

【解析】句意为:涨薪部分地取决于你的工作经验和技能。A项意为"继续;进行";B项意为"承担;接受";C项意为"依靠;依赖";D项意为"穿;戴"。根据题意,C项符合题旨要求。

33.【答案】D

【解析】句意为:您需要输入公司所在城市的名称。如果你把某物放置于(locate)某个地方,就意味着你把它放在那或建在那里。locate与company之间是动宾关系,locate相应地要用被动形式。

34.【答案】B

【解析】句意为:游客可以在我们当地导游的帮助下了解我们城市的最新情况。with the help of sb./sth.为固定搭配,表示"在……的帮助下"。注意不要受中文意思"在……下"的影响,而选C项。

Section B

35.【答案】different

【解析】句意为:患者可以在许多不同的环境下,采用不同的方法进行治疗。根据"many + *adj.* + 名词"结构,空格处需要填形容词。

36.【答案】better

【解析】句意为:上了培训课之后,他们比以前更好地履行了职责。由than可以判断出,空格处需要填比较级,well的比较级是better。

37.【答案】creating

【解析】句意为:只有通过营造一个干净的环境,我们才能真正地鼓励更多的游客过来。

介词by后接名词或动名词,create是及物动词,后面带了宾语,所以接动名词。

38.【答案】healthy

【解析】句意为:这份研究论文专注于老年人的健康生活方式。on为介词,后接名词或动名词。lifestyles是名词,前面要用形容词来修饰。

39.【答案】is expected

【解析】句意为:我们的新经理有望在明天的会议上发表讲话。在expect sb. to do sth. 结构中,expect后接复合宾语,sb.被前置后,expect相应地要变成被动语态。

2018年12月真题

Section A

25.【答案】B

【解析】句意为:如果玛丽向汤姆解释一下情况,他可能就已经理解它了。A项意为"提供";B项意为"解释";C项意为"收费";D项意为"投,扔"。根据题意,B项符合题旨要求。

26.【答案】D

【解析】句意为:很高兴收到你方4月10日要求我方提供目录和价目表的来函。现在分词asking表示伴随动作,补充说明信函上所写内容。

27.【答案】A

【解析】句意为:无论你的旅行是短还是长,我们都可以为你制作一个行程表。A项意为"是否";表示两种情况都真实,引导让步状语从句。根据题意,主句与从句之间表达一种让步的逻辑关系,A项表示让步关系。

28.【答案】C

【解析】句意为:项目组由来自公司不同部门的人组成。A项意为"开始(攀谈)";B项意为"导致,引起";C项意为"由……组成";D项意为"由于"。根据题意,C项符合题旨要求。

29.【答案】B

【解析】句意为:在调查中,我们询问了工人一些使他们的工作更难做的事情。先行词things表示物,要由that来引导,在定语从句中作主语。

30.【答案】C

【解析】句意为:我们想跟你们经理约个时间进一步讨论一下合同问题。A项意为"机会";B项意为"影响";C项意为"预约";D项意为"实验"。根据题意,C项符合题旨要求。

31.【答案】D

【解析】句意为:大约有四分之一的美国成人说,在过去的一年里,他们没看过一本书。现在完成时表示动作或行为从过去某个时间一直持续到现在,还有可能会继续持续下去。"没有看书"这一状态一直持续了过去整整一年,至今有可能已经结束或还会持续下去。

32.【答案】A

【解析】句意为:在从事外贸活动的时候,我们应该注意文化差异。be aware of为固定搭配,表示"知道,明白,意识到"。

33.【答案】B

【解析】句意为:这项研究发现了造成雇员在工作上有压力的一些关键因素。现在分词作定语,修饰 some key factors,起补充说明的作用。A 项意为"调低;拒绝";B 项意为"导致";C 项意为"拿掉;起飞";D 项意为"执行"。根据题意,B 项符合题旨要求。

34.【答案】D

【解析】句意为:这家公司现在专注于开发最新的车型。focus 表示"集中(注意力、精力等)于",后接介词 on。

Section B

35.【答案】to see

【解析】句意为:这个应用程序可以让你看到所有航班的起飞和到达。在 allow sb. to do sth. 结构中,allow 后接复合宾语。

36.【答案】be delivered

【解析】句意为:我们可以向你们保证,你们的订单将在 5 个工作日内发货。deliver 与 order 之间是动宾关系,order 被前置后,deliver 相应地要变成被动语态。

37.【答案】sending

【解析】句意为:如果你选择不接收那些电子邮件,请给我们发个信息告知一下。by 是介词,后接名词或动名词。

38.【答案】equipment

【解析】句意为:我们负责设备安装和维修。由 the 可以判断出,空格处要填名词。动词变名词,大多通过添加后缀"-ment"实现。

39.【答案】cheaper

【解析】句意为:如果你在其他商店发现有产品比我们更便宜,请跟我们联系。由 than 可以判断出,空格处要填形容词的比较级。

2019 年 6 月真题

Section A

25.【答案】A

【解析】句意为:即使机器人能有像我们一样的手,我们还是需要设计一种方式去控制它们。A 项意为"即使";B 项意为"好像";C 项意为"只是因为";D 项意为"既然"。根据题意,主句和从句之间表示的是让步关系,A 项符合题旨要求。

26.【答案】D

【解析】句意为:有时候,找一份理想的工作太难,以至于你得另外寻找一条能达成你的目标的路径。"so + adj./adv. + that"意为"如此……以至于……",表示一种因果关系。

27.【答案】A

【解析】句意为:事实上,正是这个项目让我对计算机科学产生了兴趣。"it was … that …"

为强调句型,强调主语 the project。

28. 【答案】C

【解析】句意为:我当前的目标是在一家公司找份工作,随着时间推移,我可以成长,可以接受新的挑战。at a company 是先行词,表示地点,定语从句要用 where 来引导。

29. 【答案】D

【解析】句意为:我在网上找工作时偶然看到这个网站。I 与 do a job search online 之间是主谓关系,现在分词表示主动和进行,所以用现在分词。

30. 【答案】C

【解析】句意为:参加招聘会时,记得穿着得体,注意你的外表。take care of 为固定搭配,意为"照料,爱护"。

31. 【答案】B

【解析】句意为:在你的整个求职过程中,我们会通过我们的客服中心跟你保持联系。keep in touch with sb. 是固定搭配,意为"跟……保持联系"。

32. 【答案】C

【解析】句意为:他们正在寻找在销售上至少有 1 年至 5 年工作经验的求职者。at least 为固定搭配,意为"至少"。

33. 【答案】D

【解析】句意为:在大多数情况下,当你在网上购物时,你拥有的权利跟你在商店购物时是一样的。"the same as …"是固定搭配,意为"与……一样",对同质的两件事物进行比较。

34. 【答案】B

【解析】句意为:我们的房主保险单不包括因维修不善而造成的损失。现在分词作定语,修饰 damage,对其进行补充说明。A 项意为"扔掉;扑灭";B 项意为"由……引起";C 项意为"炫耀,卖弄";D 项意为"起飞"。根据题意,B 项符合题旨要求。

Section B

35. 【答案】to provide

【解析】句意为:如果您未能在要求时提供某些信息,我们可能无法为您提供服务。fail to do sth. 意为"未能,未履行"。fail 在句中不表示"失败"。

36. 【答案】gradually

【解析】句意为:随着时间的推移,机器学习工程正在逐渐发展。gradually 在句中作状语,修饰 develop。

37. 【答案】smarter

【解析】句意为:最近一段时间,机器要比多年前更智能。由 than 可以判断出,空格处要填形容词的比较级。

38. 【答案】are asked

【解析】句意为:客户被要求对我们员工的表现和他们的技能给予反馈。在 ask sb. to do sth. 结构中,ask 后接复合宾语,sb. 被前置,ask 相应地要变成被动语态。

39. 【答案】fixed

【解析】句意为:您可以直接到我们在你们城市的连锁店找人维修这台设备。have sth. done 意为"叫/请某人做某事"。

2019 年 12 月真题

Section A

25. 【答案】D

【解析】句意为:如果你在找工作的过程中收到了几份聘书,你会如何选择最好的？A 项意为"关系";B 项意为"规则,法规";C 项意为"益处,优势";D 项意为"提供,给予"。根据题意,D 项符合题旨要求。

26. 【答案】C

【解析】句意为:这些贷款如果使用得当,可以帮你实现你的梦想。use 与 these loans 之间是动宾关系,these loans 作主语,use 要用被动语态。

27. 【答案】B

【解析】句意为:如果你想参观博物馆,你得提前至少两天去预约。in advance 为固定搭配,意为"提前"。

28. 【答案】A

【解析】句意为:这家公司呼叫中心的员工平均每小时可以挣 9～14 美元。on average 为固定搭配,意为"平均"。

29. 【答案】C

【解析】句意为:机械故障使得他们未能按时完成任务。on time 为固定搭配,意为"按时"。on duty 意为"值班,值勤",不符合题旨要求。

30. 【答案】B

【解析】句意为:就在飞机起飞前,乘客被告知飞机引擎出了问题。A 项意为"打开(设备)";B 项意为"起飞";C 项意为"出发;着手";D 项意为"写下;放下"。根据题意,B 项符合题旨要求。

31. 【答案】D

【解析】句意为:我们最终得出结论,即难以把这两项技术结合起来。同位语从句紧随一些抽象名词之后,对其进行详细说明。that 引导同位语从句,在句中不充当任何成分,但不能省略。

32. 【答案】B

【解析】句意为:面试官要求我详细地解释我为什么要应聘这个职位。in detail 为固定搭配,意为"详细地"。

33. 【答案】C

【解析】句意为:即使是他们的过错,客服还是拒绝退钱给我。A 项意为"好像";B 项意为"自从";C 项意为"即使,尽管";D 项意为"以防,免得"。主句和从句之间是一种让步关系,C 项表示让步,符合题旨要求。

34. 【答案】A

【解析】句意为:不管多么好看,任何电影我都不会看一次以上。however 后接形容词或副词,表示强调,意为"不管怎样,无论多么"。

Section B

35. 【答案】Surprisingly

【解析】句意为:奇怪的是,百分之七十的游客如果再度假还会过来的。surprisingly 作状语,修饰整个句子。surprisingly 位于句首,首字母要大写。

36. 【答案】was encouraged

【解析】句意为:那时,有人鼓励简跟她的中国朋友开始学中文。在 encourage sb. to do sth. 结构中,sb. 被前置,encourage 相应地要变成被动语态。

37. 【答案】appointment

【解析】句意为:请使用此表格向初级保健提供者申请预约。根据空格前的 an 可以判断出,空格处要填名词。动词变名词,可通过加后缀"-ment"来实现。

38. 【答案】more interesting

【解析】句意为:坦率地说,演讲要比我们预期的更加有意思。由 than 可以判断出,空格处要填形容词的比较级。interesting 是多音节形容词,其比较级为 more interesting。

39. 【答案】waiting

【解析】句意为:如果您不介意等 7~10 天,我们可以给您寄张个人支票。mind 意为"介意",后接动名词。

阅读理解

2015 年 6 月真题

Task 1

40. 【答案】B

【解析】事实细节题。根据题干中的 when shopping 定位到文章第二段第三句。该句提到,在国外购物时,可以使用信用卡。同时,本段第二句也指出,没有必要随身携带大额现金。B 项"use a credit card"与原文中的 use your credit card instead 意思相同。由此可以确定 B 项"使用信用卡"为本题的答案。

41. 【答案】C

【解析】事实细节题。根据题干中的 keep your wallet 定位到文章第二段第四句。该句提到,把你的钱包放在前面的口袋里,这样别人就无法在你不留意的时候将手伸进你的口袋里。C 项"put it in your front pocket"是对原文中的 Keep your wallet in your front pocket 的同义转述。由此可以确定 C 项"将它放在你前面的口袋里"为本题的答案。

附录二 答案与解析

42.【答案】B

【解析】事实细节题。根据题干中的 know where you are going 定位到文章第三段第三、四句。定位句提到,要了解自己所处的位置,在离开宾馆之前看一下地图,以便了解要去的地方以及如何到达那里。题干中的 To know where you are going 是对第三段第三句的同义复现。B 项"look at the map before leaving the hotel"与原文的表述 Look at the map before you leave the hotel 基本一致。由此可以确定 B 项"离开宾馆之前先看一下地图"为本题的答案。

43.【答案】A

【解析】事实细节题。根据题干中的 your valuables 定位到文章第四段。该段提到,将你的贵重物品锁在宾馆房间的保险柜里,或者宾馆的大保险柜里。A 项"In the hotel safe."是对原文地点的总结,由此可以确定 A 项"宾馆的保险柜里"为本题的答案。

44.【答案】D

【解析】主旨大意题。短文开头指出,在国外旅行,保证人身财产安全十分重要,然后具体介绍一些建议:随身携带小额现金和身份证复印件;结伴旅行,清楚自身所在位置;将贵重物品放入保险柜中;留意周围环境。D 项"Stay Safe While Traveling Abroad"与原文首句的表达"It is important for us to know how to stay safe while traveling in foreign countries."基本相同,也是这篇短文的主旨所在。由此可以确定 D 项"在国外旅行要注意安全"为本题的答案。

Task 2

45.【答案】C

【解析】事实细节题。根据题干中的 apply for a position advertised 定位到广告标题下方与其紧挨着的内容。此处提到,请将简历发送至指定邮箱,请不要打电话。C 项中的 send your resume 与原文表述一致,online 是对发送至指定电子邮箱这一方式的概括。由此可以确定 C 项"在网络上发送你的简历"为本题的答案。

46.【答案】B

【解析】事实细节题。根据题干中的 the right persons 定位到 Actively Seeking 上方的那句。该句提到,我们非常愿意培训合适的人。B 项"provided with training"与原文的表述 to train 意思相近。由此可以确定 B 项"提供培训"为本题的答案。

47.【答案】D

【解析】事实细节题。根据题干中的 be dressed professionally 定位到人物图上方的内容。该处提到,对于合格的应聘人员,将当场进行面试,还提出建议和要求:请穿着职业装。D 项"attend an interview on site"是对原文中的 Interviews will be held on site for qualified candidates 的同义转述。由此可以确定 D 项"当场参加一场面试"为本题的答案。

Task 3

48.【答案】64,500

【解析】锁定关键词。根据关键词 Workforce、about 和 employees 定位到原文第一段第二句。该句指出,我们公司在全球范围内的技术熟练工人有大约 64 500 人,其中服务站员工超过 3 200 人。通过分析题干可知,空格处考查该公司的员工总数,因此可以确定本题的答案

199

为 64 500。

49.【答案】2.6 million

【解析】锁定关键词。根据关键词 in 2013、nearly 和 oil-equivalent barrels per day 定位到原文第二段第一句。该句指出,2013 年 Chevron 公司的平均石油净产量是每天接近 260 万桶。通过分析题干可知,空格处应该填入产油的桶数,因此可以确定本题的答案为 2.6 million。

50.【答案】the United States

【解析】锁定关键词。根据关键词 about 75% of the production 和 outside 定位到原文第二段第二句。该句指出,公司大约 75% 的生产量都来自美国以外的地方。通过分析题干可知,空格处考查 75% 的生产量来自的地方,因此可以确定本题的答案为 the United States。

51.【答案】global

【解析】锁定关键词。根据关键词 production of 1.96 million barrels of oil per day 定位到原文第二段第三句。该句指出,Chevron 公司到 2013 年年底每天的全球石油生产量达到 196 万桶。通过分析题干可知,空格处应该填入句中提到的石油产量的范围,因此可以确定本题的答案为 global。

52.【答案】reliable energy

【解析】锁定关键词。根据关键词 work responsibly to develop 和 the world needs 定位到原文第三段最后一句。该句指出,公司的员工工作非常负责,努力研发世界需要的可靠能源。通过分析题干可知,空格处应该填入研发的具体产品,因此可以确定本题的答案为 reliable energy。

Task 4

53.【答案】C K
54.【答案】M J
55.【答案】F Q
56.【答案】G O
57.【答案】E H

【解析】

A —————————————— Our Business（公司业务）
B —————————————— Our Customers（公司客户）
C —————————————— Customer Training（客户培训）
D —————————————— About Us（关于我们）
E —————————————— Career Development（职业发展）
F —————————————— Select Region（选择地区）
G —————————————— Contact Information（联系信息）
H —————————————— Site Map（网站地图）
I —————————————— Privacy Statement（隐私声明）

J ———————————— Terms of Use（使用条款）
K ———————————— Company History（公司历史）
L ———————————— Campus Recruiting（校园招聘）
M ———————————— Career Guide（职业指导）
N ———————————— Press Releases（新闻发布）
O ———————————— Social Media（社交媒体）
P ———————————— Personal Investing（个人投资）
Q ———————————— Financial Reporting（财务报告）

Task 5

58. 【答案】Jim Johnson

【解析】本题考查新加入公司的人员。根据关键词 joined the company 定位到原文第一段第一、二句。定位句首先欢迎 Jim Johnson 成为公司的最新成员,并指出他从3月4日起就任公司的总经理一职。由此可见,新加入公司的人员是 Jim Johnson。

59. 【答案】The Vice President

【解析】本题考查 Jim Johnson 在 ABC 公司的任职情况。根据关键词 in ABC Company 定位到原文第二段第一句。定位句指出,Jim 曾在 ABC 公司担任的职务是副总裁。通过对比题干和原文,可以确定本题的答案为 The Vice President。

60. 【答案】introduce

【解析】本题考查员工在午餐会上需要做的事情。根据关键词 staff members、the lunch party 和 themselves 定位到原文第三段第一、二句。定位句指出,3月6日12点半将在会议室举行员工午餐会,请参加并进行自我介绍。由此可见,员工在参加午餐会时,一方面来会见新任总经理,另一方面要进行自我介绍。通过对比题干和原文,可以确定本题的答案为 introduce。

61. 【答案】next week

【解析】本题考查去总经理办公室拜访的时间。根据关键词 If one can't come 和 any time 定位到原文第三段第四句。定位句指出,如果你不能参加午餐会,你可以在下周的任何时间去 Jim 的办公室拜访。题干中的 visit the General Manager at his office 与原文中的 stop by Jim's office 意思相同。通过对比题干和原文,可以确定本题的答案为 next week。

62. 【答案】the second floor

【解析】本题考查 Jim Johnson 的新办公室的位置。根据关键词 new office 定位到原文第三段最后一句。定位句指出,他将会在位于二楼的新办公室里。由此可见,Jim Johnson 的新办公室位于二楼。通过对比题干和原文,可以确定本题的答案为 the second floor。

2015年12月真题

Task 1

40. 【答案】C

【解析】事实细节题。根据题干中的 the first step in starting a restaurant 定位到文章第二段第一句。定位句提到,首先要先了解一下将要成为你的竞争对手的餐馆。然后第二、三句又从餐馆提供的饮食和对人们的调研两个方面具体阐述如何了解你未来的竞争对手。C 项"learn much about your competitors"是对原文中的 take a look at the restaurants that will be your competition 的总结和概括。动词 compete(竞争)派生出 competitor(竞争者)和抽象名词 competition(竞争)。由此可以确定 C 项"多了解竞争对手的情况"为本题的答案。

41.【答案】B

【解析】事实细节题。根据题干中的 choosing your target customers 定位到文章第三段第二句。该句提到,选择你的目标客户有助于对将要提供的饮食类型做出决定。B 项"decide on what kind of food to offer them"与原文中的 help determine what type of food you will offer 意思相同。由此可以确定 B 项"确定为他们提供哪种类型的饮食"为本题的答案。

42.【答案】B

【解析】事实细节题。根据题干中的 when you choose a building for your restaurant 定位到文章第五段第一、二句。第一句提到确立建筑物和位置对于取得成功来说非常重要。第二句接着进行了具体的说明:要确保建筑物容易被发现,容易到达。B 项"is easy for customers to visit"与原文中的 is easily found and reached 意思相同。由此可以确定 B 项"顾客们很容易找到"为本题的答案。

43.【答案】C

【解析】事实细节题。根据题干中的 on the day of the opening 定位到文章最后一段第二句。该句提到,在盛大开业的当天,可以考虑提供一些特殊的折扣和开门奖。C 项"offer some special discounts"与原文中的 Consider having some special discounts 意思相同。

44.【答案】D

【解析】主旨大意题。短文开门见山地指出,开办餐馆可能值得做但充满了挑战。然后通过 First、Next、Finally 等过渡词分别介绍取得成功的几个步骤。由此可见,本文主要介绍如何成功地开办餐馆,所以 D 项"如何开办餐馆"为本题的答案。

Task 2

45.【答案】D

【解析】事实细节题。根据题干中的 advertised in the poster 定位到海报左上角的大字标题。由标题的内容 ST. CHARLES COMMUNITY GARAGE SALE 可知,这个海报是为 garage sale 做的广告。

46.【答案】B

【解析】事实细节题。根据题干中的 the money to be raised will be given to 定位到海报文字部分的第一句。该句提到了举行这次车库旧物出售的目的:为 STC Underground 筹集善款;句中用破折号引出对 STC Underground 的介绍,指出这是位于圣·查尔斯大街社区的一个受欢迎的青少年中心。因此可以确定 B 项"一个青少年中心"为本题的答案。

47.【答案】A

【解析】事实细节题。根据题干中的 register before April 17 定位到海报文字部分的倒数第五行。定位部分及下一行文字介绍了不同时间段的注册费用:4月17日前交费20美元,4月18日至22日缴费30美元。本题考查4月17日之前交的费用,应该为20美元。

Task 3

48.【答案】Purchasing Guide

【解析】锁定关键词。根据关键词 How to use 和 follow 定位到原文第一段第一、二句。第一句指出,使用 Best Buy Express Service 的服务很容易;第二句接着指出,只需要遵循"购物指南"即可。通过对比题干和原文可知,空格处应该填入需要遵循的对象,因此可以确定本题的答案为 Purchasing Guide。

49.【答案】1-866-Best Buy

【解析】锁定关键词。根据关键词 contact 和 call 定位到原文第一段第三、四句。第三句指出,如果你需要更多的帮助,可以联系我们;第四句接着指出,请拨打 1-866-Best Buy 询问。通过对比题干和原文可知,空格处应该填入需要拨打的电话号码,因此可以确定本题的答案为 1-866-Best Buy。

50.【答案】daily

【解析】锁定关键词。根据关键词 Prices of Products、updated 和 from *BestBuy. com* 定位到原文第二段。该段指出,Best Buy Express 产品的价格每天都会在 *BestBuy. com* 网站上更新。通过对比题干和原文可知,空格处应该填入产品价格更新的频率,因此可以确定本题的答案为 daily。

51.【答案】your purchase

【解析】锁定关键词。根据关键词 process returns 和 from the day following 定位到原文第四段第二句。该句指出,从购买产品之日的第二天开始处理退货。通过对比题干和原文可知,空格处应该填入开始处理退货的时间,因此可以确定本题的答案为 your purchase。

52.【答案】the sales receipt

【解析】锁定关键词。根据关键词 be required to process a return 定位到原文最后一段最后一句。该句指出,处理退货时,需要提供销售收据。通过对比题干和原文可知,空格处应填入处理退货时需要提供的东西,即销售收据。因此,可以确定本题答案为 the sales receipt。

Task 4

53.【答案】G C

54.【答案】J P

55.【答案】H K

56.【答案】B I

57.【答案】O D

【解析】

A ———————————— Don't follow too closely(追尾危险)

B —— Keep distance（保持车距）
C —— Accident area（事故多发区）
D —— Road closed（前方道路封闭）
E —— Road work ahead（前方道路施工）
F —— Two-way traffic（双向行驶）
G —— One-way traffic（单向行驶）
H —— Bend ahead（前方弯路）
I —— Bus lane（公交车专用车道）
J —— Electronic toll collection(ETC)（电子收费）
K —— Service area（服务区）
L —— No passing（禁止通行）
M —— No parking（禁止泊车）
N —— Dead end（此路不通）
O —— No horn（禁止鸣笛）
P —— Falling rocks（小心岩石滑落）
Q —— Slow down at exit（出口慢行）

Task 5

58.【答案】indoor and outdoor

【解析】本题考查 Public Storage 公司提供的商业单元的类型。根据 business units 和 offer 定位到原文第一段第三句。该句指出，Public Storage 公司提供室内和室外的商业单元。通过对比题干和原文，可以确定本题的答案为 indoor and outdoor。

59.【答案】online

【解析】本题考查客户预订自助存储单元的方式。根据关键词 reserve the self-storage unit 和 for free 定位到原文第二段第一句。该句指出，一旦客户找到合适的存储空间，就可以在网上预订自助存储单元。通过对比题干和原文，可以确定本题的答案为 online。

60.【答案】the property manager

【解析】本题考查建议客户在租用存储单元之前去做的事情。根据关键词 before renting the storage unit 和 To inspect the space 定位到原文第二段第二句。该句指出，在租用存储单元之前，客户可以随意地查看空间并与物业经理会面。通过对比题干和原文，可以确定本题的答案为 the property manager。

61.【答案】the moving supplies

【解析】本题考查客户准备好打包时，Public Storage 公司承诺提供的服务。根据关键词 ready to pack 定位到原文第二段第三句。该句指出，当客户准备好打包时，Public Storage 公司会提供所需要的一切设备，包括移动设备。通过对比题干和原文，可以确定本题的答案为 the moving supplies。

62.【答案】move in

【解析】本题考查客户能够得到自助存储单元的钥匙的时间。根据关键词 keep the key to their self-storage unit 定位到原文第三段第一句。该句指出,一旦客户搬进来,就可以得到自助存储单元的唯一钥匙。题干中的 As soon as 与原文中的 Once 意思相同。通过对比题干和原文,可以确定本题的答案为 move in。

2016年6月真题

Task 1

40.【答案】B

【解析】事实细节题。根据题干中的 volunteer work 和 have a chance to 定位到文章第一段第一句。定位句提到,志愿活动可以为你提供机会来锤炼在工作场所中用到的重要技能。题干中的 If you take volunteer work 是对原文中 Volunteering 的解释,选项 B 中的"practice skills"与原文的表述基本一致,needed for your work 是对原文中 used in the workplace 的同义转述。由此可以确定 B 项"练习工作中需要的技能"为本题的答案。

41.【答案】C

【解析】语义推断题。根据题干中的"stretching your wings at work"(Para. 2)定位到文章第二段。定位段提到,一旦在志愿岗位上获得了这些技能,你也许更能够 stretching your wings at work。stretching your wings 的字面意思是"伸展翅膀",在本句中引申为"大展宏图",即"充分发挥自己的能力"。由此可以确定 C 项"充分发挥自己的能力"为本题的答案。

42.【答案】A

【解析】事实细节题。根据题干中的 offer you a chance 定位到文章第三段第一句。定位句提到,志愿活动可以为你提供机会,在不需要做出长期努力的情况下尝试一种新的职业。下一句接着指出,这(志愿活动)也是在新的领域里获得经验的有效方式。题干中的 also 在第二句中出现,选项 A 中"gain experience"与第二句中的表述完全一致,in a new career 是对第二句中 in a new field 的同义转述。由此可以确定 A 项"在新的职业中获得经验"为本题的答案。

43.【答案】B

【解析】事实细节题。根据题干中的 a sales position 定位到文章第四段最后一句。定位句进行举例说明:如果你成功地就任了一个销售岗位,你就可以进一步提高演讲、交流和营销技能。选项 B 的"marketing skills"是原文中提到的三大技能之一。由此可以确定 B 项"营销技能"为本题的答案。

44.【答案】C

【解析】主旨大意题。短文开门见山地指出,参加志愿活动可以帮助志愿者锤炼工作中需要的重要技能,然后又指出参加志愿活动有助于他们在工作中施展能力,让他们有机会尝试新职业并学到一些非常重要的技能。由此可见,本文主要介绍参加志愿活动对未来工作的帮助。所以,可以确定 C 项"志愿活动的确有益于你的事业"为本题的答案。

Task 2

45.【答案】A

【解析】主旨大意题。根据题干中的 the Operation JumpStart short course 定位到海报中间方框内的第一句。定位句提到,这次 Operation JumpStart 短期课程是一个为期两天的培训课程。由此可见,这次 Operation JumpStart 短期课程为期两天。由此可以确定 A 项"两天"为本题的答案。

46. 【答案】B

【解析】事实细节题。根据题干中的 The purpose 定位到海报中间方框内的第一句。定位句提到,这次 Operation JumpStart 短期课程的目的是帮助人们创办或者扩展小型企业。选项 B 中的"start their own business"与原文中的 start or expand small businesses 有重合部分。由此可以确定 B 项"帮助与会人员创办个人企业"为本题的答案。

47. 【答案】C

【解析】事实细节题。根据题干中的 register 定位到海报最后的 Register 处。此处注明注册的联系人为 Malcolm Glover,电子邮箱为 *Malcolm. Glover@ arvets. org*。由此可见,可以通过电子邮件注册培训课程。所以,C 项"写一封电子邮件"为本题的答案。

◆ Task 3

48. 【答案】Area Sales Personnel

【解析】锁定关键词。根据关键词 to 和 Vancouver 定位到备忘录的第一行。此处指出了备忘录的发送对象。通过对比题干和原文可知,空格处应该填入备忘录的发送对象。因此,可以确定本题的答案为 Area Sales Personnel。

49. 【答案】online reporting system

【解析】锁定关键词。根据关键词 Changes made in the current client 定位到备忘录正文第一段第一句。定位句指出,根据周三举行的会议,当前的在线报告系统已经发生巨大变化。通过对比题干和原文可知,空格处应该填入发生变化的事物。因此,可以确定本题的答案为 online reporting system。

50. 【答案】improved

【解析】锁定关键词。根据关键词 Accuracy 定位到备忘录正文第一段第二句。定位句指出,它(在线报告系统)的准确性已经得到提高。通过对比题干和原文可知,空格处应该填入系统在准确性上发生的变化。因此,可以确定本题的答案为 improved。

51. 【答案】June 20

【解析】锁定关键词。根据关键词"2016"定位到备忘录正文第一段第四句。定位句指出,新的在线客户报告系统将于 2016 年 6 月 20 日生效。通过对比题干和原文可知,空格处应该填入新的在线客户报告系统的生效日期。因此,可以确定本题的答案为 June 20。

52. 【答案】username and password

【解析】锁定关键词。根据关键词 log in 和 your new 定位到备忘录正文提到的第一个步骤。该步骤指出,用你的新用户名和密码进入公司网站。通过对比题干和原文可知,空格处应该填入进入公司网站的方式方法。因此,可以确定本题的答案为 username and password。

◆ Task 4

53. 【答案】K F

附录二 答案与解析

54. 【答案】C J
55. 【答案】I L
56. 【答案】M H
57. 【答案】Q E

【解析】

A	————————————	bullet train（子弹头高速列车）
B	————————————	intercity high-speed rail（城际高铁）
C	————————————	non-stop train（直达列车）
D	————————————	dedicated rail link（铁路专线）
E	————————————	business cabins（商务车厢）
F	————————————	first-class seats（一等座）
G	————————————	second-class seats（二等座）
H	————————————	protective fence（防护栏）
I	————————————	passenger flow（客流）
J	————————————	floating prices（浮动票价）
K	————————————	real-name purchase（实名购票）
L	————————————	replacement ticket（补票）
M	————————————	on-schedule rate（正点率）
N	————————————	occupancy rate（上座率）
O	————————————	passenger rail line（客运专线）
P	————————————	run chart（运行图）
Q	————————————	vehicle type（车型）

Task 5

58. 【答案】raw materials

【解析】本题考查 CBH Manufacturers Limited 供应的材料类型。根据关键词 supplies 和 to garment manufacturers 定位到邮件正文第一段第一句。定位句对公司进行了介绍：一家向服装制造商供应原材料的公司。由此可见，CBH Manufacturers Limited 供应的材料类型是原材料。通过对比题干和原文，可以确定本题的答案为 raw materials。

59. 【答案】five

【解析】本题考查 CBH Manufacturers Limited 在这一领域的经营时间。根据关键词 For 和 years 定位到邮件正文第一段第三句。定位句指出，该公司经营原棉材料已经长达五年之久。通过对比题干和原文，可以确定本题的答案为 five。

60. 【答案】best quality

【解析】本题考查作者向 Mr. Damon 做出的承诺。根据关键词 provide、of materials 和 a reasonable price 定位到邮件正文第一段最后一句。定位句指出，该公司保证会提供最优质的材料，并且材料的价格也是合理的。由此可见，作者向 Mr. Damon 做出的承诺是以合理的价格提供最优质的材料。通过对比题干和原文,可以确定本题的答案为 best quality。

61. 【答案】a business meeting

【解析】本题考查作者在电子邮件末尾提出的建议。根据关键词 arrange 定位到邮件正文第二段第二句。定位句指出,如果对方公司能够安排一次商务会议就太好了,这样双方就能进行详细洽谈。由此可见,作者在电子邮件末尾提出的建议是希望对方能够安排一次商务会议。通过对比题干和原文,可以确定本题的答案为 a business meeting。

62. 【答案】company profile

【解析】本题考查电子邮件的附件内容。根据关键词 attached 和 A copy of 定位到邮件正文第二段最后一句。定位句指出,作者随电子邮件附带了一份公司简介。由此可见,电子邮件的附件内容是一份公司简介。通过对比题干和原文,可以确定本题的答案为 company profile。

2016年12月真题

Task 1

40. 【答案】D

【解析】事实细节题。根据题干中的 E-med service provides 定位到文章第一个小标题的内容。第一段第一句提出,网上私人医生通过电子邮件或者电话提供建议。题干中的 provides 与第一段第一句中的 offer 意思相同,选项 D "by e-mail or phone" 与原文中的表述完全相同。由此可以确定 D 项 "通过电子邮件或者电话" 为本题的答案。

41. 【答案】C

【解析】事实细节题。根据题干中的 unable to find out your problems 定位到文章第一段第二句。定位句提到,如果我们无法以这种方式解决你的问题,那么我们会向你推荐相关领域的专家。题干中的 unable to find out 是对原文中的 cannot sort out 的同义转述,选项 C 以被动的形式对原文中的 we can refer you to a specialist 进行了同义转述。由此可以确定 C 项 "被推荐到专家那里" 为本题的答案。

42. 【答案】B

【解析】事实细节题。根据题干中的 If necessary 和 ask you to 定位到文章第三段。该段提到,如果我们觉得有必要,我们可能会让你接受视频就诊来做出诊断或者进行治疗,甚至把你推荐到专家那里。题干中的 If necessary 是对原文中的 if we feel it is necessary 的省略表述,题干中的 the E-med doctor 是在具体说明原文中的 we,选项 B "have a video consultation" 与原文中的表述完全一致。由此可以确定 B 项 "接受视频就诊" 为本题的答案。

43. 【答案】B

【解析】事实细节题。根据题干中的 a hospital in London 定位到文章第四段第一句。定位句提到,如果你需要接受进一步的检查以便做出诊断,那么电子医疗医生通常会向你推荐伦敦的一家医院。题干中的 refer the patients to a hospital in London 与原文中的表述基本一致,选项 B "they think that further diagnosis is needed" 是对原文中的 you need further medical investigations to work towards a diagnosis 的简要概括。由此可以确定 B 项"他们认为需要进一步做出诊断"为本题的答案。

44.【答案】A

【解析】主旨大意题。文章开门见山地介绍了电子医疗提供的服务内容和程序,然后指出无法通过电子邮件做出诊断时的处理方法,最后指出电子医疗医生如何指导病人做进一步的医疗检查。由此可见,文章论述的主题是电子医疗服务。所以,可以确定 A 项"电子医疗服务"为本题的答案。

Task 2

45.【答案】B

【解析】主旨大意题。本题考查文章的主旨。海报上端用大字标题说明了广告的内容为青年夏季地铁实习项目,中间及下面的具体内容也都与此相关。选项 B"A youth internship program."是对海报上端标题的简要概括。由此可以确定 B 项"一个青年实习项目"为本题的答案。

46.【答案】C

【解析】事实细节题。本题考查申请人参加这个项目能够有什么收获。根据题干和选项定位到海报中间部分的第一段第二句。定位句提到,申请人将在地铁部门工作一个月,可以获得宝贵的职业经验。选项 C"gain career experience"对应原文中的 gain valuable career experience。由此可以确定 C 项"获得职业经验"为本题的答案。

47.【答案】C

【解析】事实细节题。根据题干中的 hours 和 each week 定位到海报的左下角。此处提到,这一项目每周仅需要工作20小时。由此可以确定 C 项"20小时"为本题的答案。

Task 3

48.【答案】Committee members

【解析】锁定关键词。根据关键词 and guests 定位到邀请函开头的称呼处。此处指出了邀请函的接收对象是 Committee Members and Guests。通过对比题干和原文可知,空格处应该填入邀请函除 guests 之外的接收对象,因此可以确定本题的答案为 Committee members。

49.【答案】March 7 – 11

【解析】锁定关键词。根据关键词"2017"定位到邀请函的第一段第二句。定位句指出,会议的举办时间是2017年3月7日至11日。通过对比题干和原文可以确定本题的答案为 March 7 – 11。

50.【答案】the Omni Houston

【解析】锁定关键词。根据关键词 Hotel 定位到邀请函的第二段第一句。定位句指出,会议的举办地点是 Omni Houston Hotel。通过对比题干和原文可知,空格处应该填入举办会议的宾馆名称,因此可以确定本题的答案为 the Omni Houston。

51.【答案】US $139

【解析】锁定关键词。根据关键词 Group rate for guest rooms 和 per night 定位到邀请函的

第二段第三句。通过题干可知,空格处应该填入宾馆住宿的团体价。定位句指出了宾馆住宿的团体价为每晚139美元,因此可以确定本题的答案为US $139。

52.【答案】IEEE Transformers

【解析】锁定关键词。根据关键词Group name定位到邀请函的第二段第三句。此句指出了预订宾馆房间时需要提到的团体名称。通过对比题干和原文可知,空格处应该填入预订房间的团队名称,因此可以确定本题的答案为IEEE Transformers。

Task 4

53.【答案】M D
54.【答案】Q H
55.【答案】A K
56.【答案】C I
57.【答案】E F

【解析】

A —————— Advertising Budget(广告预算)
B —————— Advertising Cost(广告费用)
C —————— Art Director(艺术指导)
D —————— Brand Loyalty(品牌忠诚度)
E —————— Brand Manager(品牌经理)
F —————— Click Rate(点击率)
G —————— Commercial Advertising(商业广告)
H —————— Consumer Behavior(消费者行为)
I —————— Customer Relation Management(客户关系管理)
J —————— Digital Marketing(数字营销)
K —————— Direct Mail(直接邮寄)
L —————— Interactive Advertising(交互式广告)
M —————— Advertising Manager(广告部经理)
N —————— Local Advertising(地方性广告)
O —————— Page View(访问量)
P —————— Senior Copy Writer(资深文案)
Q —————— Target Audience(目标受众)

Task 5

58.【答案】any network

【解析】本题考查写信人将电脑带回家后发现的问题。根据关键词when he got it back home和unable to connect定位到第一段第二句。定位句指出,当写信人将电脑带回家后,发现电脑无法连接到任何网络。通过对比题干和原文,可以确定本题的答案为any network。

59.【答案】operating system

【解析】本题考查写信人为了修理电脑存在的问题所采取的措施。根据关键词 fix the computer's problem 和 installed the latest 定位到第一段第三句。定位句指出,写信人在电脑上安装了最新的操作系统,但是仍然没有解决问题。通过对比题干和原文,可以确定本题的答案为 operating system。

60.【答案】on the receipt

【解析】本题考查写信人认为他有权退回电脑的原因。根据关键词 no such return policy can be found 定位到第二段第三句。定位句指出,收据上也没有任何关于退货的政策,而且也没有人告知写信人如果安装了操作系统就无法退货。通过对比题干和原文,可以确定本题的答案为 on the receipt。

61.【答案】very rude

【解析】本题考查写信人对店员的投诉内容。根据关键词 the staff 定位到第三段。定位段提到,写信人认为商店里的员工在拒绝退货时表现得非常粗鲁,而且拒绝让他跟商店经理交谈。通过对比题干和原文,可以确定本题的答案为 very rude。

62.【答案】copy

【解析】本题考查写信人随信附寄的东西。根据关键词 is attached 和 of the receipt 定位到第四段第二句。定位句提到,写信人随信附寄了收据的复印件。通过对比题干和原文,可以确定本题的答案为 copy。

2017 年 6 月真题

Task 1

40.【答案】D

【解析】事实细节题。根据题干中的 TSA is required to inspect your baggage 定位到文章第一段第一句。定位句提到,为了保护乘客安全,TSA(运输安全局)被依法要求检查乘客的行李。题干中的 TSA is required to inspect your baggage 与原文中的表述完全一致,选项 D "by law"与原文的表述完全一致。由此可以确定 D 项"依照法律"为本题的答案。

41.【答案】B

【解析】事实细节题。根据题干中的 the purpose of the inspection 定位到文章第二段第一句。定位句提到,在检查时,行李及所装的物品将会被检查,以便查找违禁物品。选项 B "search for prohibited items"与原文的表述基本一致,由此可以确定 B 项"查找违禁物品"为本题的答案。

42.【答案】C

【解析】事实细节题。根据题干中的 After the inspection 和 the contents 定位到文章第二段第二句。定位句提到,在检查完成以后,物品将被放回到行李中。题干中的 After the inspection 是对原文中的 After the inspection was completed 的同义转述,the contents 与原文的表述完全一致,选项 C "be returned to your bag"与原文的表述基本一致。由此可以确定 C 项"被放回到行李中"为本题的答案。

43. 【答案】A

【解析】事实细节题。根据题干中的 your bag is locked 和 the TSA security officer 定位到文章第三段第一句。定位句指出,如果因为行李上锁导致运输安全局保安人员无法打开行李进行检查,他们有可能被迫强行打开行李上的锁。题干中的 your bag is locked 是对原文中的 it was locked 的同义转述,may have to 对应 may have been forced to,选项 A "break the locks"与原文的表述完全一致。由此可以确定 A 项"强行打开锁"为本题的答案。

44. 【答案】C

【解析】事实细节题。根据题干中的 the locks of your bag are damaged 和 TSA 定位到文章第三段末句。定位句提到,因为这种必要的安全措施而导致的锁被破坏,运输安全局将不承担责任。题干中的 the locks of your bag are damaged 是对原文中的 damage to your locks 的同义转述,选项 C "not be responsible for it"是对原文中的 is not responsible for damage to your locks 的同义转述。由此可以确定 C 项"对此不承担责任"为本题的答案。

Task 2

45. 【答案】D

【解析】事实细节题。本题考查讲解员培训项目的培训时长。结合题干和选项,可以定位到海报第一个小标题"JOIN OUR DOCENT TRAINING PROGRAM …"下面的第一句。定位句提到,该培训项目是动态的,培训为期 10 周。选项 D 的内容与原文的表述一致,由此可以确定 D 项"10 周"为本题的答案。

46. 【答案】A

【解析】事实细节题。本题考查申请培训项目需要做的工作。根据题干中的 To apply for the program 定位到海报第三个小标题"APPLY NOW!"下的第二句。定位句提到,想要申请的话,需要在 *seymourcenter.ucsc.edu* 网站上下载一份申请表。选项 A 的内容与原文的表述基本一致,由此可以确定 A 项"首先下载一份申请表"为本题的答案。

47. 【答案】C

【解析】事实细节题。本题考查参加培训项目对年龄的要求。结合题干和选项内容,可以定位到海报第三个小标题"APPLY NOW!"下的最后一句。定位句提到,在 2017 年 1 月培训项目开始时,讲解员必须年满 18 周岁。选项 C 的年龄与原文的表述一致,由此可以确定 C 项"18 周岁"为本题的答案。

Task 3

48. 【答案】services

【解析】锁定关键词。根据关键词 comments and suggestions 和 helping to evaluate 定位到文章第一段最后一句。定位句指出,患者对看病过程做出的评价和提出的建议将有助于诊所对服务情况进行自我评价,提高护理水平。空格所在句表达的是患者的评价和建议有助于评估诊所的某方面。通过对比题干和定位句可知,本题的答案为 services。

49. 【答案】care

【解析】锁定关键词。参见第 48 题解析可知,本题的答案为 care。

50. 【答案】confidential

【解析】锁定关键词。根据关键词 comments and suggestions 和 be kept 定位到文章第二段第二句。定位句指出,患者的评价和建议对于诊所十分重要,诊所会对其评价和建议保密。空格所在句表达的是诊所对患者的评价和建议做出的承诺。通过对比题干和定位句可知,本题的答案为 confidential。

51. 【答案】postage-paid

【解析】锁定关键词。根据关键词 Enclosure 和 reply envelope 定位到文章第二段第三句。定位句指出,为了方便被调查人员,随信附寄了一个邮资已付的回信信封。空格处应该填入描述回信信封情况的词语。对比题干和定位句可知,本题的答案为 postage-paid。

52. 【答案】541-754-1374

【解析】锁定关键词。根据关键词 call Service Center at 定位到文章第二段最后一句。定位句指出,如果被调查人员对这次调查有任何疑问,请拨打电话541-754-1374来联系诊所的服务中心。空格处应该填入具体的联系方式。对比题干和定位句可知,本题的答案为 541-754-1374。

Task 4

49. 【答案】K F
54. 【答案】A P
55. 【答案】I E
56. 【答案】C H
57. 【答案】O G

【解析】

A	------------------------------	Warning equipment（报警设备）
B	------------------------------	Accident management（事故处理）
C	------------------------------	Protection measures（保护措施）
D	------------------------------	Risk assessment（风险评估）
E	------------------------------	Administrative controls（管理控制）
F	------------------------------	Detection technique（检测技术）
G	------------------------------	Failure analysis（失效分析）
H	------------------------------	Responsible person（责任人）
I	------------------------------	Harmful substances（有害物质）
J	------------------------------	Protection devices（防护设备）
K	------------------------------	Accident statistics（事故统计）
L	------------------------------	Safety standards（安全标准）
M	------------------------------	Accident prevention（事故预防）
N	------------------------------	Monitoring system（监控系统）
O	------------------------------	Special operation（特殊作业）

P ———————————————— Medical aid（医疗救护）

Q ———————————————— Emergency rescue（应急救援）

Task 5

58. 【答案】turn off

【解析】本题考查在实验室中应该如何处理手机。根据关键词 cell phones 和 while you are inside the lab 定位到文章第一条守则的第二句。定位句指出，在实验室里，手机和其他电子通信设备应该被关闭。通过对比题干和原文可知，题干把原文中的被动句替换成了主动句，因此空格处应该填入 turn off。

59. 【答案】non-busy

【解析】本题考查可以在实验室内开展小组学习的时间。根据关键词 group studying 定位到文章第二条守则的第一句。定位句指出，小组学习必须限制在非繁忙时段。通过对比题干和原文，可以确定本题的答案为 non-busy。

60. 【答案】10-minute

【解析】本题考查为什么要将数量多的打印任务分解成多个数量较少的任务。根据关键词 break large print jobs into smaller ones 和 printouts are limited to 定位到文章第四条守则。定位句指出，打印必须限制在 10 分钟之内——将数量多的打印任务分解成多个数量较少的任务。通过对比题干和原文，可以确定本题的答案为 10-minute。

61. 【答案】damage the printers

【解析】本题考查为什么不允许将访客的表格和纸张放入 ITaP 的打印机内。根据关键词 the customers' forms or papers 和 not permitted in ITaP printers 定位到倒数第二条守则。定位句首先指出，不允许将访客的表格和纸张放入 ITaP 的打印机内，接着解释了原因：这样做可能会损坏打印机。通过对比题干和原文，可以确定本题的答案为 damage the printers。

62. 【答案】operation

【解析】本题考查可以在实验室里使用电脑的时间。根据关键词 During the lab hours 和 no classes scheduled 定位到最后一条守则。定位句指出，电脑的使用遵循先到先得的原则，只有当实验室的电脑在运行时间内而且机房里未安排授课时才可以使用。通过对比题干和原文，可以确定本题的答案为 operation。

2017 年 12 月真题

Task 1

40. 【答案】B

【解析】事实细节题。根据题干中的 ease your fear 定位到文章第一段第二句。定位句提到，为了增加兴奋感和减轻恐惧感，你应该从一开始就做好准备。题干中的 ease your fear 是对定位句中 ease the fear 的同义转述，选项 B "be prepared" 是对定位句中 get prepared 的同义转述。由此可以确定 B 项 "做好准备" 为本题的答案。

41. 【答案】C

【解析】事实细节题。根据题干中的 making your business plan 定位到文章第二段第二句。定位句提到,在创建了目标之后,你要确保对公司有个计划。换句话说,你在为公司制订计划之前,应该先有个目标。题干中的 making your business plan 是对定位句中 make sure you have a plan for your business 的同义转述,选项 C"set your own business goals"是对定位句中 you have created your goals 的同义转述。由此可以确定 C 项"制定你自己公司的目标"为本题的答案。

42.【答案】A

【解析】事实细节题。根据题干中的 the third paragraph 定位到文章第三段。定位段首句指出,开创公司时需要考虑大量的法律相关事务,接下来举出多个事例。选项 A"legal considerations"与原文中的 There are a number of legal considerations 表述一致。由此可以确定 A 项"法律方面的考虑"为本题的答案。

43.【答案】D

【解析】事实细节题。根据题干中的 the major concern for starting a business 定位到文章第四段首句。定位句提到,在创办公司时,资金是一个大问题。题干中的 the major concern for starting a business 是对定位句中 a major concern when you start a business 的同义转述,选项 D"money"与原文的表述一致。由此可以确定 D 项"资金"为本题的答案。

44.【答案】C

【解析】事实细节题。根据题干中的 meeting business start-up expenses 定位到文章第四段首句。定位句提到,在创办公司时,资金是一个大问题,特别是放弃了收入丰厚的工作而公司启动费用数额又相当大的时候。接下来,文章详细介绍了解决资金问题的几个办法:从事全职或兼职工作,或者攒足了资金再创办公司,或者在需要资金的时候向银行申请贷款。题干中的 meeting business start-up expenses 是对原文中 if your business has considerable start-up expenses 的同义转述。选项 C"apply for a bank loan"与原文表述一致。由此可以确定 C 项"向银行申请贷款"为本题的答案。

Task 2

45.【答案】B

【解析】事实细节题。根据题干中的"coffee and cake"morning 定位到海报的第一段首句。定位句提到,我们邀请您或贵公司的一位代表参加"coffee and cake" morning 活动,时间为 4 月 8 日周三上午 11 点。由此可见,活动是在周三上午举行。由此可以确定 B 项"周三"为本题的答案。

46.【答案】C

【解析】事实细节题。根据题干中的 be invited to give a speech 定位到海报的第二段首句。定位句提到,活动将会邀请一位来自"HR Solution, Employers Advisory Service"的嘉宾发言人。换句话说,来自"HR Solution, Employers Advisory Service"的嘉宾将在活动中发表演讲。选项 C"A guest speaker from Employers Advisory Service"与原文表述基本一致。由此可以确定 C 项"来自 Employers Advisory Service 的嘉宾发言人"为本题的答案。

47. 【答案】A

【解析】事实细节题。根据题干中的 contact Debby or Elaine by phone or e-mail 定位到海报的第四段。定位段提到，请拨打电话 01564 330600 或者发电子邮件到 *debby. hares@ ubcuk. com* 联系 Debby 或 Elaine，以便确认参会。选项 A 的"confirm your attendance"与原文表述完全一致。由此可以确定 A 项"确认你来参会"为本题的答案。

Task 3

48. 【答案】33

【解析】锁定关键词。根据关键词 $8.54 a month 定位到第一段第二句。定位句说明了该险种对投保人的年龄要求，以及月保费和受益金额，即在 33 岁时每月投保 8.54 美元就可以获得高达 250 000 美元的受益金额。通过对比题干和原文可知，空格处应该填入投保人的年龄。因此，可以确定本题的答案为 33。

49. 【答案】$250,000

【解析】锁定关键词。根据关键词 coverage 和 up to 定位到第二段第二句。定位句中提到，保额可以达到 250 000 美元。通过对比定位句中的 obtain coverage of up to $250,000 可知，空格处应该填入保险金额。因此，可以确定本题的答案为 $250,000。

50. 【答案】the members

【解析】锁定关键词。根据关键词 offered、ASCE for Group Term Life Insurance plans 定位到第二段首句。定位句指出，ASCE 为其成员提供团体定期人寿保险服务。通过对比题干和定位句可知，空格处应该填入 ASCE 提供团体定期人寿保险服务的对象。因此，可以确定本题的答案为 the members。

51. 【答案】in force

【解析】锁定关键词。根据关键词 portable 和 as long as the policy 定位到第三段。该段第一句指出人寿保险的保额是可以转移的，即使改变工作也不受影响。第二句指出，只要你的保单还在有效期内，就可以完全放心。通过对比题干和定位句可知，空格处应该填入保额可以转移的条件。因此，可以确定本题的答案为 in force。

52. 【答案】insurance agency

【解析】锁定关键词。根据关键词 Contact 和 local 定位到最后一段第二句。定位句指出，如果有任何问题，可以拨打电话 800-846-3582 联系当地的保险代理机构。通过对比题干和定位句可知，空格处应该填入联系对象。因此，可以确定本题的答案为 insurance agency。

Task 4

53. 【答案】B O
54. 【答案】D F
55. 【答案】P Q
56. 【答案】E H
57. 【答案】M L

【解析】

A	Country of Citizenship（国籍）
B	Passport Number（护照号码）
C	Country of Origin（原籍国）
D	Destination Country（目的地国家）
E	City Where You Boarded（登机城市）
F	City Where Visa Was Issued（签证签发地）
G	Date of Issue（签发日期）
H	Date of Birth（出生日期）
I	Accompanying Number（同行人数）
J	Official Use Only（官方填写）
K	Business Visa（商务签证）
L	Tourist Visa（旅行签证）
M	Arrival Lobby（抵达大厅）
N	Departure Lobby（出境大厅）
O	Boarding Gate（登机口）
P	Boarding Card（登机牌）
Q	Visa Type（签证种类）

Task 5

58.【答案】Grounds maintenance workers

【解析】本题考查广告中提供的工作岗位。根据短文的标题和第一个、第三个小标题以及全文的主要内容可以看出广告中提供的工作岗位是 Grounds maintenance workers。因此，确定本题的答案为 Grounds maintenance workers。

59.【答案】outdoor environment

【解析】本题考查这份工作的职责。根据关键词 To provide a pleasant 定位到第一段。定位段指出，地面维护工人需要确保房屋、商业场所和公园的地面美观、整洁并有益于健康，以便提供舒适的户外环境。由此可见，这份工作的职责是提供舒适的户外环境。通过对比题干和原文，可以确定本题的答案为 outdoor environment。

60.【答案】all weather conditions

【解析】本题考查这份工作的工作环境。根据关键词 working environment 和 The work is mostly done outdoors in 定位到第二段第二句。该句指出，大多数的工作都是全天候情况下在户外进行。通过对比题干和原文，可以确定本题的答案为 all weather conditions。

61.【答案】on-the-job

【解析】本题考查从事这份工作将要接受的培训。根据关键词 training 和 a short period of 定位到第四段。该段开头就指出，短期的在职培训通常足以教会新聘用人员所需要的技能。由此可见，从事这份工作将要接受短期的在职培训。通过对比题干和原文，可以确定本题的答案为 on-the-job。

62. 【答案】12.90

【解析】本题考查 2016 年 5 月地面维护工人的小时工资额。根据关键词 the hourly wage 和 in May 2016 定位到第五段。该段指出,2016 年 5 月地面维护工人的小时工资额为 12.90 美元。通过对比题干和原文,可以确定本题的答案为 12.90。

2018 年 6 月真题

Task 1

40. 【答案】B

【解析】事实细节题。根据题干中的 by buying Home Solutions 和 you can get help 定位到文章第一段。该段第二句提到,保险公司理解房屋及房屋里物品的重要性,万一发生意想不到的事情,保险公司能够为你提供帮助。题干中的 you can get help 与原文中的 can help you 意思相同,选项 B"when something unexpected happens to your home"是对原文中 if something unexpected should happen 的同义转述。由此可以确定 B 项"当你的房屋出现意想不到的状况时"为本题的答案。

41. 【答案】A

【解析】事实细节题。根据题干中的 call the Emergency Homeline 定位到文章第二段。该段提到,遇到紧急情况时,可以拨打 24 小时紧急家庭电话。即使在非正常工作时间,保险公司也会安排维修人员开展维修工作。题干中的 call the Emergency Homeline 与原文中的 Call the 24-hour Emergency Homeline 意思相同。选项 A"a repairman will be sent to do the repairs"使用了被动语态,是对原文中使用主动语态的 We'll arrange for a repairman to carry out repairs 的同义转述。选项 A 中的 do the repairs 与原文中的 carry out repairs 意思相同。由此可以确定 A 项"维修人员会被派去开展维修工作"为本题的答案。

42. 【答案】A

【解析】事实细节题。根据题干中的 lose your keys 和 external doors 定位到文章第三段。该段提到,如果你丢失了钥匙,保险公司会赔付换外门锁产生的全部费用。题干中的 the insurance company 即原文中的 We,选项 A"pay for the cost of replacing locks"是对原文中 pay for the full cost of replacing locks 的同义转述。由此可以确定 A 项"赔付换锁产生的费用"为本题的答案。

43. 【答案】C

【解析】事实细节题。根据题干中的 a festival 和 your valuables limit 定位到文章第四段。该段提到在一些特殊的时间,如婚礼或者节日,保险公司会将你的贵重物品的限额自动提高 3 000 美元。题干中的 a festival 和 your valuables limit 与原文中的表述一致,选项 C "automatically increased"与原文中的表述基本一致。由此可以确定 C 项"自动提高"为本题的答案。

44. 【答案】D

【解析】事实细节题。根据题干中的 if your home is damaged by an insured event 定位到

文章第五段第一句。定位句提到,如果你家因为保险范围内的事件遭受损害而无法居住,保险公司将为你和你的宠物找到居住场所。题干中的 if your home is damaged by an insured event 与原文中的表述基本一致,选项 D 中的"find somewhere for you to live"对应原文中的 find somewhere for you and your pets to live。由此可以确定 D 项"它将为你找到住处"为本题的答案。

Task 2

45.【答案】B

【解析】事实细节题。根据题干中的 inform the golfers 定位到通知的第一段前半部分。该部分提到,很抱歉通知您,原定于 2016 年 8 月 20 日举行的"总裁杯"高尔夫球比赛将被推迟。题干中的 inform the golfers of 与原文中的 inform that 意思相同,选项 B "the postponement of President's Cup"是对原文中的"the President's Cup … will be postponed"的同义转述。由此可以确定 B 项"'总裁杯'高尔夫球比赛的推迟"为本题的答案。

46.【答案】D

【解析】事实细节题。根据题干中的 The change of the game date 和 due to 定位到通知的第一段后半部分。该部分提到,推迟比赛时间是因为俱乐部总裁的日程出现了意料之外的变化。题干中的 The change of the game date 是对原文中的 the President's Cup … will be postponed to a later date 的同义转述,选项 D "a change in President's schedule"是对原文中的 an unforeseen change in our Club President's schedule 的同义转述。由此可以确定 D 项"总裁的日程变化"为本题的答案。

47.【答案】C

【解析】事实细节题。根据题干中的 the social game will start 定位到通知的第二段第二句。定位句提到,高尔夫球比赛将于 13:15 开始,题干中的 the social game 与原文中的 the golf game 表示的内容一致,题干中的 start 与原文中的 commence 意思相同,选项 C "at 13:15" 与原文中的"at 1315h"意思相同。由此可以确定 C 项"在 13 点 15 分"为本题的答案。

Task 3

48.【答案】cheaper

【解析】锁定关键词。根据关键词 make your medicine 和 your experience easier 定位到文章第二段第一句。定位句指出了药店专家的工作目标:让患者买到更便宜的药品,让购药经历更容易。通过对比题干和原文可知,空格处应该填入 cheaper。

49.【答案】long-term

【解析】锁定关键词。通过关键词 from PrimeMail、ordering your 和 medicine 定位到文章第三段第一句。定位句指出,可以通过 PrimeMail 长期购买药物。通过对比题干和原文可知,空格处应该填入 long-term。

50.【答案】network

【解析】锁定关键词。根据关键词 a large national 和 of pharmacies 定位到文章第四段第一句。定位句指出,Prime 药品公司可以提供大型的全国药店网络。通过对比题干和原文可知,空格处应该填入 network。

51.【答案】member ID

【解析】锁定关键词。根据关键词 bringing your prescription 定位到文章第四段第二句。定位句指出,购买零售药物时需要携带药方和会员卡。通过对比题干和原文可知,空格处应该填入 member ID。

52.【答案】full-service delivery

【解析】锁定关键词。根据关键词 Prime Therapeutics Specialty Pharmacy 定位到文章最后一段第一句。定位句指出,Prime Therapeutics Specialty Pharmacy 是一家提供全方位配送服务的药店。通过对比题干和原文可知,空格处应该填入 full-service delivery。

Task 4

53.【答案】H D
54.【答案】F O
55.【答案】P J
56.【答案】A L
57.【答案】Q M

【解析】

A	School Zone（前方学校）
B	Vendors Prohibited（禁止摆摊）
C	Pass on Left（左侧通过）
D	Don't Step On（请勿踩踏）
E	Keep Away for Safety（注意安全,请勿靠近）
F	Service Area（服务区）
G	Administrative Area（办公区）
H	Watch Your Hand（当心夹手）
I	Please Don't Leave Valuables Unattended（贵重物品请随身保管）
J	Maintenance in Progress（正在检修）
K	Out of Service（停止服务）
L	Stand on Right（靠右站立）
M	Break Glass in Emergency（紧急情况击碎玻璃）
N	Don't Touch（请勿触摸）
O	Keep Clear of the Door（勿靠车门）
P	Don't Exceed Speed Limit（严禁超速）
Q	Icy Road（路面结冰）

Task 5

58.【答案】service line

【解析】本题考查煤气公司依照联邦法律需要做的检查的内容。根据关键词 required to

do by federal law、To inspect the letter receiver's 和 meter setting 定位到信函的第一段第一句。定位句指出,煤气公司依照联邦法律要求检查服务线路和仪表设置。通过对比题干和原文,可以确定本题的答案为 service line。

59.【答案】arranged an inspection

【解析】本题考查信函接收人在什么情况下可以忽略本信函。根据关键词 ignore this letter 和 If he/she has already 定位到信函的第二段前两句。定位句指出,如果你已经安排了一次检查,就没有必要再给煤气公司打电话,可以忽略这封信函。由此可见,信函接收人可以忽略本信函的前提是已经安排了一次检查。通过对比题干和原文,可以确定本题的答案为 arranged an inspection。

60.【答案】the inspection

【解析】本题考查双方的联系将会保持多长时间。根据关键词 Communications will continue until 和 has been completed 定位到信函的第二段第三句。该句指出,双方将一直保持联系,直到检查结束为止。通过对比题干和原文,可以确定本题的答案为 the inspection。

61.【答案】safe and reliable

【解析】本题考查煤气公司承诺为客户提供什么样的服务。根据关键词 promised、To provide 和 service to its customers 定位到信函的第三段。定位段指出,这次重要的安全检查是煤气公司承诺为客户提供安全、可靠的服务的一部分。由此可见,煤气公司承诺为客户提供安全、可靠的服务。通过对比题干和原文,可以确定本题的答案为 safe and reliable。

62.【答案】is not performed

【解析】本题考查煤气公司会在什么情况下停止向客户提供服务。根据关键词 stop its service for its customers 和 If the inspection 定位到信函第五段的第一句。该句指出,如果不接受检查,煤气公司将无法继续为客户提供服务。由此可见,煤气公司停止向客户提供服务的情况是客户没有接受检查。通过对比题干和原文,可以确定本题的答案为 is not performed。

2018 年 12 月真题

Task 1

40.【答案】C

【解析】事实细节题。根据题干中的 the first paragraph 和 website 定位到文章第一段第一句。定位句提到, PowerShow.com 网站是一个领先的展示与放映幻灯片的共享网站。选项 C "shares slideshows" 是对原文中的 presentation/slideshows sharing 的同义转述。由此可以确定 C 项"分享幻灯片"为本题的答案。

41.【答案】D

【解析】事实细节题。根据题干中的 Most of PowerShow.com's features 定位到文章第一段最后一句。定位句提到,该网站的大部分酷炫功能是免费的,而且易于使用。题干中的 Most of PowerShow.com's features 与原文的表述 most of its cool features 基本一致,选项 D "easy to use" 与原文中的表述完全一致。由此可以确定 D 项"易于使用"为本题的答案。

42.【答案】A

【解析】事实细节题。根据题干中的 using PowerShow.com 和 you can learn to 定位到文章第二段。定位段提到,你可以使用 PowerShow.com 查找并下载任何你能想象到的主题的 PPT 模板,免费学习如何改善自己的幻灯片及其展示的质量。题干中的 using PowerShow.com 和 you can learn 与原文的表述基本一致。选项 A 中的 "make … better" 是对原文中的 improve 的同义转述。由此可以确定 A 项"使你的展示更好"为本题的答案。

43.【答案】B

【解析】事实细节题。根据题干中的 get the industry's best online privacy 定位到文章第三段第一句。定位句提到,只需要支付少量费用,即可获取行业最好的网络隐私或者提高幻灯片的排名。题干中的 get the industry's best online privacy 与原文的表述完全一致,选项 B 中的 pay a small fee 是对原文中的 for a small fee 的同义转述。由此可以确定 B 项"支付少量费用"为本题的答案。

44.【答案】A

【解析】主旨大意题。本文主要介绍了 PowerShow.com 网站,具体介绍了该网站的主要功能和特点。由此可以确定 A 项"介绍 PowerShow 网站"为本题的答案。

📖 **Task 2**

45.【答案】B

【解析】事实细节题。根据题干中的 inform the public about 定位到公告的第二段第一句。定位句提到,经过慎重考虑,管理层决定关闭零售店以拓展批发业务。题干中的 inform the public about 是对原文中 after careful consideration, we have decided to 的解释,选项 B "the closing of a retail store" 是对原文中的 to close our retail store 的同义转述。由此可以确定 B 项"关闭零售商店"为本题的答案。

46.【答案】D

【解析】事实细节题。根据题干中的 In the future 和 the Vinjerud Family 定位到公告的第二段第二句。定位句提到,Vinjerud Family 的确计划将来在更方便的位置开设店铺。题干中的 In the future 和 the Vinjerud Family 与原文表述一致,intends to start its business 是对原文中 does plan to open 的解释,选项 D "in a more convenient place" 与原文中的 in a more convenient location 表述基本一致。由此可以确定 D 项"在一个更便利的位置"为本题的答案。

47.【答案】A

【解析】事实细节题。根据题干中的 if they have a gift card 定位到公告的第三段。定位段提到,如果你有礼品卡的话,请联系……预约退还全部的余额。题干中的 if they have a gift card 与原文的表述基本一致,选项 A "Contact the store for the remaining value." 是对原文 "please contact Olivia Costa at … to make an appointment to be reimbursed for the full remaining value" 的归纳概括。由此可以确定 A 项"联系店铺退还余额"为本题的答案。

📖 **Task 3**

48.【答案】return

【解析】锁定关键词。根据关键词 Postcards with discount information 和 attract customers to 定位到短文的第二段第一句。定位句指出,印有折扣信息的明信片是一种很好的方式,可以吸引顾客再次光临。通过对比题干和原文可知,空格处应该填入明信片能够吸引顾客去做什么。因此可以确定本题的答案为 return。

49.【答案】your/the packaging

【解析】锁定关键词。根据关键词 add them to 定位到短文的第二段第二句。定位句指出,可以邮寄明信片,也可以在包装上加上明信片,或者放到柜台上供顾客拿取和分享。通过对比题干和原文可知,空格处应该填入可以把明信片添加到什么地方。因此可以确定本题的答案为 your/the packaging。

50.【答案】easily seen

【解析】锁定关键词。根据关键词 Posters 和 eye-catching 定位到短文的第三段第一句。定位句指出了海报的特点:容易引人注意,易于被人看到。通过对比题干和原文可知,已经给出海报的第一个特点,空格处应该填入海报的第二个特点。因此可以确定本题的答案为 easily seen。

51.【答案】detailed information

【解析】锁定关键词。根据关键词 Brochures、more 和 about the business 定位到短文的第四段第一句。定位句指出,宣传册能够呈现更多关于公司业务的详细信息。通过对比题干和原文可知,空格处应该填入海报上可以呈现的内容。因此可以确定本题的答案为 detailed information。

52.【答案】photos

【解析】锁定关键词。根据关键词 use 和 clear messaging 定位到短文的第四段第二句。定位句指出,使用图片和清楚的信息把希望潜在的顾客了解的事情都传达给他们。通过对比题干和原文可知,空格处应该填入宣传册使用什么方式传达信息。因此可以确定本题的答案为 photos。

Task 4

53.【答案】C M

54.【答案】K P

55.【答案】J I

56.【答案】A O

57.【答案】Q E

【解析】

A ·················· avoid loose clothing（勿穿宽松服装）

B ·················· install safety guards（安装安全防护装置）

C ·················· keep workplace clean（保持工作区域清洁）

D ·················· know evacuation routes（熟悉疏散路线）

E ·················· know how to lift heavy loads（了解如何提升重物）

F ······················ know machine operating procedure（掌握机器操作程序）
G ······················ never reach into running machines（切勿接触运转中的机器）
H ······················ place trash in proper containers（将垃圾放入适当的容器中）
I ······················ report any unsafe conditions（任何不安全状况须报告）
J ······················ shut down machines when not in use（机器不用时请关闭）
K ······················ store chemicals correctly（正确储存化学品）
L ······················ store your tools after use（使用后保存工具）
M ······················ turn off machines in between jobs（工作间隙关闭机器）
N ······················ wash hands（洗手）
O ······················ wear protective uniform（穿好防护制服）
P ······················ wear safety glasses（戴上防护眼镜）
Q ······················ use two-handed operations（使用双手操作）

Task 5

58.【答案】insurance card

【解析】本题考查去看医生之前应该做的准备工作。根据关键词 before going to a doctor 定位到短文的第一段第一句。该句指出，在去看医生或开处方时，应该准备好保险卡。通过对比题干和原文，可以确定本题的答案为 insurance card。

59.【答案】the policy number

【解析】本题考查保险卡上可以看到哪些信息。根据关键词 information、on your insurance card、The insurance provider 和 the expiration date 定位到短文的第一段第二句。该句指出保险卡上有一些基本信息，包括保险提供商、保单号码、到期日期等。通过对比题干和原文，可以确定本题的答案为 the policy number。

60.【答案】insurance provider's website

【解析】本题考查从哪里可以查询你的保单的覆盖范围。根据关键词 find the information about what your insurance covers 定位到短文的第二段第二、三句。第二句指出，在获取保险之前，可以查询一下所买保险的覆盖范围和额度等相关信息；第三句接着指出，这些信息可以在保险供应商的网站上查询到。由此可见，查询你的保单覆盖范围的地方是保险供应商的网站。通过对比题干和原文，可以确定本题的答案为 insurance provider's website。

61.【答案】any changes

【解析】本题考查随时保持了解最新信息的原因。根据关键词 stay updated 和 To be aware of 定位到短文的第三段。第一句指出要保持了解最新信息，第二句接着指出，这样可以确保能够随时了解保险内容出现的任何变化。由此可见，随时保持了解最新信息的原因是能够了解保险内容出现的任何变化。通过对比题干和原文，可以确定本题的答案为 any changes。

62.【答案】expensive

【解析】本题考查为什么核对诊所能够接受的保险方案非常重要。根据关键词 to check

what insurance plans the clinics accept 和 Because health care can be 定位到短文的最后一段第三、四句。第三句指出,一定要认真核对诊所能够接受的保险方案;第四句接着指出,这很重要因为医疗保健费用非常高。通过对比题干和原文,可以确定本题的答案为 expensive。

2019年6月真题

Task 1

40.【答案】B

【解析】事实细节题。根据题干中的 according to the first 定位到文章的第一段第一、二句。第一句提出疑问:宾馆的费用是不是一直在上升?第二句做出回答:宾馆的费用的确在逐年上升。第二句中的 they 指的就是选项 B 中的"Hotel costs",而 increase 和 year by year 分别是对原文中的 rise 和 each year 的同义转述。由此可以确定 B 项"宾馆费用逐年上升"为本题的答案。

41.【答案】C

【解析】事实细节题。根据题干中的 One piece of advice to hotel guests 和题文同序的原则定位到文章的第二段第三、四句。定位句提到,能够帮助节省费用的通常的额外服务包括免费的早餐、免费的 Wi-Fi 和免费的儿童餐,在宾馆住宿期间,好好利用这些额外服务。选项 C 中的"take advantage of"和"the common extras"与原文的表述基本一致。由此可以确定 C 项"利用包含在房费里面的额外服务"为本题的答案。

42.【答案】D

【解析】事实细节题。根据题干中的 staying in the university district 定位到文章的第三段第二、三句。定位句提到,你也可以寻求住在城市的大学区域,因为周边的房价优惠、饮食便宜、公交方便。题干中的 staying in the university district 与原文中的表述一致,选项 D"the convenient public transportation"是对原文中 public transportation is convenient 的同义转述。由此可以确定 D 项"便捷的公共交通"为本题的答案。

43.【答案】A

【解析】事实细节题。根据题干中的 go out to eat when you are staying a hotel 定位到文章的第四段。定位段提到,要去宾馆外面就餐,原因在于宾馆菜单上的食物价格是外面饭店里同样食物价格的两倍。题干中的 go out to eat 与原文中表述一致,选项 A "Food served in hotel is too expensive"是对原文中 prices for food on the hotel menu can be twice as much as you would pay for the same food at a restaurant 的概括归纳。由此可以确定 A 项"宾馆里提供的食物价格太贵"为本题的答案。

44.【答案】B

【解析】主旨大意题。本文主要介绍了在宾馆住宿时节省费用的三个妙招:尽可能地利用额外优惠;居住在市中心之外的宾馆或者高校周围的宾馆;到宾馆外面的饭店就餐。由此可见,文章主要是关于如何在宾馆住宿时节省费用。因此可以确定 B 项"在宾馆住宿时节省费用"为本题的答案。

Task 2

45.【答案】D

【解析】事实细节题。根据题干中的 service 和 provided by the company 定位到广告的标题以及第二段第一句。由标题可知,公司提供的服务是建筑材料清理。由定位句可知,公司擅长清理不同阶段的建筑材料。题干中的 provided by the company 对应标题中的 By Jones Cleaning Services,选项 D"Construction clean-up"与原文表述一致。由此可以确定 D 项"建筑材料清理"为本题的答案。

46.【答案】A

【解析】事实细节题。根据题干中的 invite the company to bid for your project 定位到广告的第二段第一、二句。定位句提到,公司希望有机会去投标项目的最终清理工作,并给出了联系电话。题干中的 invite the company to bid for your project 对应原文中的 the chance to bid the final cleaning of your project,选项 A"Call Mike Jones"是对原文中 Give me a call at the number below 的同义转述。由此可以确定 A 项"给迈克·琼斯打电话"为本题的答案。

47.【答案】C

【解析】事实细节题。根据题干中的 guarantee 定位到广告最后一行的小字部分。此处提到了该公司的三个承诺:全保险、有担保、保证100%满意。选项 C "100 percent satisfaction"符合原文的表述。由此可以确定 C 项"百分之百满意"为本题的答案。

Task 3

48.【答案】*payment processing*

【解析】锁定关键词。根据关键词 Paying online via PayLease、a leading 和 company 定位到第一段第一、二句。定位句指出,Norris & Stevens 愿意帮助居民通过 PayLease 公司进行网上支付,PayLease 是财产管理行业处于主导地位的支付处理公司。通过对比题干和原文可知,空格处应该填入 PayLease 公司的业务范围。因此,可以确定本题的答案为 payment processing。

49.【答案】*credit card*

【解析】锁定关键词。根据关键词 Benefits、paying online via 和 electronic check 定位到第一段下的第一点。定位句指出,居民们可以享受的其中一个益处是通过信用卡或电子支票进行网上支付。通过对比题干和原文可知,空格处应该填入进行网上支付的具体方式。因此,可以确定本题的答案为 credit card。

50.【答案】*support*

【解析】锁定关键词。根据关键词 call center for 定位到第一段下的第四点。定位句指出,居民们可以享受的另外一个益处是向客户服务中心寻求支持。通过对比题干和原文可知,空格处应该填入居民向客户服务中心寻求什么。因此,可以确定本题的答案为 support。

51.【答案】*PayLease. com*

【解析】锁定关键词。根据关键词 Registration、visiting 和 clicking on "Pay Rent Online"定位到第二段下的第一点。定位句指出,注册的方法是登录网站 *PayLease. com*,然后点击"Pay

Rent Online"进行注册。通过对比题干和原文可知,空格处应该填入注册时需要登录的网站。因此,可以确定本题的答案为 *PayLease.com*。

52.【答案】1-866-734-5322

【解析】锁定关键词。根据关键词 Contact 和 PayLease Support at 定位到第三段第二句。定位句指出,如果有任何与 PayLease 有关的问题,可以拨打电话 1-866-734-5322 联系 PayLease 的客户服务中心。通过对比题干和原文可知,空格处应该填入 PayLease 的客户服务中心的电话号码。因此,可以确定本题的答案为 1-866-734-5322。

Task 4

53.【答案】C P

54.【答案】H J

55.【答案】B L

56.【答案】O E

57.【答案】K Q

【解析】

A	cost of quality (质量成本)
B	quality level (质量等级)
C	quality control (质量控制)
D	quality management (质量管理)
E	supply chain (供应链)
F	quality assurance (质量保证)
G	major defect (主要缺陷)
H	inspection certificate (检验证书)
I	check list (核对表)
J	quality engineering (质量工程)
K	sample size (样本大小)
L	inspection cost (检验成本)
M	rejection number (退货数量)
N	laboratory testing (实验室测试)
O	quality inspector (质检员)
P	consumer safety (消费者安全)
Q	appearance check (外观检查)

Task 5

58.【答案】30 days

【解析】本题考查对购买的产品不满意时退回产品的时间。根据关键词 return the product、if you are not satisfied with the purchase 和 Within 定位到第二段第一句。定位句指出,如果因为任何原因对产品不满意,可以在购买后 30 日内退回产品。通过对比题干和原文,可以确定本题的答案为 30 days。

59.【答案】in new condition

【解析】本题考查退货时对产品的要求。根据关键词 All its returned items must be 和 as it is received 定位到第二段第二句。定位句指出,所有退回的货物必须和接收到的货物一样新。通过对比题干和原文,可以确定本题的答案为 in new condition。

60.【答案】additional fees

【解析】本题考查退货时缺失附件需要进行相应的赔偿。根据关键词 any accessories were found missing 定位到第二段第三句。定位句指出,缺失或者损坏附件需要支付额外的费用。通过对比题干和原文,可以确定本题的答案为 additional fees。

61.【答案】pictures

【解析】本题考查受损的产品换货时有什么要求。根据关键词 For the damaged products 和 are required 定位到第三段第二句。定位句指出,对于受损的产品,需要提供照片。通过对比题干和原文,可以确定本题的答案为 pictures。

62.【答案】return instruction

【解析】本题考查在退回产品之前需要做什么工作。根据关键词 a RMA number 和 before return 定位到最后一段。定位段指出,退货之前可以给 sales@greennaturalsolar.com 发邮件,索取 RMA 号码和退货说明。通过对比题干和原文,可以确定本题的答案为 return instruction。

2019 年 12 月真题

Task 1

40.【答案】D

【解析】事实细节题。根据题干中的 first paragraph 定位到文章的第一段第二句。该句提到,如果你对自己的工作充满热情,这会有所帮助。选项 D "enthusiastic" 与原文中的 So it helps if you're enthusiastic about what you do 意思相同。由此可以确定 D 项"热情的"为本题的答案。

41.【答案】B

【解析】事实细节题。根据题干中的 running a business is "a big job" 定位到文章的第二段第二句。该句提到经营企业有许多困难需要克服。选项 B "You have many difficulties to overcome."是对原文中的 there have been lots of difficulties to overcome along the way 的同义转述。由此可以确定 B 项"你有许多困难需要克服"为本题的答案。

42.【答案】C

【解析】事实细节题。根据题干中的 marketing 定位到文章的第三段第一句。定位句提到,企业主为了营销,经常需要创建网站和建立品牌战略。选项 C "to build up a brand strategy"与原文的表述 develop a brand strategy for the company 基本一致。由此可以确定 C 项"建立品牌战略"为本题的答案。

43.【答案】B

【解析】语义推断题。根据题干中的 the ups and downs 定位到文章的最后一段第一句。定位句提到,她与银行家的关系支撑着她度过经营公司的起起落落,由此可以推测出她的公司经历了大起大落。选项 B"good and bad experiences"是对 the ups and downs 的同义转述。由此可以确定 B 项"好的和坏的经历"为本题的答案。

44.【答案】A

【解析】事实细节题。根据题干中的 a banker can help small business 定位到文章的最后一段第二句。定位句提到,银行家帮助小型企业融资。选项 A"financing"是对 a banker can help with small business financing 的同义转述。由此可以确定 A 项"融资"为本题的答案。

Task 2

45.【答案】D

【解析】事实细节题。根据题干中的 discover a fire 定位到开头部分的内容。选项 D 中的 leave the area 与原文表述基本一致。由此可以确定 D 项"立即离开火场"为本题的答案。

46.【答案】A

【解析】事实细节题。根据题干中的 continuous fire alarm 定位到中间部分"Leave the building by the nearest exit."。该句提到,从最近的出口离开火场大楼。A 项"Leave the building by the closest exit."与原文的表述意思一致,nearest 和 closest 是同义词。由此可以确定 A 项"从最近的出口离开火场大楼"为本题的答案。

47.【答案】B

【解析】事实细节题。根据题干中的 If smoke is heavy in the corridor 定位到结尾部分的内容。该处提到,如果走廊有浓烟,就待在你所在的区域。stay in your area 是对原文中的 it may be safer for you to stay in your area 的同义转述。由此可以确定 B 项"待在你所在的区域"为本题的答案。

Task 3

48.【答案】global startups

【解析】锁定关键词。根据关键词 select top 100 直接定位到原文的第一段第一句。该句指出,BIZSHOT 是亚洲最激动人心的深科技初创企业竞赛,旨在评选全球 100 强初创企业。通过分析题干可知,空格处考查 2020 届 BIZSHOT 的目标。因此可以确定本题的答案为 global startups。

49.【答案】11 to 13

【解析】锁定关键词。根据关键词 from 和"March,2020"定位到原文的第一段第二句。该句指出,2020 届 BIZSHOT 将于 2020 年 3 月 11 日至 13 日在天津举行。通过分析题干可知,空格处应该填入举办时间。因此可以确定本题的答案为"11 to 13"。

50.【答案】a workable product

【解析】锁定关键词。根据关键词 at least 和 with a practical solution 定位到原文的第一段最后一句。该句指出,至少需要提交一个具有切实可行的解决方案的可行性产品。通过分析题干可知,空格处考查提交的内容。因此可以确定本题的答案为 a workable product。

51.【答案】industry experts

【解析】锁定关键词。根据关键词"160"和 decision-makers 定位到原文的第二段第一句。该句指出,160 多名行业专家和决策者(主要包括投资者和公司)将对提交的资料进行评审。通过分析题干可知,空格处应该填入句中提到的评审专家的组成人员。因此可以确定本题的答案为 industry experts。

52.【答案】Participate

【解析】锁定关键词。根据关键词 click on 和 button 定位到原文的第三段最后一句。该句指出点击"参加"按钮提交材料。通过分析题干可知,空格处应该填入按钮的名称。因此可以确定本题的答案为 Participate。

Task 4

53.【答案】I E
54.【答案】F O
55.【答案】K B
56.【答案】H M
57.【答案】G P

【解析】

A ————————————	Chain store(连锁店)
B ————————————	Consumer behavior(消费者行为)
C ————————————	Consumer satisfaction(消费者满意度)
D ————————————	Direct selling(直接销售)
E ————————————	Market demand(市场需求)
F ————————————	Market research(市场调研)
G ————————————	Target market(目标市场)
H ————————————	Brand image(品牌形象)
I ————————————	Promotion methods(促销方法)
J ————————————	Telephone sales(电话销售)
K ————————————	Direct costs(直接成本)
L ————————————	Product quality(产品质量)
M ————————————	Purchase decision(购买决策)
N ————————————	Added value(附加价值)
O ————————————	After-sales service(售后服务)
P ————————————	Brand management(品牌管理)
Q ————————————	Customer loyalty(消费者忠诚度)

Task 5

58.【答案】car insurance

【解析】本题考查建议联系当地的 GEICO 的原因。根据关键词 contact your local GEICO office 定位到原文的第一段第一句。定位句指出,如果您在节省汽车保险费用方面需要帮助,请与当地的 GEICO 办公室联系。通过对比题干和原文,可以确定本题的答案为 car insurance。

59.【答案】all the discounts

【解析】本题考查 GEICO 如何帮助省钱。根据关键词 receive 和 special benefits you deserve 定位到原文的第一段最后一句。定位句指出,您将从 GEICO 获得优惠的价格,他们将确保您获得应有的所有折扣和特别优惠。通过对比题干和原文,可以确定本题的答案为 all the discounts。

60.【答案】75 years

【解析】本题考查 GEICO 运营的时间。根据关键词 For more than 定位到原文的第三段第一句。定位句指出,超过 75 年来,GEICO 一直为人们省钱。由此可见,GEICO 运营的时间超过 75 年。通过对比题干和原文,可以确定本题的答案为 75 years。

61.【答案】21 million

【解析】本题考查 GEICO 已经为多少司机提供保险。根据关键词 drivers 和 insured by GEICO 定位到原文的第三段最后一句。定位句指出,作为美国第二大个人汽车保险公司的 GEICO 为超过 2 100 万司机提供保险服务。题干中的 divers have been insured 与原文中的 auto insurance 意思相同。通过对比题干和原文,可以确定本题的答案为 21 million。

62.【答案】www. geico. com

【解析】本题考查申请索赔的方式。根据关键词 report 和 claim 定位到原文的最后一段第一句。定位句指出,你可以登录网站 www. geico. com 申请索赔。由此可见,申请索赔的方式是进入网站申请。通过对比题干和原文,可以确定本题的答案为 www. geico. com。

英译汉

2015 年 6 月真题

(每题按 3 等评分:2 分,1 分,0 分)

63.【答案】A-C-B

【解析】take advantage of 表示"利用,享受……带来的好处";"first-come, first-served"表示"先来先得到服务";discounted room rate 表示"折扣房价"。

64.【答案】B-A-C

【解析】retailer 的意思是"零售商";a wide range of products 的意思是"多样的产品"。

65.【答案】A-B-C

【解析】offer 的意思是"提供"。what car to buy and how much to pay 是两个并列的"疑问

词+不定式"短语,所以翻译成并列动词词组"买什么车和花什么钱"最妥当。

66. 【答案】C-B-A

【解析】"There be + 名词词组"是一个存在句型,表示"某地有……"。名词词组 demand for 的意思是"对……的需求"。

67. 【答案】作为一家国际性公司,ABC 集团已运营50多年。在该公司找到一份工作可以引领你达到职业生涯的新高度,因为这里有让你升到更高职位的空间。假如你希望在一家不断发展的公司里找到工作,这些工作都很适合你。

【解析】本段文字是对于一家公司的介绍性文字。第一句中,as 是介词,意思是"作为",an international company 的意思是"一家国际性公司",in business 的意思是"经营",翻译成中文时可以转换成动词短语,要注意译出 have been 表示的现在完成时态,译为"已"。第二句中,finding a job within the company 是动名词短语作主语,意思是"在该公司找到一份工作",介词短语 in your career 可以转译成定语,译为"你职业生涯的",as 在此表示因果关系,译为"因为"。第三句中,名词短语 the perfect fit for you 在翻译成汉语时可以转译成动词短语"非常适合你"。

2015 年 12 月真题

(每题按3等评分:2分,1分,0分)

63. 【答案】A-C-B

【解析】词组 developing new project 表示"开发新项目";thoroughly examined 表示"全面检查";current situation 表示"现状"。

64. 【答案】B-C-A

【解析】master the art of 的意思是"掌握……艺术";effective communication 的意思是"有效交流"。

65. 【答案】C-A-B

【解析】provide sb. with sth. 的意思是"向某人提供某物";top brand names 的意思是"顶级品牌"。

66. 【答案】A-B-C

【解析】be designed for 的意思是"为……而设计,针对……";动词词组 increase … confidence 的意思是"增强/提升信心";marketing styles 的意思是"营销风格"。

67. 【答案】我们维修所有品牌的计算机。我们为你提供专业化建议。从长远来看,这可以为你节省时间和金钱。我们团队精通技术,能使大多数计算机系统更好地工作。将你的计算机带来免费检查,我们会推荐最高效的方法来解决你的问题。只有修好了,我们才收费。

【解析】本段文字是一篇广告文字,长句较多,结构相对复杂。第一句中,介词短语 of all brands 作 computers 的后置定语,译为"所有品牌的"。第二句中,现在分词结构 saving you both time and money 作状语,译为"可以为你节省时间和金钱"。第三句中,understand … well enough 可译为"精通……"。第四句中,介词短语 for a Free Check-Up 可转译为动词词组"做免费检查"。第五句中,only … if 结构可译为"只有……才……"。

2016 年 6 月真题

(每题按 3 等评分:2 分,1 分,0 分)

63.【答案】B-A-C

【解析】book a fight 表示"预订机票";advanced 是形容词,意思是"先进的";airlines 的意思是"航空公司"。

64.【答案】B-C-A

【解析】meet the qualifications 是词组,意思是"具备……资格,满足……资质要求";application for the position 的意思是"求职申请"。

65.【答案】A-C-B

【解析】distribution network 的意思是"分销网络";supply products to customers 的意思是"供货给顾客"。

66.【答案】C-A-B

【解析】more than 的意思是"不只是";"involve + 动名词"的意思是"包括做……"。

67.【答案】请记住,绿色生活的确会使我们的生活大不一样!这对我们和我们的地球都是一种健康的选择。从长远来看,我们在生活中所做出的微小改变都会对地球产生巨大影响。正如老话所说:没有人可以做任何事,但每个人可以做一些事!

有了每一天都过绿色生活的想法,我们的"绿色环保年"就要到来了。

【解析】这是一段号召大家选择绿色生活的文字。第一段第一句中,living green 是动名词,作主语,译为"绿色生活",does make our life different 中的 does 表示强调,译为"的确"。第一段第二句中的 planet 在本段中指"地球"。第一段第三句话中的 have a great impact on 的意思是"对……有巨大影响"。第一段第四句中,As the old saying goes 的意思是"正如老话所说"。第二段中,of 引导的短语可处理为前置定语,Green Year 可译为"绿色环保年"。

2016 年 12 月真题

(每题按 3 等评分:2 分,1 分,0 分)

63.【答案】B-C-A

【解析】词组 serve better 的意思是"更好地去服务";seek opportunities 的意思是"寻找机会";open clubs 的意思是"开设俱乐部"。

64.【答案】A-C-B

【解析】changing jobs frequently 的意思是"频繁地换工作";adapt 的意思是"适应"。

65.【答案】C-A-B

【解析】be grateful for 是词组,意思是"感谢……";the arrangement for 的意思是"为……做的安排"。

66.【答案】C-B-A

【解析】assume 是动词,意思是"假设,认为";rely on 是动词词组,意思是"依靠";looks 在这里的意思是"容貌"。

67.【答案】道路施工将于2017年1月9日周一开始,预计持续一个月。第七街与第九街之间的区域将完全封闭。

对于道路施工可能给您带来的任何不便,我们表示歉意。但是,道路施工的目的是让道路更加安全。感谢您的理解。

如果您对道路施工有任何疑问,请致电(650)903-6311。

【解析】本段文字是一则道路施工通告。第一段第一句中,the road construction 可译为"道路施工",时间状语 on Monday, January 9th, 2017 可提至谓语动词之前,按照中文语言习惯,时间按年、月、日、星期的顺序翻译。第一段第二句中 is expected to 可译为"预期",last 在本句中的意思是"持续"。第一段第三句中,be completely closed 可译为"完全封闭"。第二段第一句中,apologize for 可译为"对……表示歉意",this may cause you 是 inconvenience 的定语,翻译的时候放到 inconvenience 前面,一起译为"由此可能给您带来不便"。第三段中,介词 regarding 是"关于,对于"的意思。

2017年6月真题

(每题按3等评分:2分,1分,0分)

63.【答案】B-C-A

【解析】在本句中,首先要弄清楚医疗保健和社会救助业占就业增长的三分之一,the job growth 的意思是"就业增长"。

64.【答案】A-C-B

【解析】regardless of 的意思是"不管";line of work 的意思是"行业";business invitations 的意思是"商务邀请函"。

65.【答案】C-A-B

【解析】make a special effort 的意思是"特别致力于";management and labor 的意思是"管理层和员工"。

66.【答案】B-A-C

【解析】starting a business 的意思是"创业";be right here for you 的意思是"随时为你提供(服务)"。

67.【答案】许多物品可能是危险品,邮寄时会造成严重事故。您的责任是确保您的包裹内不含任何的危险品。您的配合能避免事故发生。如发生事故,您可能得承担责任。如果您想了解是否可以邮寄某一物品,请致电客户服务部1-800-267-1177。

【解析】本段文字是一则邮寄物品须知。第一句中,items 和 goods 意思相近,都可以译成"物品",不必同时译出,避免累赘;实际状语 when mailed 是 when they are mailed 的省略形式。第二句中,It is your responsibility 可以转译成"您有责任",it 是形式主语,真正的主语是后面的不定式短语 to ensure。第四句中,if 引导的条件状语从句可以被提至句首翻译;be held responsible 可以译成"承担责任"。第五句中,whether 译为"是否",a certain item 译为"某种物品"。

2017年12月真题

(每题按3等评分:2分,1分,0分)

63.【答案】B-C-A

【解析】having trust in each other 的意思是"彼此信任";interpersonal relationships 的意思是"人际关系"。

64.【答案】A-C-B

【解析】attend the business meeting 的意思是"出席业务会议";scheduled for next Friday 中的 scheduled 表示"被安排的",因此 scheduled for next Friday 的意思就是"拟于下周五举行的"。

65.【答案】B-A-C

【解析】to show our goodwill 的意思是"为了体现我们的诚意";next order 是指"下次订货"。

66.【答案】C-B-A

【解析】complain about 的意思是"投诉";the unfair treatment 的意思是"不公平的待遇",that I received in your restaurant last Friday 是定语从句,解释说明 the unfair treatment,意思是"我上周五在贵餐馆受到(不公平的待遇)"。

67.【答案】一些老人可能因为上了年纪很难游览这座公园。现在我们的项目为这些老人提供免费服务。我们已经培训了一些志愿者做他们的司机。他们非常熟悉这座公园的历史。我们这个出色的项目是由社区捐赠资助的。我们请您对这个项目给予支持(请您支持这个项目)。

【解析】本段文字介绍的是一个帮助老年人的项目,内容比较简单,翻译时不要漏掉关键点。第一句中 find it difficult to visit this park due to old age,it 是 find 的形式宾语,真正的宾语是后面的不定式短语,due to 的意思是"由于",因此这一部分译为"因为年迈,参加这个会可能会有困难"。第三句话中,work as 可译为"担任,当……"。文字其他部分没有生词和复杂结构。

2018年6月真题

(每题按3等评分:2分,1分,0分)

63. 【答案】C-A-B

【解析】deal with 的意思是"与……交易",根据上下文语境翻译为"与……有业务往来";one of 意思是"……之一";reliable 的意思是"可靠的"。

64. 【答案】A-B-C

【解析】in seconds 的意思是"在很短的时间内,即刻";keywords 的意思是"关键词"。

65. 【答案】B-C-A

【解析】so … that 引导结果状语从句,意思是"如此……以至于,因此";be impressed with 的意思是"对……印象深刻";be pleased to 的意思是"乐于";offer 的意思是"提供"。

66. 【答案】B-A-C

【解析】control or reduce 的意思是"控制,减少";noise at work 的意思是"工作中的噪声";stopping people from 意思是"阻止或妨碍人们干某事"。

67. 【答案】如果您准备好开始您人生的下一步,我们可以提供帮助,让您的钱得到最充分的利用。您可以非正式地约见您的客户经理。客户经理会帮您找到一种办法,让您的钱更好地运作。我们还将帮助您打理您的信用卡和贷款。如需预约,请致电0345-000-888。

【解析】本段介绍的是客户经理对理财方面的一些服务,翻译时不要漏掉关键点。注意几个主要短语的翻译;make the most of 的意思是"充分利用";have an informal meeting 的意思是"随便聊聊";make your money work better 的意思是"更好地运作你的资金";book an appointment 的意思是"预约会面"。

2018年12月真题

(每题按3等评分:2分,1分,0分)

63. 【答案】B-C-A

【解析】本句为简单句,主干为 they conducted a market survey,句首的介词短语 Before setting up the business 作时间状语,说明进行市场调研的时间。介词短语 about … after-sales service 作后置定语,修饰 a market survey,解释说明市场调研的具体内容。

64. 【答案】A-C-B

【解析】本句为复合句,破折号前面的部分为主句,破折号后面的部分可视为同位语从句,对主句部分进行解释说明。主句主干为 Many Americans understand the life-saving value。介词短语 of the seat belt 作后置定语,修饰 the life-saving value。

65. 【答案】C-A-B

【解析】本句为多重复合句,主句主干为 We are building a network。介词短语 of business

作后置定语,修饰 network;who 引导定语从句,修饰 business experts;who 引导的定语从句中又包含了 when 引导的时间状语从句。

66. 【答案】A-B-C

【解析】本句为复合句,主句主干为 their demand is increasing。句首的 As 引导原因状语从句,both at home and abroad 在从句中作地点状语。主句中的 year by year 为时间状语,修饰 is increasing。

67. 【答案】我们希望您觉得本页面上的建议有帮助,并能在您下一次假期中用到它们。无论您计划乘坐飞机还是自驾,请使用我们的旅行对比工具来满足您所有的交通和酒店需求。欢迎再次访问并注册获得我们的业务通信,从而不断获得最好的消费体验和旅行建议。通过对比不同酒店的价格,您可以节省高达 70% 的费用。

【解析】本段介绍的是旅行建议方面的一些服务,翻译时不要漏掉关键点。注意几个主要短语的翻译:on your next vacation 的意思是"您下一次假期";travel comparison tool 的意思是"旅行对比工具";sign up for our newsletter 的意思是"注册获得我们的业务通信";save up 的意思是"节省"。

2019 年 6 月真题

(每题按 3 等评分:2 分,1 分,0 分)

63. 【答案】B-C-A

【解析】本句为主谓宾结构,由 not only … but also 连接两个谓语和宾语。introduction 意为"介绍",A、C 项此处都未译出;business information 意为"商业信息",A、C 项此处翻译得都不准确。只有 B 项完全正确。

64. 【答案】A-C-B

【解析】本句为主谓宾结构,包含一个 what 引导的宾语从句。check 意为"检查",B、C 项此处翻译得不准确;what 引导的宾语从句作 found out 的宾语,意为"发现缺少了什么",B 项此处翻译得不准确。只有 A 项完全正确。

65. 【答案】C-A-B

【解析】本句为主谓宾结构,包含一个 if 引导的条件状语从句。meet your expectation 意为"符合你的期待",A、B 项此处翻译得不准确,原文中并未提到"对工作感到不满意,工作的职责、权利和福利待遇"的表述。只有 C 项完全正确。

66. 【答案】B-C-A

【解析】本句为主谓宾结构,包含一个 when 引导的时间状语从句。carry their original passport and room card 意为"携带护照原件和房卡",A、C 项此处翻译得不准确;leave the ship 意为"离船",A 项此处得翻译不准确。只有 B 项最为正确。

67. 【答案】本中心 1999 年在北京成立。其目标之一是开发计算机资源并且教授企业主如何在其商业活动中使用计算机技术。本中心根据需求提供各种业务主体的培训课程。

如果您对以下任何主题的商务培训感兴趣,请拨打 701-223-0707 或者发邮件至 *info@trainingnd.com* 来联系我们。

【解析】本段文字是一则广告,翻译时不要漏掉关键点。注意几个主要词语和短语的翻译:goal 的意思是"目标";develop 的意思是"开发";based on 的意思是"基于";a variety of 的意思是"各种各样的"。

2019 年 12 月真题

(每题按 3 等评分:2 分,1 分,0 分)

63.【答案】B-A-C

【解析】本句为复合句,make sure 后接宾语从句,省略连词 that;of 后接宾语从句,由 why 引导。

64.【答案】A-C-B

【解析】本句为简单句,动名词短语 Becoming a volunteer 作主语,短语 in the process 的意思是"在……的过程中"。

65.【答案】C-B-A

【解析】本句为复合句,短语 setting up a new business 的意思是"成立一家新企业",短语 organizational structure 的意思是"组织机构"。

66.【答案】B-C-A

【解析】本句为简单句,短语 feel lonely 的意思是"感到孤独",短语 former work and colleagues 的意思是"过去的工作和同事"。

67.【答案】你选择了理想的酒店后,可以在我们的网站上预订。网站会要求你提供一些有关你个人的基本信息,以便预订:你是一家人住还是一个人住,以及你将住多久。你可以直接打电话给酒店确认你的预订。要预订会议室(的客人),请直接拨打电话到酒店前台。

【解析】本段介绍的是如何在网上预订酒店。注意几个主要短语的翻译:ideal hotel 的意思是"理想的酒店";confirm your booking 的意思是"确认你的预订"。

写作/汉译英

2015 年 6 月真题

【参考范文】

MEMO

Date：(1) June 14, 2015
From：(2) Manager
To：(3) All the staff members/employees
Re：(4) about bonus
Message：
　　Due to the company's outstanding achievement in the last year, each staff member/employee will receive a reward/bonus of $500, which will be paid with next month's wages. You are expected to/I hope all the staff members will continue to work hard and make a new contribution to the development of the/our company. Wish our company even greater achievement/success next year.
Signature：(5) Joan Blackburn

【解析】本次应用文写作考查的是备忘录。备忘录通常有固定的写作格式，一般包含收件人、发件人、抄送、发件日期、主题和正文。考生须根据所给的中文提示，将表格填写完整。考生要注意时态、语态和日期的英文表达，避免发生错译、漏译、单词拼写和语法错误。

2015 年 12 月真题

【参考范文】

Leave Request Form

Employee Information
Name：(1) Li Jun
Employee Number：(2) 120485
Department：(3) Marketing Department
Leave Type：(4) Sick Leave
Starting Date：(5) January 10th, 2016　　　　Resumption Date：January 25th, 2016
Reason for Leave：
　　I have been feeling uncomfortable in the past few weeks, but I was on a business trip in other places, so I didn't have enough time to see a doctor. When I came back, I finally got the time and came to see the doctor as soon as possible. According to the doctor, it's necessary and urgent for me to be hospitalized to get further check and treatment. So I have to take a sick leave for two weeks.
　　Signature of Applicant：*Li Jun*

【解析】本次应用文写作考查的是请假条。请假条的内容应包含请假人的姓名、请假人所属部门、请假类型、请假起始日期以及请假原因。

2016年6月真题

【参考范文】

Employment Application	
Personal Details	
Date of Application：	(1) June 19, 2016
Name of Applicant：	(2) Li Ming
Address：	50 Xinhua Road, Nanjing
Personal Contact	
Home telephone：	020-123**678
Mobile：	(3) 150****6789
E-mail Address：	(4) Liming123@163.com
Applied Position：	(5) salesperson
Expected Salary：	About 3,000 *yuan*
Education Background	
2013–2016	Dongfang Professional Technical College

Skills & Hobbies：
  I have some skills that I think are fit for the job I am applying for. I am skilled in operating computers. I am good at spoken English/I can speak English fluently. What's more, I have strong communication ability and teamwork spirit/cooperation ability.
  I have many hobbies. For example, I love reading, sports and travel. These hobbies help me widen my horizon and build up my good character and personality.
  If I could have this job, I would be willing to work overtime and travel on business/take business trips.
  I will greatly appreciate it if you can give my application a consideration.	

【解析】本次应用文写作考查的是求职申请表。求职表通常有固定的写作格式，内容应包含求职者的个人信息（姓名、出生日期、住址、电话等）、求职日期、申请职位、教育背景、工作经历、资格、技能、兴趣爱好等。

2016年12月真题

【参考范文】

Overtime Request Form

Request Date: (1) <u>March 1, 2017</u>
Employee's Name: (2) <u>Li Jianxin</u>
Department: (3) <u>Human Resources Department</u>
Date of Overtime: March 5, 2017
Overtime Needed: from (4) <u>9:00 a.m.</u> to 5:00 p.m.
Total Overtime: not to exceed (5) <u>8</u> hours
Reasons for Overtime Required:
　　Our company plans to hire different kinds of employees. The Human Resources Department published a want/job advertising a week ago, and has received many application letters. To help other departments to arrange for the interviews, I need to work overtime on Saturday to learn about the information of applicants and arrange for the interviews.

【解析】本次应用文写作考查的是加班申请表。加班申请表通常有固定的写作格式,内容应包含申请人、申请日期、所属部门、加班日期和时间、加班原因。

2017年6月真题

【参考范文】

Guest Experience Card
We value your feedback

Name: (1) <u>Zhang Jianlin</u>
E-mail address: (2) <u>zhangj1999@163.com</u>
Date of visit: (3) <u>June 15, 2017</u>
Time of visit: (4) <u>11:30 a.m.</u>
Did our Team Members exceed your expectations? Yes
If yes, please provide their names: (5) <u>John Chen</u>
Comments:
　　The staff in the hotel are very friendly and provide/offer excellent services./People here are all very kind and friendly, especially (one named) John Chen.
　　The room in the hotel is very clean and tidy, and the food (in the restaurant/dining room) is very delicious. In a word, I have a very good experience living in the hotel.
　　However, the hotel is far from the downtown area, so I suggest that the hotel should add some shuttle buses from the hotel to the subway station to provide convenience for customers.
　　　　　　　　Thank you for choosing our hotel.
　　　If you would like to talk to us about your experience today,
please contact the Guest Services Department at 1-888-601-1616.

【解析】本次应用文写作考查的是顾客意见反馈表。意见反馈表通常有固定的写作格式,内容应包含顾客的姓名、电话、地址等个人信息以及反馈的具体内容。

2017年12月真题

【参考范文】

Field Trip Report

Report to: Mr./Mrs. (1) <u>Wang Xiaolin</u>
Report from: Mr./Mrs. (2) <u>Li Junjie</u>
Date: (3) <u>December 24, 2017</u>
Trip destination: (4) <u>JUK factory/plant/firm</u>
Trip period: from December 4, 2017 to (5) <u>December 8, 2017</u>
Participants: Li Junjie & His team members
Summary:

December 8, 2017

  In order to learn about/understand water pollution, we have visited JUK factory for a week. We have learned about the main source of the problem/how the waste water mainly comes. The engineers introduced the ways/measures to deal with the problem of waste water treatment. This visit helps us to do our research work.

【解析】本次应用文写作考查的是现场考察报告。现场考察报告的内容通常包含报告人、被报告人、报告日期和时间、参加人员和具体内容。考察报告使用的语言一般比较正式。

2018年6月真题

【参考范文】

Memo

To: (1) <u>All department managers</u>
From: (2) <u>Mr. Tom Brown, Secretary of General Manager</u>
Date: (3) <u>June 18, 2018</u>
CC: (4) <u>Mr. John Smith</u>
Subject: (5) <u>Discussion on the Sales Plan of the Second Half of the Year</u>

  The marketing department has worked out our company's sales plan for the second half of the year. It is being sent to you all. Please see the attachment. The General Manager's Office will hold a meeting in the company's meeting room at 2 p.m. on June 20 to discuss the plan and listen to the opinions from all the departments. All department managers are expected to take part in the meeting. Those who can't attend it, please inform the General Managers Office in advance.

【解析】本次应用文写作考查的是备忘录。备忘录通常有固定的写作格式,一般包含收件人、发件人、抄送、发件日期、主题和正文。

2018 年 12 月真题

【参考范文】

Volunteer Application Form

Thank you for your interest in volunteering with Reading Together.
Personal Details
Name：(1) <u>Chen Daming</u>   ☑ Mr.   ☐ Mrs.   ☐ Ms.
Mobile：(2) <u>177＊＊＊＊8956</u>
E-mail：(3) <u>chendm999@163.com</u>
Birth Date：(4) <u>Dec. 15th, 1998</u>
College Information
College Name：Dongfang Technical College
Major：Computer Technology   Department：(5) <u>Computer</u>
Describe why you are interested in working as a volunteer with us.
　　I am quite interested in reading, and have read many books. I want to use the knowledge I have learned to help children in the countryside. By taking part in volunteer activities, I may have the chance to make more friends with those who love reading. In addition, I can improve my reading and communicating skills.

　　【解析】本次应用文写作考查的是志愿者申请表。志愿者申请表的内容通常包含申请人的姓名、出生日期、手机、邮箱、教育背景，以及申请理由。

2019 年 6 月真题

【参考范文】

Important Message

For：(1) <u>Ann Taylor</u>
From：(2) <u>John Smith</u>
Time：9 a.m.   Date：(3) <u>June 20</u>
Tel No.：021-77542＊＊1   Fax：(4) <u>021-7754＊＊43</u>
Please call ☐   Returned your call ■
Will call again ☐   Urgent ■
Message：
　　The material you need is prepared. Please tell Mr. Smith how many copies need to be printed and when someone will be sent to get them.
　　Their company is going to hold a training class and they want to invite you to give a talk on e-business in the class.
Taken by：(5) <u>Wang Xiaohong</u>

　　【解析】本次应用文写作考查的是电话留言(Telephone Message)。书写电话留言条是办公室工作人员必备的一项能力。当对方要找的人不在时，你需要为他找的人留言。留言条最根本的特点是行文要开门见山、简明扼要、通俗易懂，将来电者的意思清楚明白地表达出来,但又不能丢失信息。电话留言的内容通常包含来电人、收件人、留言日期、留言时间、留言内容和记录人。

2019 年 12 月真题

【参考范文】

Customer Interview

Date:(1) December 15, 2019

Information about the customer

Name:(2) John Smith

Telephone:(3) 12333311190

E-mail address:(4) JohnS@126.com

Feedback(反馈意见):

　　He likes using the ABC-1 phone very much. But he thinks it is too expensive and wishes it could be cheaper. Since the users are mainly old people, he suggests that the screen should be a bit bigger. He also hopes we would improve the after-sales service.

Interviewer:(5) Li Hua

【解析】本次应用文写作考查的是客户回访(Customer Interview)。客户回访是企业用来进行产品或服务满意度调查、客户消费行为调查、进行客户维系的常用方法,更是得到客户认同、创造客户价值的重要手段。回访记录的语言要求开门见山、简明扼要、通俗易懂,将客户的意思清楚明白地表达出来,但又不能丢失信息。

附录三　答题卡样张

请勿在此处作任何标记

下列各题必须使用黑色字迹签字笔在答题区域内作答，超出红色矩形边框限定区域的答案无效。

67 _____

Writing